THE PROMISED LAND

History and Historiography of the Black Experience
in Chatham-Kent's Settlements and Beyond

Eschewing the often romanticized Underground Railroad narrative
that portrays southern Ontario as the welcoming destination of Blacks
fleeing from slavery, *The Promised Land* reveals the Chatham-Kent area
as a crucial settlement site for an early Black presence in Canada. The
contributors present the everyday lives and professional activities of
individuals and families in these communities and highlight early
cross-border activism to end slavery in the United States and to promote civil rights in the United States and Canada. Essays also reflect
on the frequent intermingling of local Black, White, and First Nations
people. Using a cultural studies framework for their collective investi-
gations, the authors trace physical and intellectual trajectories of Blackness that have radiated from southern Ontario to other parts of Canada,
the United States, the Caribbean, and Africa. The result is a collection
that represents the presence and diffusion of Blackness and inventively
challenges the grand narrative of history.

(African and Diasporic Cultural Studies)

BOULOU EBANDA DE B'BÉRI is a professor of Communication and Cultural Studies and the ʌounding director of the Audiovisual Media Lab
for the study of Cultures and Societies at the University of Ottawa.

NINA REID-MARONEY is an associate professor in the Department of History
at Huron University College, Western University.

HANDEL KASHOPE WRIGHT is a professor of Education and founding director of the Centre for Culture, Identity and Education at the University
of British Columbia.

The Promised Land

History and Historiography of the Black Experience in Chatham-Kent's Settlements and Beyond

EDITED BY
BOULOU EBANDA DE B'BÉRI,
NINA REID-MARONEY,
AND HANDEL KASHOPE WRIGHT

EPILOGUE BY AFUA COOPER

UNIVERSITY OF TORONTO PRESS
Toronto Buffalo London

© University of Toronto Press 2014
Toronto Buffalo London
www.utppublishing.com
Printed in the U.S.A.

ISBN 978-1-4426-4717-6 (cloth)
ISBN 978-1-4426-1533-5 (paper)

Printed on acid-free, 100% post-consumer recycled paper with
vegetable-based inks.

African & Diasporic Cultural Studies

Library and Archives Canada Cataloguing in Publication

The promised land : history and historiography of the Black experience in Chatham-
Kent's settlements and beyond / edited by Boulou Ebanda de B'béri, Nina Reid-
Maroney, and Handel Kashope Wright.
(African & diasporic cultural studies)

Includes bibliographical references and index.
ISBN 978-1-4426-4717-6 (bound). – ISBN 978-1-4426-1533-5 (pbk.)

1. Black Canadians – Ontario – Chatham-Kent – History – 19th century.   2. Blacks – Ontario –
Chatham-Kent – History – 19th century.   I. Reid-Maroney, Nina Ruth, 1961–, editor of
compilation   II. Wright, Handel Kashope, 1959–, editor of compilation   III. Ebanda de
B'béri, Boulou, editor of compilation   IV. Series: African and diasporic studies

FC3099.C45Z7 2014   971.3'3300496   C2014-900417-6

University of Toronto Press acknowledges the financial assistance to its publishing
program of the Canada Council for the Arts and the Ontario Arts Council, an agency of
the Government of Ontario.

**Canada Council   Conseil des Arts
for the Arts   du Canada**

**ONTARIO ARTS COUNCIL
CONSEIL DES ARTS DE L'ONTARIO**
an Ontario government agency
un organisme du gouvernement de l'Ontario

University of Toronto Press acknowledges the financial support of the
Government of Canada through the Canada Book Fund for its publishing activities.

The University of Toronto Press acknowledges the financial support of the
University of Ottawa's Faculty of Arts as well as the financial support of the Social
Sciences and Humanities Research Council through its Community-University Research
Alliances program.

For Gwendolyn Robinson

Contents

THE PROMISED LAND

History and Historiography of the Black Experience
in Chatham-Kent's Settlements and Beyond

Introduction

BOULOU EBANDA DE B'BÉRI, NINA REID-MARONEY,
AND HANDEL KASHOPE WRIGHT

This book was born of the remarkable collaboration that was the Promised Land Project (PLP). Based on the early work of the research team, the book reflects the project's mandate, which was to create a Community University Research Alliance that would cut across disciplinary boundaries and build bridges among academics, community scholars, and students at all levels. The study of nineteenth-century African Canadian history in Chatham-Kent (formerly Kent County) was the project's point of origin, and while researchers were immediately drawn to the rich materials of the past, those materials opened pathways to wider historical discussions of race, identity, and culture. The project's grounding in particular questions about nineteenth-century African Canadian communities was balanced by its wider efforts to lift the histories and narratives of nineteenth-century Black settlement out of the narrow places where they had been pigeonholed and to open them to a national and ultimately global context.

This book's ground-breaking research develops themes that were central to the PLP. Like the project as a whole, it is about connections, place, and movement – across historical periods and national boundaries, oceans and regions, and academic disciplines. It explores the interplay between past and present, history and memory, local and global concerns. It offers fresh insights by exercising the historian's habit of suddenly shifting perspective to reveal new patterns – and, just as importantly, to reveal those places and times where the patterns blur and break.[1]

Students of recent historiography will recognize here the influence of the "spatial turn" in historical studies. The research uses the land itself – the geography of the "Promised Land" – to map settlement,

culture, and identities. Readers will also recognize that the language of
a Promised Land, even one in which the promise remains largely un-
realized, is both metaphor and reality. This understanding reaches far
back in the history of slavery and freedom. It was articulated in striking
terms by Daniel Payne, distinguished Bishop in the African Methodist Episcopal Church (AME). In the early spring of 1835, Payne was
a free man living in the slaveholding stronghold of Charleston, South
Carolina, and making his way as the teacher in charge of a small school
for Black children. Having purchased a precious book – an illustrated
atlas – for the price of one shilling from a woman in the Charleston market, he quickly added geography and map-making to the lessons he
taught his young pupils. When the South Carolina legislature passed
strict laws forbidding the education of Black students, Payne was dis-
traught. In his autobiography, he tells us:

> About this time, I had a dream which to me at that time seemed prophetic.
> It was this: I dreamed that I was lifted up from the earth, and without
> wings fled toward the North. I was clad in my pink robe, which I always
> wore in the school-room. Upon reaching the North I was all the time flying
> south of the chain of lakes which separate the United States from Can-
> ada. To and fro along this line I was still flying in my teaching robes, till
> I awoke and found myself still in Charleston, but greatly comforted in the
> midst of my troubles.[2]

Within a few months, Payne had left the South for Pennsylvania, where
he created a network of churches that linked Black settlements in Upper Canada to the abolitionist culture of the AME across the northern
United States.

Payne's vision of flight, freedom, and the Great Lakes borderlands
was as precise in its geopolitical details as it was coloured with the rich
aquatints of prophecy. In Payne's narrative, the landscapes of "Promised Lands" both real and imagined become part of a moral geography,
invested with layers of meaning that change over time. Whether the
promise of freedom was fulfilled, and when and how and by whom,
history leaves as an open question. Here, then, is a starting point. The
authors of this collection map a new understanding of Chatham-Kent's
Black settlements, using the construct, language, and experiences of the
"Promised Land" to interrogate and move beyond the boundaries of
the term itself.

Part One: Introducing the Promised Land Project

In the first section of this book, the three co-editors introduce the Promised Land Project's key research concepts and methodologies, politics of knowledge, and historiography. Chapter 1, by Boulou Ebanda de B'béri, addresses how the PLP was conceived and how it unfolded, with a focus on the structural and conceptual challenges that were faced by the project's multigenerational, international, and interdisciplinary team of researchers. This chapter opens with what is actually a political claim, one that troubles the legitimacy of the image of Canada as a Promised Land – that while the PLP is a Black historical project, it should also be seen as a project in Canadian history. This claim reminds us to consider the process of writing history. Ebanda de B'béri argues that history is written, manufactured, and constructed in the same way as many other kinds of popular knowledge. He notes that we cannot fully understand what is taken for granted in history and naturalized in national grand narratives unless we question how historical facts are collected and what kinds of politics of knowledge are being harnessed when national historical markers and symbols are created and selected. Thus, chapter 1 guides readers to understand the PLP's methodology for researching and producing a different Canadian history. Ebanda de B'béri explains how the project's partners became a team and why they were chosen. He describes the challenges they faced and will continue to face in their efforts to articulate and make sense of the Black Canadian experience in Canada.

Chapter 2, by Handel Kashope Wright, also addresses an epistemological concern – that is, how the PLP has contributed to the construction of local Black history while adding to and troubling mainstream local and national history. Wright points to the constructed nature of history, emphasizing that mainstream history in Canada is in fact raced (White) rather than racially neutral so that the articulation of Black history results in competing truths. But he does not stop at troubling mainstream history; he extends the complication of narratives to the PLP itself. He reveals that the history the PLP is constructing is not pristine and corrective; indeed, it is messy – there are competing truths even within the project. He wonders aloud how the PLP as Black history affects not only mainstream (White) history but also other histories, including Aboriginal history. In unpacking these issues, he recognizes the importance of historical materials and data to our understanding of critical cultural analyses. For example, in opening the discipline of History to non-historians like himself, he shows how some taken-for-granted historical facts and data may open up discussion to more complex, contemporary, and futuristic concepts such as mixedracedness, multiraciality, and multiculturality. He indicates that when we trouble many taken-for-granted notions such as race (Blackness, Whiteness, aboriginality), other histories emerge from History. He illustrates how the PLP refused to be contained as a spatially localized project. While the project was conceived in Ontario's Chatham and Dawn settlements, the experiences of Black were actually *rhizomatic* in nature; and this fact alone demands that the project be deterritorialized, that it follow other trajectories and address other conjunctures. In this way, the notion that the Promised Land communities and experiences have "multiple trajectories" constitutes one of Wright's contributions to the PLP. Indeed, this concept has become key to the PLP's work, having been mobilized by most of the project's partners. Finally, Wright in chapter 2 advocates that we move away from what he critiques as fairy-tale Underground Railroad (UGR) narratives to consider the possibility of competing and alternative truths, because fairy-tale endings are both incomplete and overly romanticized. Historical knowledge, he asserts, can never be sealed in eternity: different truth regimes will always be competing with one another. This explains, he tells us, how the PLP research, methodology, findings, and achievements illustrate clearly that definitive meaning can only be risky and elusive. By the same token, he concludes, the PLP continues not only metaphorically beyond the last stop of the UGR narratives, but also beyond both the Promised Land communities and the CURA program that provided the original research funds.

In chapter 3, Nina Reid-Maroney helps the reader (re)consider the relationship between Canadian historical traditions and African Canadians' historical struggles. She opens by reminding us that some of the issues and questions central to the PLP's work had already been analysed more than 150 years ago. She invites us to re-examine the actions of some nineteenth-century abolitionists and to use our findings as guiding principles for historical research. For example, Samuel Ringgold Ward's life and activities became one among many conceptual illustrations of the notion of multiple spatial and intellectual trajectories within the Promised Land communities, but they also amounted to a metaphorical invitation for all contemporary historians to adopt his pedagogical and moral activities. What might it mean for contemporary historians to acknowledge or "discover" that most Canadians have yet to "naturalize" Ward's nineteenth-century abolitionist actions? Does this amnesia not indicate clearly that we, the Canadian people, have agreed to delete certain historical facts, and that as a nation we are content to forget certain uncomfortable facts about the Black experience in Canada? As Reid-Maroney notes: "Ward was almost as well known as was Frederick Douglass ... the more telling, then, to have the call to write a sophisticated, nuanced, and complex history come to us from Ward, an unforgettable figure whose own place in the history he both lived and wrote has been all but forgotten." Indeed, when it comes to questioning the easy conclusion "that Canada was always in a position of moral superiority on the question of slavery," or that the racial prejudice historically experienced by Black people in Canada was not as severe as in other nations, contemporary historians could return to Ward's experience in order to understand and perhaps make new sense of how Canada came to be perceived as a moral lighthouse or Promised Land. Reid-Maroney finds it deplorable that the concept of Canada as a moral lighthouse has been a false light, one that hides national anxieties and that has been used in ways that have obscured rather than illuminated the histories and experiences of African Canadians in the process of Canadian nation building. Her chapter neatly concludes part one of this book by outlining some of the PLP's key achievements. She illustrates how this research has opened up new lines of historical inquiry and methodology by starting at one point and moving to another; by using the familiar to discover the complex and the untold – the competing truths discussed in chapter 2; by giving locally taken-for-granted history a new set of meanings; and, finally, by designing innovative frameworks for local and junior historians, from high school students to university undergraduates and postgraduates.

Part Two: From Fragments through Biography to History

The second section of this book takes the reader into its substance by offering three biographical case studies of notable Black figures in nineteenth-century Chatham and environs. The three figures are William Whipper, who was born into slavery but gained his freedom and an education and became a businessman, intellectual, and Underground Railroad activist; Nina Mae Alexander, a young woman born in Amherstburg, Ontario, who became a teacher at schools in Merritton and Rondeau; and Parker Theophilus Smith, a carpenter, shopkeeper, and intellectual who emigrated from Philadelphia to Dresden but stayed only some ten months. Part two's title draws attention to method and styles of historical representation. Here, the subject matter of each chapter in the section is introduced and general comments are provided about how all three contribute to this book, individually and as a whole, in terms of content, methodology, and style.

Marie Carter's chapter provides an account of William Whipper's rapid rise from slavery to freedom – to becoming a young man of letters, a newspaper editor, the founder of a library for Blacks in Pennsylvania, a successful businessman, and an Underground Railroad activist – all of this a testament to his agency and ambition. She describes how, after helping smuggle hundreds of Blacks into Canada, the "land of freedom," by rail and steamship, Whipper came to Dresden to see for himself how the refugees were doing and was so impressed that he moved to Canada himself, preceded by his brother and sister.

Carter's chapter focuses on Whipper's land purchases and business dealings and what they mean for our understanding of local history. Up until about 2003, "the Rev. Josiah Henson was often the only African Canadian mentioned in local historical accounts," and academic historians explained the Dawn Settlement from the perspective of Henson's life. Carter relates how she and other members of a research team working on the Trillium Trail Historical Walk came across records of William Whipper's land purchases in 2003 by examining Dresden land records (specifically, Van Allen Surveys 127 and 128). In part because local history has mostly been told from a White perspective and about White figures (with Henson being the token Black represented), and in part because Whipper insisted on referencing his lands only by their location on the Sydenham River (even as municipal changes meant that the river itself was moved in terms of county designation), the lives and contributions of various Black figures of the day, including Whipper, were lost to history. What Carter calls "land-based research" (work on land records) unearthed Whipper and his contributions to the community, which included lending money to both Black and White pioneers – an example of interracial cooperation and also of Black agency (thus countering the hegemonic trope that almost all Black pioneers were poor and were the sole recipients of White financial assistance in Canada). The discovery of Whipper's lands along the Sydenham provides new details about Black lives as well as a new lens through which to view local history and indeed to correct (partial, White) history.

Claudine Bonner, in her chapter on Nina Mae Alexander, describes her subject's story as "in many ways unremarkable," in that it is one of many extant narratives about the young women who took up the calling to teach in small towns in Ontario in the nineteenth and early twentieth centuries. However, almost all such narratives are about young *White* women, with the result that the history of teachers in Ontario has so far been, more accurately, the history of White women teachers. As a fully qualified Black woman teaching in White schools, Nina Mae Alexander was somewhat exceptional, and her story therefore adds to and complicates the history of teachers in Ontario.

Bonner's account draws heavily from a diary that Nina Mae kept for some four months. Bonner reorganizes its contents to articulate several themes: Education and the Family (her family clearly valued education highly – five of her six siblings were in the professions); A Full Social Calendar (Mae made many entries about her social life, which included both Black and White suitors and friends); and Nina Mae and Religion (the church was central to the Black community and attempted to dictate Mae's behaviour through its patriarchal morality).

Nina Mae's diary covers only four months of her life, but what does exist is surprisingly comprehensive, although lacking important details. In that regard, Bonner's exasperation is almost palpable – she wonders, for example, how her family could afford to send her to Normal School and her brother to medical school at the same time. Bonner's chapter is the one that most closely follows the life and daily activities of its subject; but she also follows Reid-Maroney and Carter in making her account a case study, in this case one that provides insights into the life experiences of African Canadians and a snapshot of life in a small Ontario town at the beginning of the twentieth century.

Nina Reid-Maroney, in her chapter, tells the story of Parker Theophilus Smith's move from Philadelphia to Dresden, his life during his ten-month stay in Canada before declaring that "in Canada I will not stay," and his return to Philadelphia. She describes Smith's life in both Philadelphia and Dresden, including snippets of information about his wife and family. In his pre-emigration days in Philadelphia, Smith was a man of accomplishments. A carpenter and drugstore owner, he held real estate worth some six hundred dollars by the time he was thirty-eight. He was also a prominent intellectual – a member and later president of the Banneker Institute, a Philadelphia-based literary and debating society for Blacks. On first sight of Dresden, he thought he had found a utopia, and he quickly involved himself in the intellectual life of the village, and in its church and choir, while establishing himself in business. All of this is interesting, but it is not his life that is Reid-Maroney's primary concern but rather his movements from Philadelphia to Dresden and back and his reasons for them.

The identification of Canada (more specifically, the southern part of what was then Canada West) as the final destination on the Underground Railroad, as Dawn, "the Promised Land," and so on, suggests a form of symbolic closure. But in Smith's day, that closure was somewhat imperfect – indeed, many Black individuals and families who had reached Canada chose to return to the United States. In her chapter on Smith, Reid-Maroney provides one carefully nuanced example of this. Smith returned to Philadelphia mainly because he was homesick, not just in a purely emotional sense but more so in an intellectual sense: he longed for the larger and more erudite Black intellectual society of Philadelphia (the intellectual life of Dresden was a poor substitute). While he might have migrated physically to Dresden, his was a failed migration in terms of his intellectual and political concerns, which remained fixed on the situation in the United States and especially in Philadelphia. Dresden's ethnoscape only stimulated his longing to immerse himself in American racial politics and the abolition struggle. Dresden was a faraway outpost of the British Empire from which it was hard to get the latest news from the United States and from Philadelphia in particular; paradoxically, the village was also too entangled in American racial politics, given that it was packed with American refugees to the point that all existence was political. Dresden had forced him out of his intellectual comfort zone and compelled him to confront actual refugees from American slavery. And, of course, the problem of racism did not disappear once he crossed the border: some local Whites were tolerant and even abolitionist in their politics, but he and other Blacks in the area also faced everyday and intellectual racism (which he had to forcefully confront and address on several occasions), giving the lie to the idea that Canada was a land of freedom where Blacks could be free from racial discrimination. All of these factors rekindled his republican spirit as well as a renewed interest in racial politics, one that went beyond intellectual engagement and embraced explicit abolitionist activist politics. As a result, he felt a pull back to Philadelphia that he could not resist.

The three chapters in part two delineate one important moment each in the lives of three noteworthy individuals. They also shed light on the everyday lives and activities of African Canadians in mid- to late-nineteenth-century Chatham and environs, as well as on the issues of the day, which included the struggle for freedom and equality on both sides of the Canada-US border; the movements of Blacks between the United States and Canada and within Canada and the reasons for those movements; identity formation and identification with and against places of origin and places of arrival; and the sociocultural differences within the multicultural communities (and indeed, within African Canadian families and communities) that those individuals helped create. And, finally, all three chapters speak to how local histories are told and retold. Thus, each biography in this section outlines an important moment in the life of one individual (rather than an entire life story), using that moment as an portal to broader historical sociocultural and political issues and thereby suggesting what the everyday lives and concerns of these individuals mean for our understanding of the local (and indeed intellectual, political, social, and national) history.

All three chapters are historical case studies, but they also diverge in terms of both process and presentation. Reid-Maroney's case study of Parker Smith is a smooth-flowing narrative, told in the third person, with little but the references to primary and secondary sources, all neatly tucked away in the endnotes, to give any indication of the research undertaken and the historian's role. Though also written in the third person, Carter's chapter on William Whipper is a study in meticulous documentation that makes the research method transparent, inviting the reader to follow the process by which fragments of data were found. The chapter also sets out the effect that such findings had on the narrative being constructed. References to the author's previous work and its relationship to the present case study not only make the author present but also make plain the process of constructing the historical account. Finally, by writing in the first person but with long stretches of description that draw our attention more to the story and away from the author's voice and presence, Claudine Bonner in her chapter on Nina Mae Alexander strikes a middle ground in terms of making plain the work of data collection and the hand of the researcher in constructing the historical account.

Part Three: Mapping Transgeographical Trajectories and Identity Formation beyond the Underground Railroad

The third section of this book shifts the focus away from particular people towards discussions of place. While acknowledging the importance

of the Underground Railroad to Black migration from slavery to freedom, the chapters in this section recontextualize that history by expanding the discussion to consider other narratives of Black abolitionist
migration and the role those narratives have played in shaping concepts of race, freedom, and identity. The section's focus on mapping
returns us squarely to the Promised Land but sets that metaphor in motion. Trajectories crisscross the map of the Promised Land communities;
each connection traced here leads somewhere else, doubles back, until
together they form the web of associations that sustained the work of
Black abolitionists in Canada. The three chapters fit together as views of
the Promised Land through three lenses that frame the scene, each with
a different focal length.

   In chapter 7, Olivette Otele takes a long view, moving back in time
to consider the history of the Black Atlantic and its influence on the
colonial history of Upper Canada. As Christopher Brown has argued,
British anti-slavery movements were a response to the moral challenge
of the American Revolution, as a consequence of which early Black
abolitionists in Britain gained a wider public hearing.[3] By reminding
us of this eighteenth-century background to the nineteenth-century
communities at the centre of the inquiry, Otele's chapter anticipates the
direction of subsequent PLP research, which would explore the links
between Chatham-Kent and the Nova Scotian communities founded in
the first foment of Black abolition in the Atlantic world.

   Otele's main focus is on the connections, sometimes easily made,
sometimes weighted with tension, between White and Black abolitionists in Britain and in North America. She traces those links through
shared ideologies, institutional networks, and religious traditions. Using the example of Josiah Henson, she explores the idea of Black abolitionists using a "narrative pedagogy" in which their preaching in the
evangelical Christian tradition and the narratives of their own lives
constituted a powerful and liberating form of instruction for sympathetic Whites. Her chapter highlights the agency and power of Black
abolitionist voices. In her analysis of Henson, the familiar trope of the
Promised Land becomes both story and history – personal, political,
and spiritual. Black narrative pedagogy creates a common ground
or "religious kinship" with Whites, even though, as the chapter concludes, "the tie proved to be confrontational at times." In making this
argument, Otele draws attention to the complexities underpinning the
seemingly familiar story of Josiah Henson, placing his religious life at
the inquiry's centre.

Peter Dalleo's chapter is also set against the backdrop of the Atlantic world. His account takes us to the colonial foundations of the state of Delaware, tracing the establishment of slavery there and the origins of a powerful anti-slavery movement that would eventually flow directly into the Promised Land communities of Chatham-Kent. We are not accustomed to thinking of Delaware as a slave state, yet its history of slavery goes back to the period of Dutch settlement in the seventeenth century and would last all the way to 1865 and the end of the American Civil War. As Dalleo points out, the existence of an active Black abolitionist community in the heart of a slave state created particular pressures on the anti-slavery movement that gave Delaware a large role in shaping anti-slavery movements elsewhere.

In tracing their kinship connections with Delaware's influential free Black community, Dalleo places well-known African Canadian figures in a new light. Mary Ann Shadd, perhaps the best known of the Delaware émigrés, is situated in the context of her extended family and the intellectual currents that ran through free Black Wilmington. Given the strong involvement of Delaware's Black abolitionists in discussions about Liberia, Shadd's efforts to encourage immigration to Canada West in the 1850s take on a fresh aspect. William Whipper and Parker Smith are also discussed, as part of the political activism led by Delaware's Black abolitionists. The chapter tracks this political engagement over much of the nineteenth century, creating a clear picture of a complex network whose direct ties to Canada have just begun to be explored. Dalleo provides new insights into the politics of the Promised Land communities, reaching beyond anti-slavery to the broader struggle for civil rights and full racial equality.

In the final chapter, Marie Carter uses extensive research of local land records to answer the question, "What was the Dawn Settlement?" The question is important, she argues, because in local histories and academic accounts the term has been widely adopted to frame Black settlement as a declension narrative in which hints of the old racial framework of the nineteenth century lurk behind stories of failure. The stakes in reimagining the Dawn Settlement are high.

Carter begins by distinguishing between the British American Institute (BAI) – the school founded by Josiah Henson and Hiram Wilson with the support of the American Missionary Association and others, including James Canning Fuller – and Black settlement in the rich farmlands that surrounded the school property. While it is clear that the BAI had been organized as part of the Black abolitionist vision of moral and material progress through education, and was meant to support the goals of independent settlement, landownership, and prosperity, it was not a utopian or planned community called the Dawn Settlement.

Carter's paper goes on to explore the history of the term "Dawn Settlement," setting out the context in which the mapping of nineteenth-century settlement was conducted. With political boundaries being drawn and redrawn, with lands changing hands first through treaties and then through gradual shifts in local government, and with the imposition of a certain kind of order on the map as a key part of the colonial project itself, the assigning of place names was ideologically charged and open to inconsistencies. Omissions and errors have been absorbed into the canon. Dawn Mills, Dawn Township, Dawn Settlement, and plain "Dawn" all played a part in the confusion of names, and Carter's sifting of local sources and appreciation for the nuances of changes on the ground – details that are lost at a distance – lay the groundwork for her broader argument. She argues that the Dawn Settlement was and remains as much a shifting construct as a discrete geographic place. "It may be," she concludes, "that attempting to put borders around Dawn will prove as elusive a goal as trying to define the borders of the dreams and hopes of a people." The final chapter, in returning to one of the PLP's first research questions, points towards new questions and highlights the importance of process over final answers. The third section of this book invites new interpretations and opens rather than closes questions about method, the politics of historical knowledge, and the implications for Canadian culture. All of those questions are addressed in the Epilogue by the distinguished historian Afua Cooper.

NOTES

1 Gaddis, *The Landscape of History.*
2 Payne, *Recollections of Seventy Years,* 34.
3 Brown, *Moral Capital.*

PART I

Introducing the Promised Land Project

1 The Politics of Knowledge: The Promised Land Project and Black Canadian History as a Model of Historical "Manufacturation"?

BOULOU EBANDA DE B'BÉRI

To Kenzo!

Introduction

In this chapter, I use the Promised Land Project: The Freedom Experience of Blacks in the Chatham and Dawn Settlements (hereafter PLP) – a Black Canadian research project – as a tangible object that can guide our understanding of some of the processes of knowledge production. Specifically, I investigate the process of writing history, focusing on the ways in which specific tensions can lead to the production of historical knowledge. One of my key arguments is that history – and Canadian cultural and social history in particular – is inescapably linked to a specific "geography of identity." According to Brian S. Osborne, the notion of "geography of identity is premised on the assumption that peoples' identification" with specific symbols, places, space, and time "is essential for the cultivation of an awareness – *an a-where-ness*" that would lead them to secure a sense of belonging.[1] Indeed, I suggest that our sense of Canadianness – indeed, anyone's sense of belonging, whether micro or macro – is secured through the same kinds of markers. Nowadays, the Canadian geography of identity is poorly defined; it remains a complex articulation of multiple tensions, largely because it involves many floating signifiers that extend far beyond the known two politically claimed founding fathers, the First Nations of Canada, and the marketing concept of Canadian multiculturalism. In other words, articulations that Handel Wright refers to in this book as "presentist," and futuristic notions such as "mixedracedness" and "multiraciality," as well as cosmopolitanism, transnationalism, and multiculturalism, all of which constitute multiple conditions of possibility of "Canada's multiculturality," have been absent if not deleted from the Canadian geography of identity.

Thus, as I make my demonstration follow the structures of immediate history, the main methodological position I want to take is genealogy. My key assumption is that the PLP's genealogy offers an excellent means to highlight the parallel frameworks of the Canadian grand history and of other "sideline" histories that are yet to become Canadian. This genealogy will illustrate how the PLP was established as well as the processes of writing, organizing, producing, and disseminating this Black history as real Canadian history. I hope this methodology will help us outline tangible processes of knowledge mobilization, along with some key concepts that comprise Canada's uniqueness – for example, our strong sense of multiculturalism, which nurtures the mythical-ethnic sense of "Canadianicity."[2]

The Promised Land Project: What Is My Name?

The idea of the PLP was born by accident on a hot summer day in 2005. An article published in the *Ottawa Citizen* more than two years later, in October 2007, captures this fortunate accident very well: "Some people return from camping trips with poison ivy. [I] returned with an idea. A million-dollar idea."[3] Clearly, the PLP's narrative had already begun to articulate specific national symbols and gestures that the project would need to contextualize. Poison ivy, camping trips, and million-dollar ideas are not, and *cannot* be, innocent signifiers in this Canadian context of public funding accountability and performance measurement, especially in academia. Although these concepts have been naturalized in most people's minds, their meanings are not clear-cut. Those concepts do, however, capture the essence of any process of knowledge production, for in fact, the PLP started on the day I decided to temporarily free my only son and myself – the two men in the house – from the five women in our household – my three daughters, my wife, and my mother-in-law – to spend some manly time together in southern Ontario.

We drove along the Loyalist Parkway and ended up in Amherstburg, near Canada's southernmost point, on Lake Erie. From the patriots' fields and highways to the statues of celebrated Native warriors and pioneers, to the re-enactment of Fort Malden's musketeers assaulting an American position on Bois Blanc Island, I was exposing both my five-year-old son and myself to a portion of Canada's Grand History, which was loaded with symbolic signifiers. In places like these, the Canadian identity follows a naturalized geography that is both specific and unspoken. It is symbolically represented as that memory we need to keep. It is factual history, our Canadian history.

Yet in Amherstburg, another kind of Canadian history that I had until then only glimpsed was also opening up to me. I took Kenzo, my son, to the North American Black Historical Museum, on King Street in Amherstburg. There, we visited the museum's permanent collection of artefacts. In the church, seated on wooden benches, we watched a documentary about the Underground Railroad (UGR) showing how Blacks fled slavery in the United States. We bought souvenirs and books to enrich our knowledge of the UGR, which is part of the Canadian grand narrative, albeit on the margins. Among other things, the documentary explained how some poor Blacks from the US South found a safe haven in Upper Canada (now Ontario). It described the wonderful creativity of the community that helped these Black people. It talked about specific strategies these people used to cross the Canada–US border. And it talked about the North Star and the Underground Railroad as geographical metaphors that Blacks used in order to reach Canada. These stories, however, are not part of the Canadian grand narrative; rather, they cling its margins as minor episodes, perhaps because the people who experienced this portion of Canadian history do not have highways and statues named after them. They were poor, mostly nameless, and "of little account." They were erased symbols who could not be part of the national landscape. According to Denis Cosgrove, "landscape constitutes a discourse through which identifiable social groups historically have framed themselves and their relations with both the land and other human groups, and this discourse is related epistemically and technically to ways of seeing."[4] Delle's work on spatial dialectics maintains that humans possess a "social space" as a result of their relationships with other people and with the physical landscape.[5] Hence, the physical landscape can be used when analysing a culture within a historical framework.

However, as I will illustrate throughout this chapter, nowadays it is no longer enough to designate various points on the national landscape as showcases of Canada's cultural and historical diversity. As Marie Carter shows in chapter 9 of this book on the Dawn Settlement, our work must be bold and strategic if the totality of this cultural diversity, in all its complexity, is to be fully integrated into the local and national grand narrative.[6] Yet at the same time, any process of cultural integration that leads to a sense of national identity runs the risk of erasing cultural differences. Strategically, therefore, careful and thoughtful planning must be done, and a serious conversation must be held among those who have particular mandates for and interests in cultivating and enriching Canada's cultural and historical content. For example, national institutions such as Parks Canada, the Canadian Museum of Civilization, and the Historic Sites and Monuments Board of Canada[7] (to name but a few) should team up with communities to integrate heretofore invisible narratives into the national panorama. One goal for a project like this one is to build bridges between institutions and the peoples and communities that hold particular knowledge. On the academic side, we see this sort of strategy emerging in some of the chapters that new scholars have produced for this book. A good example is Claudine Bonner's chapter on Nina Mae Alexander, an unknown player in Canadian history whose life no longer exists in isolation; Bonner links of Alexander's story with those of other African Canadians and in doing so illustrates how a national history might be written.

While my son and I were travelling from Sandbanks to Amherstburg and back to Ottawa, we discussed what we had seen, what cultural geographers refer to as "material culture," that is, human-made material forms that frame specific historical and cultural discourses.[8]

This discourse is historical because it essentially re-enacts history by selecting particular artefacts and historical moments. Examples of this include the young men who play musketeers at Fort Malden and the young women who play their wives, cooking in a space that represents an eighteenth-century kitchen. This discourse is also cultural, in that the landscape on which this history is being re-enacted showcases specific traditional and homogenous cultural symbols that resist integration with *other* national markers. Culture, as Stuart Hall argues, is a site of struggles and is consequently political because people inevitably make sense of the world through cultural discourses that are narrated again and again and thereby become valued and naturalized in the national grand narrative.[9] While Kenzo, myself, and other Canadians and tourists were witnessing the musketeers' re-enactment at Fort Malden, we all learned about and made sense of a particular Canadian historical moment. That moment was portrayed with specific symbols and articulated specific values standing for the "Canadian thing"; it also challenged my contemporary understanding of Canada's multiculturalism and cultural diversity. Any effort to rearticulate such a representation – for example, to integrate Canadian Black Loyalists into the musketeers' forces – will not succeed without a struggle, that is, without encountering resistance from traditionalists. Traditions are not going to die out any time soon, even in our growing global landscape of consumption.[10] Traditions channel themselves through multiple exclusionary practices whose aim is to solidify the their own grand narrative. In this regard, museums, festivals, and other venues for cultural representation merely articulate traditional markers and symbols. Rarely do museums, national parks, and cultural festivals serve as windows for cultural complexity.

After Amherstburg, Kenzo and I started back to Ottawa. Our first stop was a campground north of Tilbury. During an after-dinner conversation around the fire with a neighbouring camper, the PLP was born when he told me, "You should visit the WISH Centre in Chatham – there's a sort of office called the Heritage Room."

We drove to Chatham the next morning with the idea of stopping for lunch and visiting the WISH Centre. We parked at 4th and King Streets, had lunch in the downtown mall, and walked from there to the WISH Centre. It was just after one o'clock, and I was thinking that Kenzo had had enough of me. He wanted to get home soon and tease his sisters, mom, and grandmom about his boy's adventure. He asked, "We will stay only a couple of minutes, won't we, daddy?" I promised, "Just two or three minutes, just time to see what is in there." I lied! Indeed, I had no control over what happened next. As we entered the little room dedicated to Black history in Chatham, a large banner above the display cupboards grabbed my attention. On it was inscribed, "Chatham: The Coloured Man's Paris." That sentence challenged not only my visual experience but also my critical faculties. I asked myself, "How could they write a statement like that?"

Kenzo and I spent the next three hours listening to Gwen Robinson, a local historian who helped preserve this Canadian heritage. All that time, she described to us the contribution that Black people had made to the local economy and to the cultural and social life of Chatham-Kent. And she told us "little-little" people's stories about the blacksmith, the doctor, the churches, the Freemasons, the links between Chatham and John Brown of Harpers Ferry, and on and on.[11] I learned that between 1840 and 1880 more than 28 per cent of Chatham's residents and most of those in the Dawn Settlement were of African descent (compared to around 21 per cent in Windsor and only 2.2 per cent in Toronto). Indeed, "in the decade before 1861, Chatham's Black community increased dramatically and during this ten-year period, Chatham was home to many Black doctors, along with many affluent community leaders and shopkeepers ... Many organizations were started and the churches grew significantly; the John Brown Convention was held in Chatham during this era."[12]

I learned that the Black abolitionist Samuel Ringgold Ward had described this region as the great moral lighthouse on the North American continent. Canada in the nineteenth century was viewed as morally and politically superior to its southern neighbour and as such became the logical destination for those who wished to leave the United States.[13] Indeed, Canada did offer a safe haven, especially to fugitive slaves. Unlike in the United States, "no loophole could be found in the Canadian law that would permit the rendition of a slave."[14] I learned that Chatham, Chatham Township, and Dresden drew people of diverse social, cultural, and economic backgrounds whose resources, education, and skills had a profound effect on the region's development and helped create extraordinary multicultural communities. This book is about their stories.

I concluded that the story of the UGR, which my son and I had been hearing throughout our journey in southern Ontario, was overly romanticized and did not tell all. The UGR was only dots in the official memory, a means of promoting Canada's reputation as a multiculturally open society. The stories Robinson told us that summer day in 2005 – and many other stories I have since uncovered – made it clear that the UGR was merely a signpost to a much more complex historiography that had yet to be explored.

In any process of knowledge mobilization, the known stories that together constitute big stories (i.e., a national grand narrative) are naturalized and elevated to the status of factual legitimacy. Thus, Canada's extraordinary heritage is seen as an ending rather than a beginning, and as something that – like the musketeers' narrative at Fort Malden – needs to be re-enacted over and over in order to solidify the national grand narrative. The prevailing Canadian grand narrative on the UGR continues to represent the Blacks of nineteenth-century Canada as "fugitives slaves," even though they had a profound effect on the abolitionist movement in the United States, on civil rights in modern Canada, and on the social, cultural, and economic development of many Canadian regions.[15] As Dorothy Williams argues, the history of her ancestors, like that of many other Black Canadians, has been literally deleted from the national landscape, even though Blacks were the sixth-largest population group when Canada became a nation in 1867.[16] In this book, Marie Carter reveals as much when she provides a "new lens with which to view the familiar" but deleted story William Whipper and his key role in founding the Dawn Settlement.

The Black population in nineteenth-century Canada was far from inconsequential; indeed, it was prominent. To illustrate this, when we read between the lines of S.G. Howe's 1863 report, *The Refugees From Slavery in Canada-West*, we learn that Ontario's Black people were hardworking, industrious, and thrifty (104), peaceful (97), and determined to educate themselves (77–8). This report, produced for the US Freedmen's Inquiry Commission, provides us with key questions related to our analysis: Why, in 1860, did the United States strike a commission to investigate the condition of Black people in Canada? And to what extent did the experience of Blacks in nineteenth-century Ontario serve as a model for community building? As Nina Reid-Maroney points out in chapter 3 of this book, Black settlements in Canada were important sites for not only civil rights activism in the mid-twentieth century, but also for social justice struggles long before, in eighteenth and nineteenth centuries. Twentieth-century "legal challenges to racial segregation in Chatham and Dresden" led to Ontario's passage of the Fair Accommodation Practices Act in 1954; they also stand as irrefutable proof that Black communities had by that time sunk deep roots in Ontario and throughout the country. These missing stories of Black people in Canadian history and their dispersed markers on the Canadian landscape have yet to be uncovered. That is why I later returned to Chatham on my own, but this time with a clear idea in mind: the Promised Land Project.

The Making of the *Promised Land Project*

It's commonly believed that the visual-spatial is more germane to the infantile and adolescent mind than to the mature intelligence. Whether such is indeed the case may be for the psychologist to decide. However it is easy to see how arguing from the ontogenetic to phylogenetic visualism may turn pedagogical principles into political programs.

Johannes Fabian (2001)

Robinson's talk at the WISH Centre and the statement on the banner in the Heritage Room haunted me. In fact, they became an obsession, a project. I wanted to know more about the Black community in

Chatham-Kent. It astonished me that in the 1850s, a woman named Mary Ann Shadd Cary owned a newspaper in Chatham, the *Provincial Freeman*, especially since most editors of Black newspapers at that time were wealthy, educated Black men.[17] The *Provincial Freeman* was Shadd Cary's instrument for advocating for the equality, integration, and self-education of Black people, not only in Canada but also in the United States.

While "Mary Ann was the editorial voice of the [*Provincial Freeman*] ... due to the anti-feminist views of the day, she used only her initials when writing."[18] In addition, she often "employed masculine language commonly used among Black activists" so that her views would not be belittled, given the male domination of the press at that time.[19] I became fascinated by Shadd Cary – I wondered how she had been able to break through the social and intellectual walls that had previously been breached only by men.[20]

Hello? – a little voice exclaimed inside me – *a Black lady, a newspaper editor, in the mid-nineteenth century, in Canada?* And I had received my Communication Studies PhD where? How much did my professors, who were so keen about human rights, human agency, and feminist thought, know about Mary Ann Shadd Cary? Would they appreciate this particular feminist-human agency: a Black woman in 1860s Canada West, editor-in-chief and owner of a newspaper? As a Black and a woman, she was not even viewed as a human being. Nineteenth-century society was *White* society, and any variance from this was outside the mainstream. As Jane Rhodes points out, Blacks were "disavowed" or "discounted" during the nineteenth century; only Whites were meaningful and valuable and had something to say.[21] Shadd Cary was considered a privileged Black because of her freeborn status; nevertheless, she was subject to "a racist social order in an era in which the question of African-American rights stood at the forefront of politics."[22] Her voice had been erased from any national dialogue – she could not vote like her White male counterparts; indeed, she had no rights at all.

Today, she is still on the margins of Canadian history. Sadly, she is never mentioned in journalism studies in Canada, nor is she referenced in books about women journalists in Canada, such as *Women Who Made the News (1880–1945)* and *News Worthy: The Lives of Media Women*.[23] "Hello," I asked myself, "how can this discovery become a pedagogical program? How much about Shadd Cary is in the official national narrative? How might we learn from her actions, which preached the intellectual emancipation of all Black people and their integration into

Canadian society – especially at this time of growing hopelessness that has driven some individuals in Toronto, and in Halifax and elsewhere in Canada, to call for segregated Black schools?" In January 2008, the Toronto District School Board – Toronto being the largest and most multiracial city in Canada and one of the most multicultural cities in the Western world – could not take it anymore; its members voted to create an Afrocentric school system.[24]

Canadian scholarship has long been viewed as liberal, open-minded, and non-ideological. But as Reid-Maroney argues in this book, the notion that Canada is a moral lighthouse hides national anxieties and has been used in ways that obscure rather than illuminate contributions of Black Canadians to Canadian nation building. This remains true in Canadian scholarship today. In Canada, as in most of the West, the same dominant ideologies frame not only *what* to know, but also *how* to know what you should know. In Communication Studies, this process of framing knowledge is known as agenda setting. Even the Cultural Studies perspective, which is presented as a tool for overcoming dominant ideologies, especially in studies of minorities, fails to be inclusive. Indeed, the Canadian university departments that claim to be producing new knowledge in Cultural Studies are located within (perhaps inescapable) dominant exclusive paradigms of knowledge – for example, the ideological process of *Whiteness-ing* knowledge. I learned nothing about Mary Ann Shadd Cary during my studies mainly because my professors could hardly be expected to talk about something to which they had not been exposed themselves. They were trapped in the Eurocentric framework of the university system. This suggests a failure in the domains of knowledge production in Canadian scholarship. In turn, this leads me to link the lack of knowledge of Black history to the current state of the Black community in Canada.

Delle suggests that histories can "say as much about present realities as they do about past societies." There is a causal law to be drawn from this.[25] For example, while Shadd Cary envisioned a Canadian society in which Blacks could successfully integrate themselves into various institutions, "few White Canadians were willing to allow their children to be educated alongside fugitives," and this hampered integration in the Canadian education system during the nineteenth century.[26] Similarly, the education system fails, even today, to bring together complex and challenging knowledge produced by all Canadians regarding the formation of a multicultural Canada. As demonstrated by my own experience, this national system reflects a grand narrative with which not all Canadians identify (especially Black students). The high failure rate among Black students in Canada today – the same failure rate that seems to legitimate a separate Afrocentrist school system – is a direct result of the failure of the Canada's education system to encourage intellectual integration.

Knowledge has colour, indeed! Knowledge is political, never neutral!

If Shadd Cary's life story was known and taught with the same vigour as those of courageous White Canadians, if all Canadian students were exposed to her actions as they have been exposed to other grand narratives, if they knew that she fought for emancipation, freedom, human rights, social integration, and more, Black Canadians would not feel as if they didn't belong in Canada. Black Canadian students would not be able to justify failure on the grounds that all the knowledge they were being taught was Eurocentric. The White students in my classroom would know about slavery in Canada and would later expose their own students to the history of slavery and civil rights here; they would know about Mary Ann Shadd Cary and many other now-faceless eighteenth-, nineteenth-, and twentieth-century Black intellectuals in the country. Indeed, they would learn not only that Shadd Cary developed specific strategies for combating the colonial and imperial mentalities that oppressed her fellow Blacks, using her newspaper and many other tools, but also that she was – and still is, to me at least – an exemplary model of feminism in mid-nineteenth-century Canada. Although subjected to what Prestage terms "dual oppression," Shadd Cary excelled in a world in which, as a Black woman, she had been doubly disenfranchised.[27] This, at least, should be presented in school textbooks.

This suggests a process for ensuring that Canada's symbols are recognized by all. The would be little need for the PLP if Canada's politics of knowledge mobilization had integrated all of the layers and symbols that might contribute to the national identity.

These were some of the my thoughts as I returned to Chatham. Indeed, they are my thoughts today. The experience of Blacks in Chatham-Kent promised me a multitude of questions about an unknown and uncelebrated Canadian history. One of my goals in returning to Chatham was to launch a discussion on these issues.

In 2007, after two years of phone calls, several meetings, and exchanges with Robinson about the Blacks of Chatham-Kent, the PLP arranged funding from the Social Sciences and Humanities Research Council of Canada through one of its strategic programs: the Community–University Research Alliance (CURA). Before the money came through, questions the PLP would ask had to be selected. This process was important, for it would determine the quality, quantity, and relevance of the knowledge the project would produce. Knowledge mobilization is discriminatory – indeed, it has to be, because it is so difficult to frame a complex research topic such as the historical amnesia about Black Canadian history without wielding a sharp knife. For example, I had to find people who, like Robinson, had information for the PLP to gather. Who was out there who could help compile and disseminate knowledge about Blacks in nineteenth-century Ontario, whether it was through memories, archives, or artefacts? And if such people existed, how could I convince them to share what they had with the PLP?

Robinson and I started to reflect on these questions, and we invited Marie Carter to join us. We three prepared the ground for a final team of sixteen community organizations and a dozen or more individuals, all of whom considered it important to explore and record the lost narratives of Black people in various settlements we had identified, from 1775 to the present. This research team spans provincial, national, and international boundaries and has the support of partners and collaborators in Canada, the United States, and Europe (see Figure 1.1). This project is a true example of articulation, in that one of its aims is bring to light the spatial and temporal linkages between cultures, nation-states, and geographies. My colleague Handel Kashope Wright came up with a term for this: "multiple trajectories." The broader PLP community we are investigating encompasses people who are "affectively" connected to Chatham, whether or not they have ever been to Chatham (and many have not).

Chatham in the mid-nineteenth century was a crossroads and headquarters for human rights activists, who were branded as outlaws or outcasts. Many did not stay long. When they left, it was for two principal reasons: (1) the impact of economic depression on small, Black-owned businesses, and (2) the American Civil War.

Even so, between 1850 and 1860, Chatham was the focal point of Black abolitionist militancy in North America, a place where many campaigns against slavery were planned. When the US Congress passed the Fugitive Slave Act in 1850, slave masters acquired the right to recover fugitive slaves and free slaves alike. As a consequence, many slaves fled to Canada to avoid slave catchers.[28] In addition, freedom fighters from all races came to Chatham to build an international effort to fight slavery and to work with early Black fugitives and settlers. Among them were Martin Delany, Mary Ann Shadd Cary, Austin Steward, Levi Coffin,

William Lloyd Garrison, John Brown, Josiah Henson, Osborne Anderson, Mary Anne (Whipper) Hollensworth, James C. Brown, and Frederick Douglass. "By crossing this divide on the Underground Railroad, African-Americans fled a nation that upheld chattel slavery for a land where the dread institution had become illegal."[29]

A group when faced with injustice must often collectivize itself politically and effect new patterns of consciousness.[30] The anti-slavery movement of the nineteenth century can be viewed in this light. African Americans who fled slavery did so autonomously, and this action on their part "can be characterized as self-liberation by flight in which the entire migration process was directed by the enslaved people themselves."[31] The same period saw the emergence of organizations for Black self-determination – for example, the True Band Societies, which were voluntary associations founded in 1854 with the mandate to improve social, economic, and intellectual conditions for Blacks in Canada.

The actions of these key figures helped shape contemporary Canadian politics and human rights as embodied in legislation such as the Canada Fair Employment Practices Act, the Fair Accommodation Practices Act of 1954, and, ultimately, the Canadian Charter of Rights and Freedoms. The Promised Land communities contributed directly to this progress, yet their efforts have been deleted in the national grand narrative and are rarely mentioned in textbooks.[32]

The PLP team assembled in the fall of 2006 and decided that the primary goal of its investigation would be to recover, document, analyse, and disseminate the fullness, interconnectedness, and significance of Black history in the Promised Land communities. This program is huge, and perhaps political, for the PLP's findings will also highlight the importance of the Promised Land communities as an unrecognized yet pivotal part of Canada's history. In particular, the team hopes to bring to light earlier models of multiculturalism by researching the connections between the Black communities of the Chatham area and other anti-slavery movements in the United States, Europe, and the rest of Canada. We want to understand how these national and international connections were forged, as well as how they survived and evolved over time. We also want to outline the ways in which such an assembly of forces, peoples, and cultures can inform our present-day discussions of multiculturalism and national community building. These continue to be the primary goals of the PLP.

Figure 1.1. Institutional partners and individual collaborators

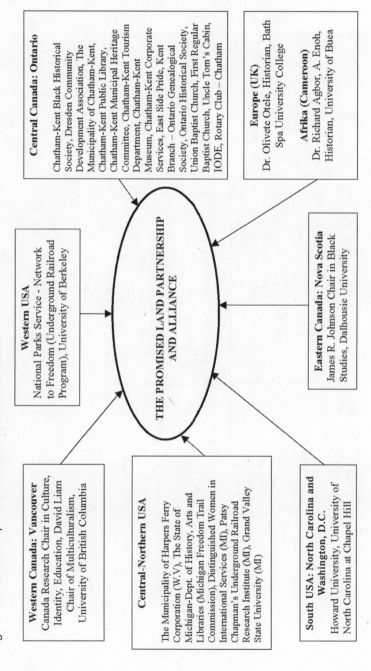

Central Canada: Ontario

Chatham-Kent Black Historical Society, Dresden Community Development Association, The Municipality of Chatham-Kent, Chatham-Kent Public Library, Chatham-Kent Municipal Heritage Committee, Chatham-Kent Tourism Department, Chatham-Kent Museum, Chatham-Kent Corporate Services, East Side Pride, Kent Branch – Ontario Genealogical Society, Ontario Historical Society, Union Baptist Church, First Regular Baptist Church, Uncle Tom's Cabin, IODE, Rotary Club – Chatham

Europe (UK)
Dr. Olivete Otele, Historian, Bath Spa University College

Afrika (Cameroon)
Dr. Richard Agbor, A. Enoh, Historian, University of Buea

Western USA
National Parks Service - Network to Freedom (Underground Railroad Program), University of Berkeley

THE PROMISED LAND PARTNERSHIP AND ALLIANCE

Eastern Canada: Nova Scotia
James R. Johnson Chair in Black Studies, Dalhousie University

Western Canada: Vancouver
Canada Research Chair in Culture, Identity, Education, David Liam Chair of Multiculturalism, University of British Columbia

Central-Northern USA

The Municipality of Harpers Ferry Corporation (W.V), The State of Michigan-Dept. of History, Arts and Libraries (Michigan Freedom Trail Commission), Distinguished Women in International Services (MI), Patsy Chapman's Underground Railroad Research Institute (MI), Grand Valley State University (MI)

South USA: North Carolina and Washington, D.C.
Howard University, University of North Carolina at Chapel Hill

Figure 1.2. A sample of multiple trajectories

Central-Northern USA: Pennsylvania, Michigan, and Ohio

Jennie Johnson; James Henry Johnson, Hallie Quinn Brown, Merchant, the Hyers Family, Nathaniel Murray, Samuel Watson, Dr. Martin Delany, James Maddison Bell, W.H. Day, Mary Smith, Josiah Henson, Hiram Wilson, Whipper family (William, Alfred, Mary Ann, and Benjamin); John Brown....

Canada West and Central Canada

John Brown, Addison Smith, William Harvey, Dennis Hill, Rev. William Newman, J.C. Brown, Mary Smith, Josiah Henson, John Scoble, Thomas Hughes, Hiram Wilson, Jennie Johnson; James Henry Johnson, Hallie Quinn Brown Merchant, the Hyers Family, Nathaniel Murray, Samuel Watson, Dr. Martin Delany, James Maddison Bell, W.H. Day, Mary Smith, Whipper's family (William, Alfred, Mary Ann, and Benjamin). Rev. William King, J.B. Hollensworths' family, Dr. T.R. McInnes and family, Maddison Bailey, James and Cornelius Charity....

Western Canada

Maddison Bailey, Cornelius Charity, Dr. T.R. McInnes and family

FROM ONTARIO TO MULTIPLE TRAJECTORIES

Europe and Beyond (Great Britain, Africa, Caribbean)

Mary Branton Tule (South Africa and Liberia); George Cary (Haiti); William Newman (Jamaica); Dennis Hill, Rev. William Newman, Josiah Henson, John Scoble, Thomas Hughes, Martin Delaney and W.H. Day, James and Cornelius Charity (Caribbean and Africa)....

USA

North Carolina, Baltimore, Mississippi, and California

Samuel Davis, Issac D. Shadd, Mary Ann Shadd, J.B. Hollensworths (and family); Rev. William Newman, Mary Smith, Josiah Henson, John Brown, Sophia B. Jones, Mary Pleasant, Jesse Binga, James and Cornelius Charity....

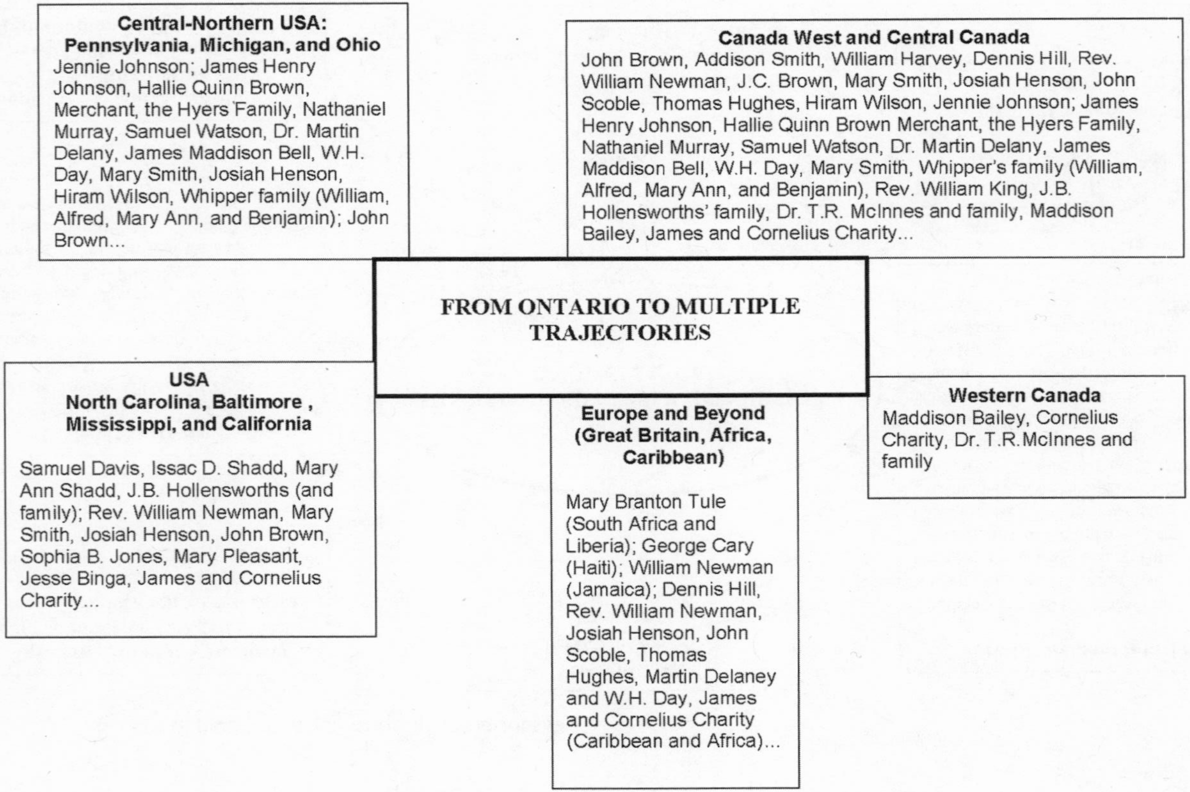

The Promised Land Project: A Political and Affective Research Program

The key challenges I have had to face as leader of this research program relate to (1) the political aspects of knowledge, and (2) the "affective" (and perhaps personal) links each individual on the team has with particular objects of the research. The first two sections of this chapter outlined several situations and models of questioning that lead to the production of particular kinds of knowledge. My analysis has suggested that knowledge is political, and the genealogy of this project indicates that the Canadian experience of cultural diversity is *profoundly* political.

My experience as the PLP's chair illustrates that any process of knowledge mobilization that involves a group of individuals needs to consider another important factor: affectivity. The production of collective knowledge is *political* because the process must first secure certain cultural authorities in time and space, in specific imagined territories and trajectories, before a solid research team can be formed. Furthermore, this production of knowledge is profoundly *affective* because it must accommodate the connections the actors involved in the project have with the objects of research. For example, I was affectively astonished by the invisibility of Mary Ann Shadd Cary in the Canadian grand narrative, and that astonishment compelled me to act. Delle has noted that "it is through human agency that material culture is given meaning, and through human agency that material culture in turn serves to create new meanings."[33] However, this sort of affective activism runs the risk of producing partial knowledge – in this case of Shadd Cary, the risk of focusing too strongly on her to the detriment of many other figures in the communities the PLP is examining. This threatens to render further invisible the work of many other unheralded individuals who were also creating a better society. And this is not all: the affective connections that individual PLP members and cultural authorities have with the research objects must be taken seriously. It is the cultural authorities who legitimate the symbols used to frame historical knowledge, in that they insist on a particular "language" for representing a precise geography of identity. For example, during the 2008 general meeting of our research team, one of the university collaborators reminded everyone that the names of the people we were about to start researching were not fictitious or conceptual: "We should remember that these people were made of blood and flesh." In other words, the legitimate affective connections between research collaborators and the objects of this project must be considered, and so also must be the language used when framing the project's findings. This approach to the objects of research provides the space for individuals to claim a particular cultural status, which I call "cultural authority."

That cultural authority is an articulation of many elements that affect the knowledge generated by a project like this one. These two factors – the politics of knowledge and individual affective connections with research objects – challenge CURA's goals and raise questions of structure, administration, and trust.

The PLP has not escaped structural struggles, despite the tremendous goodwill of all team members. Some of the questions we faced in our early years landed on me like a tsunami. I had to make tough choices in reconfiguring the research team, the administrative structure, and the dissemination strategy. Most of these problems were related to the researchers' affective connections. For example, the PLP protocol had been written in plain language with input from all members of the team, yet months later, some key members were still requesting special accommodations for cultural and affective reasons. The project spent its first year managing crises that ensued from this. There was nothing in CURA's assessment criteria to help us address these issues, and theories of knowledge mobilization provided little clear direction for managing diversity on teams. Finally, the PLP hired a community coordinator, someone who knew little about the project but who did know the community, and this ameliorated some tensions. This brought some stability to the team so that it could focus on research instead of individual interests.

It is worth noting that the external assessors and the CURA committee anticipated these challenges. They admired the PLP team, and one external assessor forecast that

> if the team is able to execute the project as planned, and with the evidence of careful planning done since the Letter of Intent was submitted ... the alliance will be a role model for those of us who would like to do similar project work. In fact, I think a reflective piece on their collaboration is missing from the dissemination plans. (External Assessor #3, CURA 2007 *Committee's commentary*)

Generating team spirit was the key challenge the PLP faced, and in the end, half the members did not participate to their full potential, with some choosing to abandon the project. Strong individuals do not necessarily make a strong team; affective connections with the research have a powerful impact on success. Knowledge is politics, and individual connections to the research are also political. This raises questions about the quality of the knowledge produced by a project like the PLP, given that knowledge is generated through tensions that must continually be revisited. Those tensions have an important impact on team cohesion and on the knowledge produced.

Individual connections to research objects – to people, physical spaces, cultural symbols, ideologies, and so on – affect the process of knowledge mobilization. This articulation between the geography of individual identity and the objects of research represents precisely the politics of knowledge.

The politics of knowledge are highly affective because the individuals involved in producing it have their own legitimate interests that must be accommodated, and because a complex project like the PLP inevitably starts with affective connections. For example, at my first working meeting with my close partners, I asked everyone to tell me where to begin: Should we should each pick *one* key figure and investigate how his or her actions could help us answer some of the research questions framed in the PLP protocol? Or should we begin with a historical time frame and focus on what occurred within it? Neither of these approaches is a "best" one; each is methodologically valid and relevant. That said, this question compels a focus on the "procedure" or the Foucauldian "dispositive" through which particular ideas can become valid objects of knowledge.

Valid knowledge is comprised of articulations, which underscores that "fabrication" is part of historical knowledge production. And valid knowledge is also affective, for in the case of the PLP, each individual team member was choosing a key figure or concept on which to focus. Based on this, I suggest that history cannot be written without taking into account the genealogy of affective articulation that constitutes knowledge production. Indeed, our understanding of Canadian history relies on these articulations, for history is inevitably a form of fabrication, in the sense – here – that each member of the PLP has an affective connection with the research object. Our knowledge of Canadian history or Black history in Canada will therefore always remain incomplete, because the process of articulation cannot but involve selecting, framing, connecting, producing, and reproducing subject matters that need not *belong together*.[34] As suggested earlier, this is more than a methodological positioning; it is also a political claim because it engages different epistemologies.

Nietzsche helps illustrate this process of knowledge production. His line of reasoning in *Genealogy of Morality* can be applied to the PLP's efforts to mobilize, write, produce, and disseminate a new Canadian history. For example, when I asked my research collaborators to tell me where to start, I was indicating that *all* histories entail a process of artic- ulation. For Nietzsche, the process of articulating or "manufacturating" history follows specific *historiographical* procedures, which ultimately involve at least six factors, with their own pre-existing political affects that must be considered:

(1) Individual politics or collective authors interested in a subject matter
(2) Research and selection of particular sources of data
(3) Interpretation of data
(4) Mediated reproduction (writing, audiovisual, etc.)
(5) Mobilization of particular aesthetics (style, bias, etc.)
(6) A reader or audience

These six seem to bring out the natural process through which all know- ledge is produced. As well, they seem to represent a natural genealogy that can guide our reproduction and understanding of Black Canadian history today, and of Canadian history as a whole. Nietzsche's philo- logical line of reasoning still seems impressively enlightening and con- temporary. In developing his theory of articulation, he argues that there are two facts to consider for any politics of knowledge. The first is that "primordial facts of all history" are linked to "the will of power" of the group of people who possess the ability to write a particular his- tory. The partners and collaborators I have invited to help me with this project cannot escape this. In inviting them, I have constituted a will of power that will allow certain kinds of voices and knowledge to be heard. Second, for Nietzsche, no historical fact can exist apart from an interpretation, just as no text can speak for itself. This points to the production/reproduction/consumption that is central to the PLP's dissemination practices. Nietzsche's early theory of articulation (i.e., the production and reproduction of knowledge, or, literally, the pro- cess that leads to producing historical facts, disseminating them, and consuming them – what I tentatively call the "the politics of knowl- edge") exemplifies the PLP's overall strategy of researching, writing, and disseminating its historical findings. In building and organizing this strategy, I was engaging my researchers to explore their individual affectivity. This articulation reflects what the PLP is really about and has helped us generate and disseminate a particular kind of knowledge in a variety of venues.

Individual members of the PLP are engaged in a variety of knowledge mobilization activities in the broader community, in schools at all levels, and in academia. Regarding this last venue, the PLP has benefited from the creation of the first academic book series in Canada to focus on the African diaspora, created and chaired by two PLP members.[35] This University of Toronto Press series, together with academic conferences and a permanent PLP website, are the windows through which PLP findings are being disseminated in the academic community.

Another strategy we have adopted is community/student-based historical performance. The PLP plans to team up one of its members who specializes in theatre with students in a classroom setting or with the broader community to research a particular key figure, write a script, and perform it. On the basis of that performance, the PLP will produce a mobile exposition or photo-documentary, which will be permanently displayed at Chatham and Dresden; also, documentaries and theatrical scripts will be posted on the project's website. As examples, the Readers Theatre[36] and Group Performance[37] have long been respected as approaches to understanding literature and history; their works are not traditional plays. In recent years, various community-based performances have helped promote community healing and public memory.[38] Clearly, performance is vital to communicating the PLP's findings to the community and to schools, and also for encouraging different generations within the community to engage with the PLP. In partnership with the Chatham-Kent Guild of Writers, we have formed a panel of volunteer judges from the wider community – most of them retired teachers – to coordinate the Freedom Experience Writer's Competition, a contest for high school students in Chatham-Kent. In addition, the PLP team has been helping some churches with lectures, archival days, and re-enactments. One of these, on 4 October 2009, celebrated the founding of the church of the noted abolitionist the Reverend Thomas Hughes with a dramatic performance and a special service presided over by the Bishop of Huron. At the end of 2012, this disseminating strategy was crowned by an online presence using the Arc-Gis geomapping technology as a platform. Indeed, the PLP has made heavy use IT: students and the research team have established a website, which includes a permanent wiki-style geomapping database (visit http://plp.uOttawa.ca). The PLP has also resorted to documentary films, radio and television programs, books, and magazine articles to reach as many people as possible.

Conclusion

My goal in this chapter has been to use the PLP as pretext for discussing the process and strategy of historical knowledge production and the politics of knowledge in the context of the Canadian multicultural landscape. I began this discussion by outlining the project's genealogy as well as my own experience with Black Canadian history. I argued that this particular Canadian history requires several concrete actions as well as a long-term strategic plan that will make it a viable national object of knowledge. I also argued that within the community/university alliance, knowledge mobilization faces unique challenges that require us to reimagine the structural procedures and interventions necessary to secure valuable knowledge. I suggested that the PLP has done much more than present a revisionist account of the Underground Railroad or of Canadian history. Rather, the PLP is working to end Canada's amnesia about Canadian Black history by exploring, representing, and disseminating it.

There is still a lot of history to be found today in the basements of Chatham-Kent's houses and churches and in people's hearts. There is a great deal of history that has yet to be told, but most of it is embedded in people's memories and experiences – sometimes conflicting – and will never be brought to light. A project like this one can, however, pick up bits and pieces here and there and assemble them into coherent truths. Indeed, the PLP can illuminate a great deal. Through this project, we now know that the Promised Land communities were connected to the politics of race and freedom across the Atlantic world and that Chatham was the centre of multiple trajectories of Blackness. And this Black experience did not start or end in southern Ontario; rather, it began with the people who came together in the Promised Land communities, where new models of interracial cooperation were developed; those ideas were then disseminated to multiple Canadian, American, Caribbean, and other international locations. So in many respects, the Promised Land communities are true examples of "transgeographical practices of belonging."[39] That is, these locations were rhyzomic in terms of their links with other locations. Our limited sense of brotherhood, race, class, time, and space cannot really express the complex affective connections that have forged the communities in Chatham. That is why the PLP's main goal has been to learn from those communities and to understand how they generated their own geography of identity through multiple national and transnational trajectories. Our goal has also been to use the new knowledge we have generated to frame current discussions of ethnoracial identity, social justice, migration, and Canadian multiculturalism. This work is political in that it is attempting to integrate new cultural symbols into the naturalized geographies of identity that currently constitute our knowledge of Canadian history, thereby reconfiguring that history.

This is the main intervention that the PLP's researchers have conducted. And it has produced new information, as well as tools such as permanent websites, lectures, books, and book chapters; all of this has contributed to a paradigm shift vis-à-vis the history of the Promised Land communities. This intervention in Canadian history has moved Black identity from the margins to the centre, from speculative possibility to certainty. It has allowed Black Canadians to integrate themselves on library shelves without resistance, from kindergartens to universities to Parliament Hill, and around the world. The PLP, in other words, has helped release Canada's hidden memory.

NOTES

1 Osborne, "Landscapes, Memory, Monuments, and the Commemoration," 39–40.
2 Here, I explicitly use "Canadianicity," not *Canadianness* or *Canadianity*, to highlight that Canadian identity (like many other national and cultural identities) is a notional process; it is not fixed and sealed for eternity. I have extensively demonstrated this process of identity formation – for example, in *Mapping Alternative Expressions of Blackness in Cinema*, and in "Transgeographical Practices of Marronage in Some African Films" – by coining the word "Africanicity" and showing how different this notion is from previous articulations of "Africanity" and "Africanness."
3 See the Dec. 2007 scan-copy of the *Ottawa Citizen*, http://lamacs.arts .uottawa.ca/lamacs_in_the_news.htm (accessed 18 December 2013).
4 Cited in Osborne, "Landscapes, Memory, Monuments," 47.
5 Delle, *An Archaeology of Social Space*, 39.

6 With her contribution on William Whipper, Marie Carter reminds us of the marginalizing of Whipper and the centralizing of Josiah Henson as the founding father of Dresden, even though both men were anti-slavery activists and were equally active on the UGRR.

7 Particularly in Ontario, this kind of work is now being carried out by several historical groups and individuals, whose goals include locating historical sites, producing scholarly materials, and organizing disseminating practices such as expositions and theatre performances. See, for example, Shadd et al., *The Underground Railroad*.

8 Delle, *An Archaeology of Social Space*, 37.

9 Hall, "The Culture Gap."

10 See Ebanda de B'béri, "Transgeographical Practices."

11 John Brown was a White anti-slavery crusader who was hanged in 1859 after leading an abolitionist raid on the US federal arsenal at Harpers Ferry, Virginia (now West Virginia).

12 Robinson and Robinson, *Seek the Truth*, 3.

13 Olbey, "Unfolded Hands." On Samuel R. Ward, see Nina Reid-Maroney in this collection.

14 Fred Landon, "The Negro Migration to Canada," 36.

15 Quamina, *All Things Considered*. See also the works of Robin Winks and James Walker, listed in the bibliography.

16 Dorothy Williams, in *Looking for My Pygmalion: Memoires*, dir. Boulou Ebanda de B'béri, Globe des Arts / Orphelin Films, Montreal, 2001.

17 Jun, "Black Orientalism," 1054; Yee, "Finding a Place." See also Peter Dalleo's account of the Shadd family in chapter 8 of this book.

18 Robinson, *Seek the Truth*, 106.

19 Yee, "Finding a Place," 5.

20 Jensen, "Not Only Ours but Others," 17.

21 Rhodes, "The Contestation over National Identity," 176.

22 Faires, "Going Across the River," 119.

23 These two books deal with the history of women and the media, or women in journalism or newsmakers.

24 See Robert Dei's interview in the University of Toronto Magazine http://www.magazine.utoronto.ca/leading-edge/afrocentric-schools/ (accessed on 18 December 2013). On the same topic, you may also consult the CBC, "The 1st Afrocentric School Set to Open," accessed on 18 December 2013 at http://www.cbc.ca/news/canada/toronto/toronto-s-1st-africentric-school-set-to-open-1.809455.

25 Delle, *An Archaeology of Social Space*, 5.

26 Olbey, "Unfolded Hands," 163.

27 Prestage, "In Quest of African American Political Woman," 90.
28 Lechner, "Black Abolitionist Response."
29 Faires, "Going Across the River," 119.
30 Everitt, "Public Opinion and Social Movements," 748.
31 Schwalm, "'Overrun with Free Negroes,'" 158.
32 Hundey, *Canada: Builders of the Nation*; Martinello, *Call Us Canadians*; Apple, *Ideology and Curriculum*; Poole, *And Nobody Wondered and Nobody Understood*.
33 Delle, *An Archaeology of Social Space*, 6.
34 See Hall, "The Culture Gap."
35 Visit the Promised Land Project and the African and Diasporic Cultural Studies links on http://lamacs.arts.uottawa.ca. See also the following permanent websites with links dedicated to this project: http://plp.uottawa.ca and http://www.lamacs.uottawa.ca.
36 Coger and White, *Readers Theatre Handbook*.
37 Long, Hudson, and Jeffrey, *Group Performance of Literature*.
38 Haedicke and Nellhaus, *Performing Democracy*.
39 Ebanda de B'béri, *Mapping Alternative Expressions of Blackness in Cinema*.

2 Multiculturality before Multiculturalism: Troubling History and Black Identity beyond the Last Stop on the Underground Railroad

HANDEL KASHOPE WRIGHT

Introduction: The Promised Land as Historically and Geographically Comprehensive, Open-Ended Project

By the media and perhaps even more importantly by the researchers and partners involved, the Promised Land Project (PLP) has often been loosely portrayed as a history project focusing on the Chatham area's nineteenth-century designation as "Dawn," as a "Promised Land" for the Blacks who settled there, as a Canadian terminus of the Underground Railroad, with an emphasis on the biographies of the Black people involved.[1] That is, the PLP has been viewed as a Black history project focused on Chatham and environs, the purpose of which has been to snap a missing piece into the jigsaw puzzle of Canadian history by articulating an aspect of Black history. This contribution to Black Studies would thus trouble "official" Canadian history for another of its exclusions.

All of this is accurate enough. However, this snapshot of the PLP elides its expanded, almost open-ended spatial and temporal scope. For example, it is more accurate to describe the PLP as primarily but not exclusively a history project. The PLP is concerned not only with those early-nineteenth-century settlers but also with the lives and accomplishments of their twentieth-century descendants; not only with producing a specific history but also with addressing the implications of that history for historical, contemporary, and future identity categories and for the national project in general and sociocultural diversity in particular, a diversity that is still being generated, engaged, and portrayed both locally in the Chatham area and farther afield, in Canada *and* the United States. In terms of (historical) geography, the

PLP began with a strong focus on Chatham, but partly because of sub-sequent interest in descendants and movements of figures of interest, and partly because of the fortuitous/planned location of some of its members,[2] it quickly spilled over into Kent County (see Marie Carter's chapters in this book – for example, for a discussion of Dresden as part of the Dawn Settlement) and then into Ontario as a whole and on to the United States and to other areas of Canada, from Nova Scotia to British Columbia, and then much farther, to West Africa, the Caribbean, and the United Kingdom (see Olivette Otele's chapter in this book on governance, trade, and religious links between Upper Canada and England and, in particular, on the role of Blacks in these links).[3] Finally, in terms of the combination of history and geography, at least one aspect of the project – that one that explores the Black presence in British Columbia – has examined early Black settlement right up to present-day Blackness. And in terms of its subjects, the PLP is about Black lives and the emergence of the Black presence in Canada, but it is simultaneously and indeed inextricably also about the history of racism in Canada, about what Samuel Ringgold Ward referred to at the time as "Canada's Negro hate" (see Reid-Maroney's chapter in this book about history and historiography in the Promised Land). As I shall argue later, the PLP could be said to be about other histories as well, including the history of interracial relationships, multiracial subjectivity, and the making of a multicultural local and national community, even though these, understandably, remain tantalizingly underexplored by the PLP.

Thus, as it evolved, the PLP refused to be contained within its initially identified parameters in terms of spatiality and temporality and, in turn, its subjects and focus. In this chapter I reiterate this expansiveness and open-endedness as a significant characteristic of the PLP and account for the evolution of this characteristic and my own role in some of these developments. I also discuss not so much findings but rather some rereadings and implications of and projections from the expanded, open-ended PLP. More specifically, following this introduction, I address my own role as an example of how the locations, interests, and areas of specialization of the project's researchers contributed to the PLP's temporal and spatial expansiveness and provided a concrete illustration of that expansiveness and the production of conceptual frames that have made the PLP meaningful and viable. I then undertake what I hope is a productive troubling of two core aspects of the PLP, which normally would be taken for granted – namely, the type of history we conduct (from naive realism to social history) and the racial identity of the project's subjects (from Blackness to mixedracedness). I undertake these rereadings to further illustrate the expansiveness of the PLP, a characteristic that was almost inevitable given that some figures, including the principal investigator, Boulou Ebanda de B'béri, and myself are not historians but Cultural Studies scholars who therefore lean towards interdisciplinary work and to more open-ended projects.[4] In sum, this chapter is meant to be an alternative introduction to the PLP, one that points to characteristics, approaches, contributions, rereadings, roads not taken, and potential future directions that are not highlighted or in some cases are not readily apparent in the present collection.[5]

A Non-Historian's Contributions to a (Primarily) History Project

I am a cultural studies and education scholar who is strongly aware of the crucial importance of history for various projects, and as an interdisciplinary education scholar, I have both conducted historical research and engaged history and historiography.[6] Given that the PLP is principally a history project, I do play hard at being a historian within the project. I mean this in several senses. First, I play the traditional role of historian by conducting research on early Black settlers in British Columbia and supervising and collaborating with three doctoral students undertaking this work with me at the University of British Columbia. The results of our individual and collective work have been several essay-biographies of noteworthy Black settlers in British Columbia (with an emphasis on women and feminist struggles) and overviews of the community making of Black settlers in BC (with an emphasis on interactions with other races and the evidence of what I am calling pre-multiculturalism, or multiculturality before multiculturalism). Some of these essays have been presented at conferences, and some will be included (together with selected presentations from a two-day conference I organized on Black British Columbia in April 2012) in a book I am co-editing with Afua Cooper (Cooper is author of the introduction to this book).[7] Even as I undertake this work, however, I still consider myself an ardent *student* of history and historical methods and, importantly and more specifically, a student of the "real" historians involved in the project (who have much more expertise and who have undoubtedly produced more fine-grained history than I have produced or could produce).

My primary commitment is not to history as such; nor is it to histo-riography; rather, it is to the politics of historicizing and the way that history is linked to, informs, and troubles the present. The two-day conference I organized in April 2012 as part of my contribution to the PLP reflected this fascination with the links between past and present. Titled Black British Columbians: Race, Space, and Historical Politics of Difference at the US/Canada Border, this conference brought together community and academic historians as well as education scholars and university students. The specific topics of the papers presented on his-torical and contemporary Blackness in BC (and the US Pacific North-west) ranged from an autobiographical essay about growing up Black in Seattle in the 1960s to the current work of a student organization on raising awareness at UBC regarding issues facing the African continent and students of African descent in Vancouver; from the lives and works of pioneer Black women settlers in the British Northwest to the politics of identity, group solidarity, and factionalism among contemporary Af-rican Canadians in BC; and from putting Blacks' experiences in early BC and Western Canada in perspective to the erasure of Black presence in historical and contemporary accounts of the province. In short, while history played a strong role, the overall goal of the conference was to cover both past and present and to illustrate what we might refer to as a "continuity of Blackness" in BC.[8] Interestingly, continuity proved elusive, since a key point emerging from the conference was that little systematic literature had been produced on Black lives in and contribu-tions to BC between history texts on pioneer Black settlers and socio-logical interest in recent immigrants and refugees from Africa.[9] Part of what the forthcoming edited text attempts to address or at least high-light is precisely this chasm in the literature, this "absent presence" of Blackness between nineteenth-century and present-day BC.[10]

I am a researcher who is not invested in the construction of a co-herent, comprehensive history but rather in the awkward and odd pieces of data that trouble coherence, whether those data invoke the official account, which has largely excluded the figures and contribu-tions of the people we are studying in the PLP, or the new one the PLP is putting forward. In a sense, my approach involves replicating the PLP itself in relation to Canadian history, albeit to alternative or at least adjacent ends. As Reid-Maroney points out in chapter 3 of this book, much of the PLP's work has involved literally piecing together Black history and the Black historical geography of Dawn and the Promised Land from scraps from primary sources – photos, surveys, newspaper articles – and from brief or longer passages in secondary sources. Even as these scraps were pieced together to carefully map specific locations where Black individuals and families lived and businesses were established in the Chatham area, my attention was drawn to other scraps that told of individuals and families moving back to the United States or away to other parts of Canada or overseas; while many of my colleagues focused on interpreting the presence of Blacks of various hues in the area and marriages among them and between them and Whites and Aboriginals as proof of Blackness taking root in Canada, I as a scholar interested in multiraciality/mixedracedness reinterpreted these data as the history of racial mixing, multiracial subjectivity, and early multicultural community making – alternative perspectives that on the one hand pointed to the possibility of other histories in the PLP project and on the other contributed historical substance to areas of interest I had hitherto conceived in hegemonically presentist terms.

In short, in the PLP I am the insider/outsider who, when not playing the role of primary historian and supervisor of others' historical research (in the BC aspect of the PLP), is content to play (in a serious way) with odd findings, the chaff data (from the Chatham side of things), convinced that they too tell a story or, better yet, tell other stories or trouble the narrative we are busy constructing. While I realize that veracity and rigour are crucial in historical research and writing, I am drawn even more to discerning purpose and engaging the overt and covert politics of the historical account, and I focus much of my effort on doing so. When it comes to the project's primary work – the work on the Chatham area – I am the marginal researcher who engages in Barthesian *juissance*[11] or the joyful yet serious and, hopefully, productive play that refuses the traditional, "disciplined" reader subject position and instead repeatedly approaches the data as "writerly" texts – an approach that is multi/inter/antidisciplinary and that contributes not to the construction of a coherent historical narrative but rather to multiplying and troubling histories and perspectives on contemporary issues and to keeping the project open-ended and self-reflexive.

When I am not conducting and supervising research on the BC aspects of the PLP, I am engaged with developments in the research on Chatham and environs. My role does not involve conducting original research on Chatham (this is already being done most ably by the community and academic historians based in the area and specializing in it). Rather, my interest is variously in using bits of data they produce that they might consider marginal to trouble coherence and meaning (both historical and contemporary); in exposing the taken-for-granted politics of our work; in not drawing hard and fast conclusions (about origins or contemporary states); and in discerning to what alternative histories other than Black history the data might be contributing. More specifically, I am interested in how the PLP as a whole might give the lie to the curiously taken-for-granted presentist and futuristic conceptions of notions I work with such as cosmopolitanism, transnationalism, multiculturalism, and mixedracedness or multiraciality. I am also interested in troubling the premises and building blocks of these concepts and indeed of the PLP itself – namely, categories such as Blackness and Whiteness, the nation-state, and community. Finally, while I endorse our overall perspective that this is an important project that needs to be undertaken to tell a scandalously missing story of Black Canadian (and American) history, I also have a strong interest in the politics and purpose of history and historiography – in our motives for undertaking this history project, the use we are putting it to, and how we engage in this exercise in revisionist history and to what end.

What Manner of History Is This? Beyond Naive Realism in the PLP

When we launched the PLP, we decided that community historians in the Chatham area would take the lead in the primary substantive work – namely, the development of Black family histories, starting with certain prominent families. These historians decided on the Jones (A.B. "Gunsmith" Jones's line) and the Whippers (William Whipper's line) as initial family case studies.[12] Note that we generated a long list of figures to explore, since the idea was not to select only a few figures who were particularly outstanding in their intellect and/or accomplishments. Boulou Ebanda de B'béri points out in chapter 1 that he resists fetishizing highly accomplished figures such as Mary Ann Shadd Cary, for a focus on exemplary Black figures can only be double-edged, in the sense that it provides proof of extraordinary accomplishments even while keeping other, ordinary Black lives hidden from history (and, I would add, it contributes to racist, token-based representations of Blackness). Once we threw ourselves into the lives of various figures, the PLP veered towards becoming a genealogical study, a mere compilation of family histories. But at the same time, there was considerable interest in specific locations of the homes and businesses of the figures and families as well as in the contours and details of the Black settlements. Especially influential in generating this interest was community historian Marie Carter's argument that changes in geographic and political place names in the 1850s created lasting confusion over the Dawn Settlement's true nature and scope.[13] Largely because of her interventions, the PLP added historical geographical mapping as another approach.

Thus, the PLP developed a dual approach: family histories, and the mapping of Black homes and businesses. The focus was on the Chatham and Dawn Settlements in Ontario, and much of the early work involved identifying specific businesses and institutions in the Dawn Settlement (which suggested a one-place study). This combination of place study and family history is exactly the approach that Gwendolyn Robinson, that veritable living historical archive of Chatham, and a former PLP member, took in her 1989 book *Seek the Truth: A Story of Chatham's Black Community*. Ostensibly for the PLP, as for Robinson, the purpose of the project has been to correct (official) history by recovering and telling the neglected story of Chatham and the Dawn Settlement. This purpose emanates from a Black race-conscious politics, and the result is an unabashed anti-racist and Black-affirming project involving the representation and assertion of early Black presence in Canada, the insertion of Blackness into a Whitewashed history of Canada, a project that "speaks truth to power." The PLP project is about a past that has been sidestepped and buried, and its unearthing reflects what Khaled Hosseini says about the past in his novel *The Kite Runner*: "It's wrong what they say about the past, I've learned, about how you can bury it. Because the past claws its way out."[14] There is a comforting concreteness, correctness, straightforwardness, and justness to this conception that the PLP is helping the Black past claw its way out. We can characterize this as realism, indeed – and I intend this characterization to be a positive one – as naive realism.

Things are more complicated than this, however. The Promised Land Project has gone well beyond naive realism. First, in terms of spatiality, the project has proven to be decidedly expansive; it has been impossible to limit the study to one place. As we started to map it, we ascertained quickly that the PLP could not limit itself to the town of Chatham; it was going to spill over into nearby Dresden and rural Chatham Township. As it turned out, it started out far afield, in the United States (where the Underground Railroad originated) and from Chatham would later extend itself to other locations in Canada and the United States and even to South Africa, the Caribbean, and the British Isles. I introduced the notion of trajectories to the project as a way of capturing the movement of Blacks, radiating from the pivotal location of Chatham/Dawn to BC, Nova Scotia, the State of Washington, and so on (places to which PLP figures or their progeny migrated), and to England, South Africa, and the Caribbean (places where PLP figures travelled or that had influence on local developments, which points to what Reid-Maroney in chapter 6 calls "intellectual migrations").

Second, while we may have started off with family histories, we proceeded to add geomapping and to merge the two in a mutually informative way. This is an example of what Sherene Razack has described as the racial mapping process through which "place becomes race."[15] And while we could have simply reported our findings in traditional historical essays, we ended up producing a wide variety of texts. What could have stopped as a genealogical project, with the product being a neat collection of genealogies of Dawn and Chatham Township, has mushroomed into a global endeavour that challenges the received outlines and contents of the local. We have not restricted ourselves to traditional essays, such as the present collection and presentations at annual PLP symposiums and other national and international conferences; instead, we have produced a wide variety of "texts," including interviews (on radio and television as well as internal PLP interviews with one another to document the project);[16] dramatic scripts (with performances by students at local schools); write-ups of spoken-word poetic autobiographies of contemporary Black youth (in the BC contributions to the PLP); and websites, one of which offers a geomapping database.

In conducting different types of research and producing texts for a variety of audiences (academic, local, school and university, radio and television), factual work has been crucial. Some of us, though, myself included, have stressed that contexts are also important. Family historians and the descendants of the nineteenth-century figures at the heart of the project are excited about the specifics of names, spaces, places, movements, lineages, and so on, and throughout the project they have unearthed and enthusiastically shared their findings with one another or have asked for help from one another. Fine-grained archival work and carefully constructed and meticulously supported family histories have resulted from these efforts. Some of us have argued that this sort of factual work needs a context to give it meaning. In my case, I have been particularly interested in how we might read these family histories today and in what they are trying to tell us about contemporary times and the politics of engaging in their very construction.

Theodor Adorno, in *History and Freedom*, succinctly articulates the interrelatedness of fact and context when he asserts that "it would ... be just as foolish to demand of history that it should concentrate solely on the so-called context, the larger conditioning factors, as it would be for historiography to confine itself to the depiction of mere facts."[17] In this statement he goes beyond an earlier point he made that history is more than a collection of facts – it necessarily should have a context to be meaningful – and that historiography cannot be mere speculation and projection but needs facts to substantiate and ground it. He is warning us in the excerpt quoted that the exhortation to include the historiographical in history should not ironically reduce history to bad historiography, nor should the exhortation to include historical facts and data in historiography be allowed to reduce historiography to bad history. His point is that there is a dialectal, mediated relationship between fact and context, between history and historiography, between the universal and the particular, between the course of history and the individual.

My point, following Adorno, is that to be comprehensive, the PLP has required elements of both – that is, contextualized facts and factually informed historiography. The fact that we have ended up producing an online data bank, dramatic scripts and performances, educational narratives, conference presentations, theoretical chapters, and so on, aimed at a variety of audiences, is evidence that the project has taken on a multiplicity not only of forms but also of contexts, and thereby underscored the importance of the contextual.

Third, if we put these observations together (and, indeed, add others that I will make shortly), we find that the conceptualization of the PLP as a project of naive realism cannot be sustained. Rather than being limited to a specific location, it is characterized by potentially innumerable worldwide trajectories, only a few of which can be reasonably traced within the project. In terms of historiography, we have produced a neat collection of family histories that add missing pieces to the local history, thus providing representation and continuity, but this work has ended up being more complex. We have worked with a combination of genres that constitute a social and cultural history that is discontinuous and revisionist regarding not only the local but also national history. And as I will illustrate in the next sections, the very premises on which the search for truth in the project is based (Black identity, the nation-state, community) can all be shown, through alternative interpretations of the PLP data, to be distinctly unstable and contestable. In short, the Promised Land Project might have started out seeking *the* truth, but our findings could be said to reveal (or rather construct) several related and even competing truths. It could be said that the work has produced definitive meaning, but read otherwise, it could be said that the PLP illustrates that definitive meaning is elusive.[18] In fact, precisely *because* it is a Black identity politics project, it is on the one hand a project of representation, continuity, and meaning making, but on the other hand, always already what Eelco Runia describes as a project of "presence," a project of discontinuity, of "the unrepresented way the past is present in the present." As Runia puts it, "presence" is "being in touch" – literally or figuratively – with people, things, events, and feelings that made you into the person you are."[19] He goes on to say: "It is a desire to share in the awesome reality of people, things, events, and feelings, coupled to a vertiginous urge to taste the fact that awesomely real people, things, events, and feelings can awesomely suddenly cease to exist."[20] Surely there are few things like slavery that have made North American Blacks who we are. And surely there are few phenomena like the disappearance of a broad knowledge of the Promised Land communities (of the Black figures and families, buildings and businesses, entire settlements, lives lived, experiences and accomplishments, and those very strong feelings of connection to the past they evoke in us) to help us realize how crucial, concrete, awesome parts of "our" history can be lost.[21]

"Are You Light or Very Dark? ... Are You Dark or Very Light?" What Is This Black in the Presumed Black Promised Land Project?

In the title of this section I have combined two lines from Wole Soyinka's 1962 poem "Telephone Conversation" with a play on the title of an essay by Cultural Studies theorist Stuart Hall, "What Is This Black in Black Popular Culture?"[22] The PLP figures we are investigating have an assumed racial identity; furthermore, the project is underpinned by an assumed corresponding racial politics. It is Blackness: most of us researchers in the project are Black, and for us and "our people," this is a Black history project about documenting and celebrating Blackness: a resistant Blackness, a resilient Blackness, in short, a life-affirming and inspirational Blackness. At the same time, for many Whites of the day and even today and indeed for hegemonic mainstream Canadian history, this is about avoiding Blackness: a discomfiting Blackness, a threatening Blackness, a guilt-producing and defence-inducing Blackness, in short, a very troubling Blackness.

Thus, even if we take an essential Blackness as given, Blackness in this project is always already contested (as positive and negative). Indeed, the very category Black itself cannot be taken for granted. From the vantage of contemporary race and ethnic studies in general, and with the strong introduction of the notion that multiracial and multiethnic are distinct identity categories marking the contemporary discourse on identity politics,[23] it becomes interesting to trace examples of racial and ethnic mixing – of interracial marriages between Blacks and Whites and between Blacks and Aboriginals and between various Aboriginal ethnic groups both within and beyond Chatham and the Dawn Settlement. Using the American one-drop rule, we would continue to consider the resulting racially mixed people Black: mulattoes, quadroons, octoroons – those racist calculations of degrees of pollution of pure White blood. In many cases it might be difficult to trace these Black people, since some "light-skinned" descendants would have chosen to "pass" as White and therefore are lost to our present-day data on a Black settlement. Alternatively, however, we can move beyond the stark White/Black binary and begin to identity these people of both Black and White ancestry (and in some cases, Black and Aboriginal or indeed, Black, White, and Aboriginal) as biracial or multiracial, and see the PLP as offering an opportunity to begin documenting much earlier examples of those supposedly cutting-edge contemporary identity categories: biracial, multiracial, multiethnic, interracial.[24]

Robinson's book does not focus on interracial or interethnic marriage or multiracial identity; nevertheless, it provides several passing illustrations. She reports, for example, that "Rev. Thomas Pinckney, a Black missionary, married a White missionary woman (Elizabeth King from England)."[25] Thus, over strong opposition from local Whites, interracial relationships and marriages did take place, and the children of such unions, while they would have been considered Black, can also now be considered mixedraced or biracial. Presuming for the moment that both the bride and the groom were racially pure – however unlikely this was – the Pinckney–King union provides an example of the start of the process of racial mixing in the Chatham area – a mixing that would become compounded in succeeding generations.

Aware of my specific interest in multiraciality (and here is an example of historians sharing facts with each other), Marie Carter pointed out to me several other examples of interracial unions among Dawn and Dresden figures and their descendants on the various trajectories. She pointed out that the Whippers, Hollensworths, and Shadds were all mixedraced families.[26] To me this was quite significant and ironic, since these were three of the presumed Black families that we had selected to focus on as we launched this project of Black revisionist history. Carter provided me with another interesting tidbit when she mentioned that keeping my interest in multiraciality in mind had caused her to notice multiraciality she would otherwise have ignored or to which she might not have paid much attention:

> In particular, I'm finding that using Whipper's case study in this way would allow me to get at that curious case of the Spanish South American, who is married to the Black woman from the U.S. who end up here. I found a land record document the other day that lists him as Whipper's real estate lawyer … Most curious.

In another e-mail, she mentioned someone she thought I might be interested in interviewing:

> Incidentally, there is a man here that I would love you to chat with at some point … He grew up identifying himself as "Black," but has blue eyes and freckles and when he recently had genetic work done, found that he is primarily First Nations and European, with only a small percentage of African heritage. He's had an interesting struggle with identity his entire life, and eventually he had to break free of the community here where he was "known to be Black" to find himself.[27]

This last example shows how we have inherited and been limited by the old racist obsession with definitive, singular racial identities. This man was identified as Black and so self-identified as Black, even though he had blue eyes and freckles. In the stark dualism of race politics, the only alternative open to him would have been to identify or "pass" as White. His actual genetic make-up was more accurately one of multiraciality (predominantly White and Aboriginal but also Black). It is ironic that the racist obsession with racial purity and definitive, singular identity continues to be the basis on which the vast majority, including Blacks, self-identify racially and assign racial identity to others.

If Blackness and Whiteness are more complicated than we usually allow, it is tempting to retreat to considerations of Aboriginality, which presumably can be relied on for distinctiveness and even purity. In reality, identity is not so clearly essential here either. As most historical accounts do, we have tended in the PLP to assign an ethnic distinction to the local Native population (and contrast it with the supposedly distinct White and Black populations). Yet there are examples of considerable interethnic and even interracial mixing in the Native population. One example from *Seek the Truth*, namely Joseph Brant, is illustrative. This is how Robinson describes his parents: "His father was a full-blooded Mohawk Indian and his mother was at least half-blooded Indian." Robinson further observes that "around 1765, Joseph Brant married the daughter of an Oneida Indian chief and settled at Conajoharie ... His wife died in 1771 leaving him with the charge of a son and daughter. Brant had two subsequent marriages; the second was childless and the third produced seven children."[28] What we have in Brant, then, is someone we can identify not simply as Mohawk or even Native but as an always already multiracial and multiethnic person who went on to marry someone of yet another ethnicity and produce even more complexly multiracial/multiethnic children.

In sum, the very racial and ethnic categories we utilize generally and in the PLP are rather messy and far from discreet, and this has opened the project to other categories of difference, such as those relating to interracial relationships and multiracial and multiethnic subjectivity. Multiculturalism as a discursive and social policy response to sociocultural difference in the nation-state is relatively new (originating in Canada in the 1960s and first put forward by a national government – again in Canada in 1972 – by then Prime Minister Pierre Trudeau). And in a version of what Daniel Rosenberg and Susan Harding refer to as "nostalgia for the future," its focus is usually on a utopic future of diversity (read, for example, the *Vancouver Sun* on mixedraced unions and interracial children as a de facto future solution to the problem of racism).[29] However, what David Theo Goldberg describes as the multicultural condition (which I prefer to identify as multiculturality) – namely, various ethnicities and races living in close proximity or making up a strongly mixed community – is in fact a rather old phenomenon.[30] This fact appears to be conveniently forgotten in the highly presentist and futuristic emphasis of the discourse of multiculturalism and its alternatives.[31] The PLP is investigating the movement of Blacks into an area already complexly crisscrossed by both White (especially Scots-Irish) and Aboriginal occupants. Although they forged their own settlement, Dawn, others settled in rural areas (e.g., Chatham Township) that were more difficult to demarcate neatly into distinct ethnoracial communities. Also, whether they were relatively segregated or allowed to blend together, the Black, Native, and White communities intermingled and interacted to varying degrees and for various purposes. This constituted early multiculturality (well before multiculturalism), which was governed by practices, mores, and laws that constituted what I call pre-multiculturalism.

Conclusion: The Promised Land – Righteous Black History and Beyond

It is interesting how much like a fairy tale the American version of the Underground Railroad reads. In the same way that most fairy tales end with "and they lived happily ever after," American tales of the Underground Railroad end with the gist "and they went to Canada." The railroad metaphor in itself suggests Canada as a final destination, a last stop, a terminus. Canada is not simply an end point in these narratives; it is a *blissful* end point, "Freedom's Land," or – as we ourselves now call it, in biblical and providential terms – the Promised Land. The Dawn Settlement specifically was described as "the Black man's Paris."

But what happens after the last words in those fairy-tale lives supposedly lived happily ever after? Almost no fairy tale discusses that, but in the materialistic world of Hollywood sequels we have the irreverent *Shrek 2* and *Shrek 3* to tell us what life was like for Shrek and Fiona and Donkey and the Dragon beyond that magical kiss at the end. So, what happened to Blacks who came to Canada once they got off the train at that last stop on the Underground Railroad? Perhaps Americans can afford to construct Canada as a magical faraway land where enslaved Africans gained freedom and lived happily ever after, but surely it behooves Canadians to tell the story of what really happened to them once they arrived. In contributing to the telling of *that* story, the PLP is helping construct Canadian history, extend American history, and blur the boundaries between two supposedly distinct national histories. That is, it is helping reveal that things were much more complex: Dawn was Freedom's Land, yet it was also marked by what Sara Ahmed describes as the "stickiness" of emotion.[32] In other words, Dawn and Canada were simply two more locations where Blacks felt the too familiar fear, rage, sorrow, embarrassment, incredulity, and character-building or -defeating facts of marginalization, segregation, and racism all over again.

And for me, the smaller things, the odd passing details, also matter greatly. For example, in *Shrek*, the story is about the evolving relationship between Shrek and Fiona and how the awkwardness of their difference (he is an ogre, while she has a dual identity – beautiful princess by day and ogre by night) is resolved when Shrek's kiss firmly establishes her identity as an ogre and makes them a distinctly compatible couple. However, while everyone else paid attention to this romance, I was struck by the fleeting depiction of the female dragon's attraction to Donkey – an apparently doomed attraction since they were so completely divided by difference. My curiosity about this minor, indeed throwaway detail in *Shrek* was rewarded in *Shrek 3* when we learned that Donkey and the female dragon had become a couple, despite their differences, and had a brood of darling little donkey–dragon kids. Similarly, while the PLP is really about the big picture of the lives of Blacks (freedmen and freedwomen, escaped enslaved Blacks) who came together and established the Dawn Settlement, the little details of the intermarriages and multiracial descendants complicate the story and indeed tell alternative or additional stories/histories that we might otherwise miss.

In terms of historiography and the politics of history, I seize the privilege of being a naive non-historian to work against the grain: I refuse to fully embrace the construction of a new, corrected, coherent historical narrative; I act as a caution against substituting a new metanarrative of truth – even a Black one whose politics I endorse wholeheartedly – for an older and readily acknowledged racist, exclusionary narrative of truth. As we speak truth to power, I ask as a non-historian playing earnestly at being a historian, "What version of whose truth are we speaking, and who is speaking what truth to us?"

In terms of race politics in our historiography, I trouble Blackness and indeed racial and ethnic categories in general, not to undermine the Black politics of the PLP but to extend it. While this project can be conceptualized as a Black narrative and a Black intervention in the national history of Canada, it is also in many ways the history not just of Blacks but of various races and of how we are interconnected and at times have intermingled. For example, while binary White/Black and wrong/right views on history would call upon my BC team to work with the accepted mainstream history that asserts there was an early Black settlement on Salt Spring Island in the 1860s, and while Walker and Irby's revision would have us abandon this narrative as a White myth, I am excited by the "third way" that is opened up when we focus on an 1800s pre-multicultural community that included Blacks.[33]

In other words, the PLP is not one but several history projects. It is definitely a Black history project and in that sense adds to Canadian

Black history and Black Studies an important story that has already been valiantly partially told by local historians like Gwendolyn Robinson. It is also a story that has remained too long on the margins of Canadian grand narratives, as Ebanda de B'béri argues in this book. At the same time, by the very fact that it is Black history, it is also revisionist history that adds to and troubles local and national history (and helps reveal that official Canadian history is not to be seen as neutral and complete but rather as partial and White and contestable). We can also legitimately and simultaneously see the PLP as a project of multiraciality, multiethnicity, and transnationalism, one that troubles, extends, and complicates not only Canadian but also American history and indeed helps reveal the porousness of those imagined communities that are nation-states;[34] one that introduces an early practice of multiple and transnational identities; and one that, in a cautious and modest manner, speaks generally to the complexity and interconnected nature of the human condition.[35]

The Promised Land Project started *in medias res*. While in the introductory chapters to this book, Ebanda de B'béri, Reid-Maroney, and I speak of the start of the PLP, it is more accurate to say that the PLP proper started by taking up work that had already consumed many years for historians in Chatham and environs. Ostensibly, work on the PLP has now come to an end: the CURA grant is running out, and this book is one of the principal end products of our work, another marker of the project's end. However, with two other books in process, many trajectories yet to be discovered and followed, and innumerable stories of the lives of ordinary Black settlers in the Chatham area (and in Nova Scotia and BC) to be (re)told; with new data to be generated and multiple rereadings of existing data to be undertaken; with exciting alternative histories of interracial unions and multiracial subjectivity being unearthed; with spatiality, race, and place making to be explored; with gaps in Black continuity in BC and other places to be filled in; with the lessons that pre-multicultural communities have for contemporary multicultural Canadian local and national communities to be passed on; and so on, and so on, this feels like we are also ending *in medias res*. Perhaps this is only fitting. I asserted at the start of this chapter that the PLP is local, national, and global in scope; that it is primarily but not exclusively historical; and, importantly, that it has proven in many ways to be openended. I want to reiterate that and say in closing that given its scope and multiplying foci, the Promised Land Project is not complete and indeed cannot be completed.

NOTES

1 The full title of the PLP – The Promised Land: The Freedom Experience of
  Blacks in Chatham and Dawn Settlement – underscores this notion of a historical project about nineteenth-century Blacks in Chatham and environs.
  By the time a midterm report was submitted to the Social Sciences and
  Humanities Research Council in 2010, the project had been covered in nine
  local, national, and international radio and television interviews, including on CBC television, ISLAND 102.9 FM in the Bahamas, and Télévision
  Francophone de l'Ontario, as well as in sixteen newspapers and magazines
  in both English and French, including the *Michigan Citizen*, the *Chatham
  Daily News*, *La Rotonde*, *Le Droit*, and the *Ottawa Citizen*.
2 I indicate the location of members as fortuitous/planned because the locations and thus their effects were indeed fortuitous in some cases, while in
  others they were planned. For example, initial member David Divine and
  later Wanda Thomas-Bernard were both based in Halifax, Nova Scotia,
  while I was based in Vancouver, British Columbia; this meant that Black
  presence from the east coast to the west coast of Canada (sometimes with
  vague but tantalizing links to the Chatham area) cropped up repeatedly as
  a topic of discussion and potential area of investigation by the PLP. Once
  researchers ascertained that some Chatham-area Blacks had moved to or
  had connections as far-flung as South Africa and England, Olivette Otele of
  Bath, UK, an expert on British Black history, was invited to join the project
  (see Figure 1.1).
3 Peter Dalleo's chapter in this book perhaps best illustrates the far-flung
  international migrations and familial links that characterize the people and
  ideas involved in a project such as the PLP.
4 The ideas that Boulou Ebanda de B'béri and I share as Cultural Studies
  scholars engaging history – that history is not found but constructed, that
  the PLP is open-ended, and so on – are captured succinctly in the following
  quote from "The Politics of Knowledge: The PLP and/as Black Canadian (Social) History," a talk he gave in 2009 at UBC's Centre for Culture,
  Identity, and Education for the Black History Month Lecture Series. He
  declared: "My presentation [on the PLP] is fully illustrative of the work
  of theory in the process of selection, framing, production and reproduction of history. Indeed, coming from a Media and Cultural Studies field
  of investigation, I have learned that I can articulate a selection of objects
  within a particular frame of mediation to produce – at the end of this chain
  of linkage – invaluable knowledge; that is why I like to use the best tools of
  this field – audio and image – to make my presentation."

5 It should be mentioned that this collection is the first of three planned co-edited books from the PLP. The second will focus on historical gender issues in the Chatham area; the third will cover the historical and contemporary Black presence in BC.

6 For example, although I am not a curriculum historian, the journal *Curriculum Inquiry* nonetheless invited me as an interdisciplinary education and Cultural Studies scholar with a strong background in curriculum studies to respond to an essay by curriculum historian Peter Hlebowitsh, "Generational Ideas in Curriculum: A Historical Triangle," *Curriculum Inquiry* 35, no. 1 (2005): 73–87, in which the author argued for a radical revision of the history of the field based on links he had unearthed between three founding figures who constituted a "triangulation" of early curriculum thought. My approach in my response essay, "Does Hlebowitsh Improve on Curriculum History? Reading a Re-Reading for Its Political Purpose and Implications," *Curriculum Inquiry* 35, no. 1 (2005): 103–17, was not to argue facts and figures and the accuracy of quotes and references with the author. Rather, I chose to reread his rereading of the texts, tease out his ideological stance (and hence aspects of the received history he favoured and of those he was predisposed to be against), and ask, in effect, what purpose and whose ideological agenda his triangulation served and in turn what effect his newly triangulated history was likely to have on both our historicizing of the field and perhaps more importantly on the legitimacy (or otherwise) of the foundations of myriad contemporary stances on issues in curriculum studies. The approach I take in this chapter is similar to the one I take in the PLP and in my work in general. My concerns in the PLP are, variously, these: What sort of history are we undertaking/producing? What other histories does ours underscore or disrupt? And what are the links between the past we are producing and a present that not only is the vantage point from which we are constructing the past but also is in turn troubled by the very past we are producing?

7 Wright and Cooper, *Black British Columbians*.

8 For the idea of "Black continuity," I am drawing on the useful notion of "African continuity" developed and utilized in African Diaspora Studies; see, for example, Adetugbo, *African Continuities in the Diaspora*. However, instead of focusing on cultural survival across geographical (dis)location as in the original notion of African Diaspora, Black continuity emphasizes the very existence of Blackness, manifested through generations of ascendants and descendants in the same location.

9 For example, Gillian Creese's sociological studies, from her *Negotiating Belonging* (2005) to her latest, *The New African Diaspora in Vancouver* (2011), are

noteworthy contributions to the sparse literature on the lives of migrants from sub-Saharan Africa in Vancouver.

10 Because literature on the Black presence in BC from the Black pioneer settlers to recent immigrants is sparse, some contributions presented, such as Sherry Edmunds-Flett's "'There Ain't Nobody Going to Do It for You': The Work and Life Struggles of Black Working-Class Women in British Columbia, 1910s to 1930s," took on a particular significance at the two-day conference, as they will in the planned co-edited book.

11 Of the several interpretations and uses of the term *jouissance* (in psychoanalysis, philosophy, literary studies, etc.), I employ it here following the literary critic Roland Barthes, who in *The Pleasure of the Text* (Toronto: HarperCollins, 1975) uses the term to suggest that unlike "readerly" texts, which encourage enjoyment through *"plaisir"*(i.e., taking up the traditional reader role), "writerly" texts encourage *jouissance* – the rejection of the traditional reader subject position in favour of deriving more complex pleasure from reading, against the grain of literary (or in this case historical) codes.

12 While there was consensus about focusing on these two families, merely listing them does little to indicate the amount of research involved or the depth and breadth of knowledge that community historians displayed in undertaking this work. For example, for the town of Chatham alone, a list of some thirty-five figures was generated, any one of whom could have made for an interesting family history case study. Some examples: Nathaniel Murray owned a china shop on King Street West; Alfred M. Lafferty was a lawyer and a principal at Wilberforce Educational School; Henry Weaver was a store owner and alderman; Isaac Holden was a store owner and early alderman; Dr Amos Aray was a doctor; Henry Blue was a store owner; Cornelius Charity was a cabinetmaker and had a boot and shoe establishment on King Street East between Fourth and Fifth Streets; William Needham kept a store at King and Princess Streets; Stanton Hunton, who came from Virginia in the 1840s, was a businessman and built the Hunton Block; Sally Ainse purchased a huge tract of land extending from Lake St Clair to Chatham in the 1790s from her Indian brothers; Dr Anderson Abbott was an early coroner, a Civil War Veteran, and assistant editor of the *Missionary Messenger;* and James C. Brown came to Chatham in 1849 and was very active in bringing artisans there from the south, who were instrumental in building early structures.

13 Marie Carter develops those arguments in her contributions to this book. For example, the Whippers comprise a substantial part of her chapters.

14 Hosseini, *The Kite Runner,* 1.

15 Razack, ed., *Race, Space, and the Law.*

16 In my case I was interviewed on approaches to historicizing sociocultural difference in general as well as representations of travel and movement. I described how "trajectories" might help us conceptualize travel and movement and how multiculturalism (or, more specifically, what I was developing as notions of pre-multiculturalism, multiculturality before multiculturalism) might help us address difference and the making of communities marked by sociocultural diversity and how all of this could be linked to the contemporary project of making and maintaining a nation.

17 Adorno, *History and Freedom*.

18 One example of competing truths and elusive meaning is the Black colony on Salt Spring Island (off the southeastern coast of Vancouver Island). All members of the BC research team already "knew" of this Black colony, and we quickly decided it would be one of the examples of Black presence we would document and discuss in our BC contribution to the PLP. We easily found references to this colony, which was established in the 1860s. However, further research generated assertions that brought us up short. Charles Irby, in "The Black Settlers on Salt Spring Island in the Nineteenth Century," and Peggy Walker (quoted in Irby), assert that there was no such thing as an initial "Black settlement" on Salt Spring Island in the 1860s: it is simply a myth, albeit one that has become accepted as the truth. According to Walker and Irby, the first settlers on Salt Spring were seventeen in number; they came from Victoria, and only four were Black. Thus, even if all four Black individuals established holdings – and it is quite possible not all did – this hardly constituted a "Black colony." Irby, somewhat ironically, holds that the myth of the Black colony emerged because the narrative of settlement was first told from a White perspective, from which *any* number of Blacks would have been considered large and noteworthy. We were left with an interesting quandary: competing facts, competing truths. Should we go with the flow of received history and general folk knowledge, which asserts Blacks were the first to "settle" Salt Spring Island (leaving aside for a moment the problematic notion of settlement with respect to Aboriginal people who had always been there)? Or should we go with the revisionists, Walker and Irby, who dismiss this as myth and as an example of how racial perspective distorts even as it constructs history? Ironically, (White) mainstream history provides us here with one more example and proof of a quite consequential early Black presence, even while revisionist history illustrates that mainstream history is raced and that myth can solidify into history. Thus, we are robbed of a tale of substantial early Black presence, so that Salt Spring Island no longer holds special meaning for Black history in BC.

19 Runia, "Presence."

20 Runia, "Presence," 5.

21 My mention here of the loss of "our" history is a woefully inadequate reference to the strong and almost visceral connection (what Ebanda de B'beri refers to as the "affective connection" in his chapter in this collection) that various parties feel with the lives of the nineteenth-century Blacks. The contemporary "our" in this sense refers to the PLP researchers and Black people in the Chatham area, but it extends to *all* PLP researchers and to many members (of all races) of the communities in Chatham and environs.

22 Soyinka, "Telephone Conversation," 750; Hall, "What Is This 'Black' in Black Popular Culture?," 1.

23 Lawrence Hill, whose father was Black and mother White, both American immigrants to Ontario, has made a huge Canadian contribution to this international, multidisciplinary exploration of interracial relationships and mixed-raced identity. Those contributions have included essays – for example, "Zebra: Growing Up Black and White in Canada" – and several best-selling books, including novels (*Any Known Blood*) and non-fiction (*Black Berry, Sweet Juice*).

24 Others in the project have taken up my interest in reinterpreting the data from the PLP as also being about pre-multiculturalism and the history not just of Blackness but of multiraciality. This is evident in the title of Marie Carter's "The Dawn Settlement: Black Utopian Colony or Early Experiment in Multiculturalism," a contribution to the book that Afua Cooper and I are co-editing (which is primarily about historical and contemporary Black BC but includes one or two essays that link back to the PLP project in general, including to Chatham as the primary PLP site).

25 Robinson and Robinson, *Seek the Truth*.

26 See Marie Carter's account of the Whipper and Hollensworth families in this book's "William Whipper's *Lands along the Sydenham*."

27 Marie Carter, e-mail to the author, 17 September and 1 October 2007.

28 Robinson and Robinson, *Seek the Truth*, 9.

29 There have been several articles in the *Vancouver Sun* over the years that highlight Vancouver's multiraciality and multiculturality. One prominent example is a series of articles by Douglas Todd on ethnic enclaves ("Ethnic Enclaves Series: Visible Minorities, Lively Communities," 2 May 2012), which points to the rise of ethnic enclaves and the mixing of ethnicities that is producing a more tolerant and mixed Vancouver.

30 Goldberg, *Multiculturalism: A Critical Reader*.

31 Official multiculturalism has only been around since the 1970s, yet it has already been eschewed as passé by the EU countries as well as by several

Latin American countries (e.g., Bolivia and Mexico) in favour of intercul-
turalism. This has led to what I have referred to as a moment of danger for
multiculturalism; see my "Between Global Demise and National Complacent Hegemony."

32 Ahmed, *The Cultural Politics of Emotion.*

33 Irby asserts: "The early settlement of the Island created a mosaic of mixed
colors and nationalities. Pioneers who came to the Island were Black from
Victoria, colored from Hawaii, White from Australia, Canada, Great Britain, the United States and other countries." Irby, "The Black Settlers," 369.
Whether this initial "settlement" is considered Black, White, or multicultural, the idea of "settlers" and the impact on the Aboriginal population is
usually not discussed. Besides attempting to pinpoint the racial identity
of the supposedly initial "settlers," I have become interested in what the
arrival of non-Aboriginals on the island meant for the Hul'qumi'num
First Nations who had lived there for some five thousand years, and
who included the Cowichcan, Chemainus, and Saanich. See Kahn, *Salt
Spring: The Story of an Island,* on the process and politics of the making of
pre-multicultural community on Salt Spring Island.

34 Anderson, *Imagined Communities.*

35 For a detailed account of the PLP in relation to the complexities of historical method and contemporary historiography, see chapter 3 of this collection: N. Reid-Maroney, "History, Historiography, and the Promised
Land Project."

3 History, Historiography, and the Promised Land Project

"But scholars deserve no such extenuation ..."

Over a century and a half before the Promised Land project was conceptualized, African American and African Canadian abolitionists confronted some of the same historiographical questions that engage us now. Among the most perceptive of these people was Samuel Ringgold Ward, the self-emancipated author of *Autobiography of a Fugitive Negro* and founder of the *Provincial Freeman*.[1] In 1854, Ward travelled on the anti-slavery lecture circuit through Britain and worked on his autobiography, published the following year. Throughout his personal travels, which included his passage out of slavery, his journeys to free communities in Canada, and his tour through Britain and the West Indies and back to the United States, Ward was a prototype of the Promised Land figure who has drawn so much attention in the course of our research project. He reminds us of the importance of "trajectories," in Handel Wright's term, of movement in and out and through the Promised Land communities.[2] Ward's travels through the transatlantic community of anti-slavery work and his simultaneous act of writing about them are perhaps what explain his interest in the importance of narrative, the shape of history, and the claim that history creates and holds identity.

It is easy to imagine Ward turning to the problem of history from the immediate circumstances in which he found himself. He was addressing British audiences that, while sympathetic to his political cause, nonetheless expected him to explain himself. He also encountered a wider public that remained indifferent to anti-slavery agitation. In the eyes of the White English men and women who came to hear him,

Ward was an articulate and self-emancipated slave whose very presence in the lecture hall tested the limits of their most cherished ideas about the narrative of racial slavery. Ward's use of history in this context is even more interesting because he was travelling on the same lecture circuit that winter as Harriet Beecher Stowe. Some of his sense of the importance of history was surely informed by his understanding of the power of Stowe's fiction.

Towards the end of his account of his British tour, Ward turned explicitly to the problem of history and slavery:

> It is not to be denied that a history of the Negro race is unwritten; no, it is written in characters of blood! It is a very compact, succinct chronicle: it comprises but one word and its cognate – *slavery, slave trade*. There is the history of the Negro, at least for the last seven centuries, while what is said of him before that time is interspersed among the annals of other peoples. It would seem from this fact, at first sight, that those who know nothing of the Negro, except as they see him in slavery and in menial positions, are quite excusable. But scholars deserve no such extenuation.[3]

For me, Ward's insistence that scholars "deserve no such extenuation" speaks with the power of truth. More than 150 years after Ward's time, we are still trying to write African Canadian history in ways that recognize the cost of oppression and to balance that recognition with the awareness that slavery was neither the beginning nor the end of the story. This effort is all the more powerful in the writings of Ward, who knew the African Canadian landscape well, who travelled through the Promised Land communities in the 1840s and 1850s, and who contributed so much to the development of the Black Canadian press – in his own time, Ward was almost as well known as Frederick Douglass. It is all the more telling, then, that the call to write a sophisticated, nuanced, and complex history comes to us from Ward, an unforgettable figure whose own place in the history he both lived and wrote has been all but forgotten.

A second aspect of Ward's discussion of history relates directly to the objectives of the Promised Land Project. Having made the point that the history of slavery was inclined to overshadow all else, he went on to say that slavery had exacted another sort of historical price: the destruction of evidence. "Our condition," he noted with a modulated tone of bleak understatement, "is far from favourable for the furnishing of historical data. Scraps, patches, anecdotes – these are all that bear record of us." This observation, too, has a ring of familiarity for anyone who has read the PLP's objectives. More than 150 years later, we are still gathering scraps, patches, and anecdotes and reading them for interpretive patterns they might disclose, or conceal.

Elsewhere in his work, Ward provides us with two seemingly conflicting yet equally powerful images that have shaped much writing about the African Canadian past. The first is that of Canada as "the great moral lighthouse for Black people on this continent." Recent African Canadian historiography has taken great pains to dispel this description of a Canada that never was – indeed, the title of our project was chosen deliberately to join in questioning the easy conclusion that Canada was always morally superior on the question of slavery. The second is that of racial prejudice in Canada: "Canadian Negro hate," Ward wrote, was "incomparably meaner than the American article," strong enough to dim if not extinguish the great moral lighthouse.[4] Both of Ward's statements carried particular resonance for the "Promised Land" communities of Dresden and Chatham and their rural hinterlands. He was talking about *us*.

Beyond the local communities in which both images are rooted, the ideas Ward articulated about Canada circa 1854 have had a powerful effect across the sweep of Canada's national history. For Ward, both images of race in Canada were part of lived experience, a complex reality in which both could be true at the same time. Since his time, however, the extremes of "moral lighthouse" and "Canadian hate" have been used in such a heavy-handed way that they obscure rather than clarify the history of African Canadian freedom. This problem in historiography is not unique to Canada. A generation ago, in his now classic chapter on American history and the "master narrative," Nathan Huggins exposed the dangers of treating concepts of race, slavery, and freedom as though they were "frozen" in time.[5] In Canada, ideas about race, slavery, and freedom have been just as solidly frozen, albeit in distinctive patterns embedded in the historiography of national identity.

Each of these three questions raised in the writings of Samuel Ringgold Ward – the problem of contextualizing the history of slavery, the problem of sources, and the problem of interpretation with respect to Canada's national identity – is addressed in the PLP research. Given his demand that historians be held to account, what would Samuel Ringgold Ward make of the work we have done so far?

As Boulou Ebanda de B'béri noted in chapter 1 of this book, when the PLP began, we turned to the problem of "historical amnesia." Against the backdrop of the recent proliferation of studies of cultural memory, we defined historical amnesia in a way that draws attention to the conscious action that the passivity implied by the term can often mask. Forgetting, in this sense, is as much a sin of commission as a sin of omission. Afua Cooper writes of this in the *Hanging of Angelique* – of a Black past in Canada not just forgotten or buried, but bulldozed, except for those parts that can be celebrated.[6] In Cooper's book, the emphasis is on restoring the knowledge that there were slaves in Canada, that there was slave resistance to Canadian slavery, and that Canada during its colonial past was deeply implicated in the Atlantic slave trade. In the Promised Land communities, we faced a related problem: here, the African Canadian past was not absent, but its presence had taken the form of celebrating the heritage of the Underground Railroad. Here was the great moral lighthouse, brightly and boldly illuminating the historical landscape – a suitable metaphor for a presentist understanding of the past: monumental, monolithic, and blinding.

David Blight's recent work on the Underground Railroad in American history and memory makes a related point. In the public's appetite to make a vital connection to the Underground Railroad, Blight sees a "sometimes contentious battle between learning and lore" that goes to the heart of national guilt about slavery. In a land in which slavery is cast, in President Barack Obama's language, as America's original sin, narratives of redemption become all the more important. In Canada, we have relished the vantage point afforded by the moral high ground of the *Promised Land*, but the questions are still the same. We should ask, along with Blight, "Why do we need this story?," and "Why now?"[7]

In the case of the Promised Land communities, a kind of selective amnesia has robbed historical accounts of much of their complexity and power. Even now, we find ourselves, like Ward, having to crack through old assumptions that have been lifted straight from the moral and narrative universe of *Uncle Tom's Cabin* and layered over the events of the past. There are pockets of memory that are wide enough to accommodate particular figures, such as Josiah Henson, Harriet Tubman, and more recently, perhaps, Mary Ann Shadd and Henry and Mary Bibb.[8] Each of these important figures has somehow been made to stand for the whole. This kind of postage stamp approach to historical memory reveals a great deal about the packaging and consumption of history in the present, but little about the past.

The PLP has been informed by the opposite or corrective tendency to emphasize the reality of racial prejudice in Canada. Robin Winks's

The Blacks in Canada is shot through with this sense of disappointment in the Canadian experience. The book sets out to uncover and explode the "myth of the North Star," which Winks locates in a Canadian sense of moral superiority over Americans with regard to slavery. *The Blacks in Canada* deflated the scholarly version of the myth (its life in popular culture has been longer and stronger), but as James St G. Walker has pointed out, Winks's "depressing story" of Canadian racism has obscured Black history in other ways. "From a different perspective, one that emphasizes the positive achievements of Black Canadians in the face of overwhelming difficulties, it is not Black history, but the history of White racism, that is 'depressing.' Black history itself is nothing less than heroic." Other scholarship has clarified that racial prejudice in Canada has systemic and legal components that are much more difficult to address than the capricious de facto racism to which Ward was referring when he decried "Canadian Negro hate."[9]

All of this has particular relevance for the PLP because the Promised Land communities were important sites of civil rights activism in the mid-twentieth century. Legal challenges to racial segregation in Chatham and Dresden, mounted by the descendants of the men and women whom Ward knew in the 1850s, led directly.to the passage of the Fair Accommodation Practices Act by the Ontario legislature in 1954.[10] At the same time, it is worth remembering that our contemporary interest in exposing the "colour-coded" nature of Canadian legal history is tied to our present-day preoccupations. To the extent that they are linked to an emerging narrative of the "ugly Canadian," histories of racism in the Promised Land tiptoe along a fine line between corrective and polemic. That line reveals as much about our current national anxieties as it does about the African Canadian past.

Our initial manoeuvring between the more rigid explanatory frameworks led us to James Walker's call that Black agency be recognized through community history – one of the five "orientations" in African Canadian historiography that he identified in his 1997 article on Africville.[11] The recognition of Black agency as a first principle was also commended to us by our colleague, David Divine, former James Robinson Johnson Chair in Black Canadian Studies at Dalhousie and co-investigator on the PLP. The positioning of historical actors at the centre of study, defined in their own terms, was meant to counter the tendency, as Divine put it, to place Black historical subjects "like models on a catwalk, observed, commented upon, put upon from time to time, shaped and in part shaping, continuously on display."[12] The recognition of historical agency through nuanced community history made sense in theoretical terms; however, a new set of problems emerged when we turned to the communities at hand. The PLP opened the region's history to investigation by those not necessarily tied to local communities by proximity, racial identity, personal experience, or family connection; from this, it soon became evident that local history sometimes carries assumptions about proprietorship over historical materials. The issue was often simply trust, the lack of which was based on the very real and painful experience of racism in the Promised Land communities. The fear of appropriation was meant to guard family history, recollection, memory, and ancestral loyalties, but in the process it rendered vulnerable the very history it was meant to protect.

This was complicated by the nature of the project. The program architecture called for academic historians and community historians to work together in a community-university alliance; this was bound to run up against the sort of challenge described by David Lowenthal in *The Heritage Crusade and the Spoils of History*. Heritage and history, he argues, share an interest in the past but not the same purpose or practice. We do not have to accept his distinction between heritage and history uncritically to see that some aspects of the PLP have borne out his prediction that "the aims of these two enterprises, and their modes of persuasion are contrary to each other. To avoid confusion and unwarranted censure, it is vital to bear that opposition in mind."[13]

From the beginning of the project, we understood that the particularity of place mattered. For this reason, one of the first steps in the research involved historical geography – that is, the mapping of settlements based on original land records. The importance of place, and of settlement, was counterbalanced by the idea of movement, of setting the world of the Promised Land communities in motion. That is why Handel Wright's concept of trajectories suited the project so well, and indeed, this has turned out to be an important balance to maintain. Particular places, artefacts, and even people have become "sites of memory," to use Pierre Nora's term – places "where memory crystallizes and secretes itself."[14] As Nora argues, sites of memory protect memory from history. They are "moments of history torn away from the movement of history." The PLP has tried to respect the present value of those crystallized moments, even while working to reintroduce them somehow to the world beyond their protection.

If we think of meaning and memory in the Promised Land as collected in tidal pools, as rich in treasure but cut off from sea changes in

historical scholarship, it is not difficult to recognize that the interdisciplinary nature of the project introduced its own set of challenges. The
strength of the project is its interdisciplinary character, but that character also points to the ways in which historical *materials* are used, both
outside and within the academy, independent of recognizable historical
method. This is not necessarily a problem, but it does impose additional
pressures. In chapter 1, for example, Ebanda de B'béri's evocation of
Nietzsche's *Genealogy of Morality* to describe the manufacture of history
makes the point about the politics of knowledge. It also leaves us just a
breath away from catching the contagion described by Jacques Derrida
in "Archive Fever." This malady of the historian is a problem of vision.
Blinded by the unattainable goal of objectivity, dazzled by the mythic
notion of unassailable truths that lie waiting to be unearthed in the archive, the historian, Derrida argues, is left in a sad state. To suffer from
archive fever is "never to rest, interminably, for searching the archive
right when it slips away. It is to run after the archive, even if there is
too much of it, right where something in it anarchives itself."[15] Any
large project that begins with historical analysis may well seek to guard
against such an outcome, but it is also important to remember that
while historians deal in the dust, they also lift their heads from time to
time, long enough to know an epistemological crisis when they see one.
In some ways, the debates about history and the meaning of historical knowledge in the PLP signal African Canadian history's emergence
from the fiery trials of postmodernity in reasonably good shape –
critical, sceptical, and aware of the limitations as well as the power of
the knowledge the project can create.

Precisely because the PLP's historical work has been forced at times
into an almost hyperbolic state of self-awareness, we have been able to
open up new lines of inquiry, using the familiar in the Promised Land
communities as our starting point. By the time the project formally concluded in June 2012, the full scope of those new inquiries had begun to
emerge more clearly. The project focused attention on the experiences
of women as well as men. It produced intellectual as well as social history. It drew from the insights of genealogists and family historians, and
it connected particular people to broader demographic and ideological
patterns. It took up the study of political resistance, activism, religious
radicalism, and the wide North American and transatlantic networks
that made these pursuits possible. It extended itself into twentieth-century history, collected oral histories, and supported ground-breaking
comparative histories of Nova Scotia, British Columbia, and Ontario.

The PLP created new research databases and explored the multiplicity of ways in which that collected data might be interpreted. Although we did not initially call it a project of public history, it is to the emerging field of public history that the PLP has made some of its most valued contributions. Secondary school students, undergraduates, and graduate students were directly engaged in project research, and this sparked new pedagogy and new models for community-based research. Most significantly from the point of view of a practising historian, the project provided a framework – solid, complex, and utterly compelling in its construction – for integrating all of these themes in undergraduate classrooms.

"Approaching African-Canadian history," James Walker has written, "is a political act, deliberate or not. How you approach it will determine the lessons you derive from it. You can even shape the future." No one understood the political imperatives of historical consciousness more keenly than Samuel Ringgold Ward. To recall a history that was more than "that of the chain, the coffle gang, the slave ship, the middle passage, the plantation-hell!" was to imagine a future beyond these things. The chapters in this book highlight some of the historical work undertaken by the PLP; they are the first fruits of that process. Even more important than their particular conclusions, however, is the way in which they illustrate that the PLP has tried to open a vast repository of historical material to the light of historical imagination. There are risks as well as possibilities in this sort of exposure, but the historiography of the project draws us back to Ward's central tenet: history is important because it affirms our common humanity even as it describes particular identities, experiences, and oppressions. Small wonder that nineteenth-century historians of the Promised Land have linked the writing of history to liberation.[16] Lest we miss Ward's point that historical imagination has the power "to cheer, encourage and stimulate" – and, I would add, to assert the contingency of human experience – we have the echo of Ward's judgment that "scholars deserve no such extenuation" to call us to account.

NOTES

1 For biographical background on Samuel Ringgold Ward, see Ripley et al., *Black Abolitionist Papers* (*BAP*), vol. II, 292n7.
2 See Handel Kashope Wright's discussion of trajectories in "Multiculturality before Multiculturalism," in this book.

3 Ward, *Autobiography of a Fugitive Negro*, 269–70.
4 Ward to Henry Bibb and James Theodore Holly, October 1852, in Ripley, *BAP* II:224–8.
5 Huggins, "Deforming Mirror of Truth."
6 Cooper, *The Hanging of Angélique*.
7 Blight, *Passages to Freedom*.
8 Heike, in "Out of Chatham," places the Chatham community and the analysis of its history in a broader international context. This is a welcome addition to work on the familiar figures of Shadd, William King, and Martin Delany.
9 Walker and Thorvaldson, *Identity*, 3; Winks, *The Blacks in Canada*. See also Walker, *"Race," Rights, and the Law*; Backhouse, *Colour-Coded*; and Barrington Walker, *Race on Trial*. In an insightful assessment of African Canadian historiography, Carmen Poole argues that recent works drawing on feminist and labour history, while offering important new insights, have at the same time "effectively appropriated Canadian Black history in an effort to shed light on their specific concerns. Simply stated, Canadian Black history has been fractured before it ever had the opportunity to fully come into its own as a sub-discipline within the wider Canadian historiography" See Poole, "'And Nobody Wondered and Nobody Understood,'" 23. Many of these questions are addressed in Este, "Black Canadian Historical Writing, 1970–2006," 388–406.
10 The civil rights challenges to Dresden's segregated restaurants in the 1950s are chronicled in the documentary *Journey to Justice* (NFB, 2000). On the National Unity Association's civil rights work and the background to the installation of an Ontario Heritage Trust plaque in Dresden in June 2010, see James Walker, "Hugh Burnett and the National Unity Association" (http://www.heritagetrust.on.ca/CorporateSite/media/oht/PDFs/Hugh-Burnett-NUA-ENG.pdf).
11 Walker, "Allegories and Orientations in African-Canadian Historiography."
12 Divine, "Voices Waiting to Be Heard and Acknowledged."
13 David Lowenthal, "Preface," in *The Heritage Crusade and the Spoils of History*.
14 Nora, "Between Memory and History," 7.
15 Derrida and Prenowitz, "Archive Fever."
16 This is the central argument in Ernest, *Liberation Historiography*.

PART II

From Fragments through Biography
to History

4 William Whipper's *Lands along the Sydenham*

MARIE CARTER

In 2007, at the start of the Promised Land Project, Boulou Ebanda de B'béri asked us to begin our explorations of the freedom experiences of Chatham and the Dawn Settlement by choosing a single person we believed worthy of a case study. For me, William Whipper was the obvious choice from the perspective of Dresden. The 2003 project called the Trillium Trail Historical Walk had revealed the extent of Whipper's investment in land in Dresden, which was part of the Dawn Settlement.[1] His accomplishments were a largely unknown aspect of local history prior to that discovery. The discovery of Whipper provided a new lens through which to view the familiar story of the Dawn Settlement.

Up until 2003, the Reverend Josiah Henson was often the only African Canadian mentioned in local historical accounts; indeed, many academics investigated the Dawn Settlement almost exclusively from the perspective of his life. That year, discoveries made by the Trillium Trail Historical Walk Project changed this. The committee overseeing that project devoted nearly half its grant money to original research to ensure that the history it gave was based on the most accurate information available. That included primary source materials, especially land records. The committee and my husband and I, who had been hired to do the research and writing, concluded that for the trail to include the histories of women, Native people, and people of African descent, it would be essential to challenge the predominantly male and Eurocentric lens through which Dresden's community history had long been viewed. These individuals, we felt, must have accounted for most of the community's early population. The year we began, it was estimated that in Dresden's early years, 40 per cent of its people were of African descent (the actual percentage may in fact have been much

Figure 4.1. William Whipper was a prominent landowner in Dresden, Ontario, in an area along the Sydenham River popularly known as the Dawn Settlement.

higher). So it seemed logical to assume there were other people of African descent, besides Rev. Henson, who had made contributions that merited them an interpretive plaque on the Historic Walk. We set out to identify some who could be subjects of further research – perhaps an early minister or educator. In the end, we found evidence of a multitude of individuals who had been largely absent from previous historical accounts. In fact, our land-based approach to research revealed that most of the properties in our area of study along the Trillium Trail had been owned by African American investors between 1852 and 1874 and that one man in particular, William Whipper, could be counted a "founder" of the community for his investment in the town's development, economic and otherwise.[2] Whipper's presence as an investor and developer would call into question many well-worn "truths" about the Dawn Settlement and its founding. It would also lead to an exciting new understanding of the contributions of African Americans and African Canadians to our local history and, it followed, to the history of Canada. The initial discoveries resulted in three years of intensive work leading up to and including the Promised Land Project.

There is not enough space here to detail the full extent of our discoveries. I will, though, attempt to highlight our key findings about the Van Allen surveys (127 and 128) of Dresden. We have concluded from our research that these lands were what William Whipper referred to as his "lands along the Sydenham" in the account he provided to William Still, published in the latter's 1871 history *The Underground Rail Road*.[3]

It is believed that Whipper was born in Pennsylvania, the son of a house servant named Nance and a White farmer or lumberman. He was born into slavery and became a labourer. He somehow managed to gain his freedom and secure an education. As a young man, he rose rapidly as a leader in Pennsylvania's African American community. He distinguished himself as a writer and editor and encouraged literacy in others by founding a reading room and library for African Americans. He also became a leading spokesperson for the Moral Reform movement and editor of the National Moral Reform Society's newspaper, *The National Reformer*.[4] For much of the 1830s and 1840s, he held the view that there ought not to be separate institutions or movements to improve the lives of African Americans. Rather, he believed that creating integrated institutions concerned with the moral advancement of all people was a sounder strategy for improving their lot. This ran counter to the view held by other leaders that the special problems of Africans in America warranted the founding of institutions focusing on their special needs.[5]

Whipper was also a successful businessman. He was married to Harriet, the adopted daughter of Stephen Smith. (Harriet was also the niece of Smith's wife, Harriet Lee.)[6] And he was one of Smith's business partners and ran the Whipper and Smith coal and lumber industries in Columbia, Pennsylvania.[7] He grew his fortune through investments in real estate and railway "rolling stock" and, later, through banking and

Figure 4.2. Close-up of survey map 127 – Dresden. Collection of the Kent Genealogical Society.

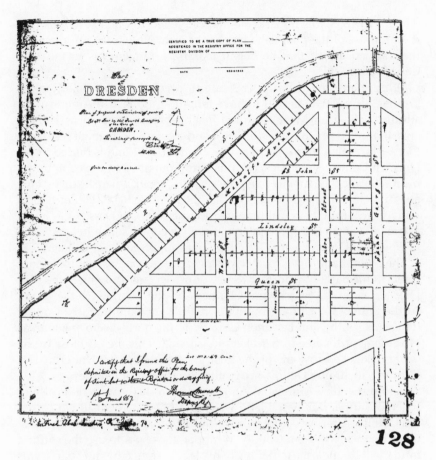

Figure 4.3. Close-up of survey map 128 – Dresden. Collection of the Kent
Genealogical Society.

money lending.[8] By the late 1840s, he had placed his fortune and his life
at the service of the Underground Railroad. His house in Columbia was
located at an important ford along the Susquehanna River across from
Virginia (now West Virginia). By his own account to Still, he smuggled
hundreds of freedom seekers north to Canada, the place he called "the
land of freedom."[9]

Whipper and Smith are said to have owned a steamboat and are
thought to have transported freedom seekers both by rail and by

water.[10] In 1853, this remarkable man travelled to Canada to look into the progress of the people he had sent north. He was so impressed at their advancement that he began making arrangements to move to Canada himself.[11]

Other members of Whipper's family preceded him, including his brother Alfred, who is said to have taught at the British American Institute.[12] His sister Mary Ann and her husband James Burns Hollensworth moved to Dresden after 1854 and took up permanent residence there. Mary died tragically of an aneurism in 1864 and is buried in the Dresden Cemetery.[13] James, her husband, remained in the community until 1895. He then moved to Appleton, Wisconsin, where he died at the age of eighty, at the home of his daughter Annie.[14] J.B. Hollensworth reinvented himself several times during his years in Dresden as a real estate lawyer, an entrepreneur, and finally a confectioner. In later years he operated Dresden's first ice cream parlour, Sweet Briar Cottage.[15]

The Sydenham River, formerly Bear Creek, is one of two important rivers in the part of the former Kent County we are studying in the PLP. Dresden is on the Sydenham, Chatham on the Thames, to the south. At the time of the Underground Railroad, Kent County, Essex County (to Kent's south), and Lambton County (to the north) were major areas of settlement for freedom seekers in Canada. This area is close to the Great Lakes and to some of the busiest crossings of the Underground Railroad, including Detroit, sixty miles southwest of Dresden.

Before the 1850 Municipal Act, the stretch of the Sydenham River where Whipper purchased land was part of Dawn Township in Lambton County. After 1850, this area was redistricted to become Camden & Gore Township in Kent County. Whipper chose not to use the shifting municipal boundaries to delineate his lands; rather, he did so in terms of a more constant geographic feature: the Sydenham River. Because there was no reference linking Whipper or his land investment to the now famous Dawn Settlement, his reference to "lands along the Sydenham" remained obscure. Despite being mentioned in so prominent a work as William Still's history, his properties remained a virtually "undiscovered" component of the Dawn Settlement.[16]

In 1857, in a letter to the Dawn Settlement's Emancipation Day organizers, Whipper wrote glowingly about the prospects for the lands in which he had invested. "From the spot, where you are now assembled," he told them, "you can cast your eyes over the broad landscape and point to a bright and glorious future." A visionary, he anticipated the industrial, rail, and shipping developments that would take place in the area over the next thirty years. He praised the area as "the garden of the West. A paradisiacal Eden to many a weary traveler."[17] But setting aside his prophetic grasp of the region's business possibilities, why did Whipper purchase these particular "lands along the Sydenham"? Why did he not invest instead in land in Chatham, which was more accessible after the Grand Truck Railroad arrived there in 1854 (nearly thirty years before rail service to Dresden began)?

All of Whipper's lands discovered to date are concentrated in the two earliest surveys of Dresden, 127 and 128 (with the exception of three lots on the northern extreme of the Fairport Survey and two late purchases in the BAI Survey of 1871). It is tempting to assume that Whipper settled in Dresden because of the British American Institute's presence, and this could indeed have been what first attracted him to the area, especially if his brother was teaching there. However, the institute's presence may be only one of a number of factors that made Dresden an attractive choice for investment.

Another compelling reason for settling in Dresden may have been the availability of large blocks of affordable land. Dresden's second survey (128) had been surveyed for the sale of lots only the year before Whipper arrived. Examination of the primary land records in Surveys 127 (Dresden's first) and 128, both completed by the Van Allen family, suggests that these early townsite developers may have suffered a reversal between 1849 and 1852 that made them anxious to divest themselves of their Dresden properties.[18] This would have created plentiful real estate investment opportunities on unsold and repossessed lots in 1853 and 1854. Dozens of town lots were up for grabs at precisely the time freemen began flooding the area as a result of the US Fugitive Slave Act of 1850. Having cash available after selling real estate in Pennsylvania, Washington, DC, and elsewhere, Whipper and his associates were uniquely positioned to make multiple lot purchases. Nowhere is this more dramatically illustrated than in Survey 128. Of the 136 lots in this survey, all but 14 were purchased, initially by Dennis Hill and a partnership of several Whipper associates, and later by Whipper, his family, and his business associates and one other African American family, the Charity family (the brothers James and Cornelius and their wives).[19] The only historical data on Whipper's activities in Dresden in previous local history accounts erroneously note only that "a colored man named Whipple ... own[ed] considerable Main Street Property, [and] started the building of the Tiffin or Shaw House."[20]

Whipper's part in the history of Dresden and the Dawn Settlement is one of many lost stories waiting to be recovered through land records and related documents. Finding Whipper's name on abstracts inspired a lot-by-lot "inventory" of other early survey properties, as well as a cross-referencing of names on land abstracts with census and other documents in order to determine which purchasers had been freedom seekers or freemen, and to learn more about these individuals.

Another major property owner in Survey 128 was the Charity family. The Charitys were involved in at least one land deed with a close associate of the Whippers, Absalom Shadd. Independently, they made many real estate purchases, and they began developing these holdings in both Chatham and Dresden before losing all of them around 1855. The Charitys were bootmakers. After arriving in Canada they became prominent businessmen in Chatham. On their Dresden block of properties they established rental housing, a crockery store, and a corn milling business. The Charitys also owned a ship, the *City of Detroit*, which on at least one occasion docked at Dresden.[21] James and Cornelius Charity also owned farmland on the south side of the BAI and in north Dresden totalling about four hundred acres. In Chatham they owned the Charity Block, on which was built a brick structure that housed the *Provincial Freeman*. Sometime after losing their property, they joined with local agents of Richard Redpath and immigrated to Haiti; after about three years, they moved on from there to British Columbia.[22]

By 1857, nearly all the lots in Survey 128, except for the Charity properties and a handful of lots owned by the founder of neighbouring Fairport, William Wright, and his son-in-law Alex Trerice (later mayor of the consolidated villages of Fairport and Dresden), were owned by William Whipper. However, Whipper was not the first African American owner. Several abstracts show "Dennis Hill et al." to be the owners of much of Survey 128 prior to Whipper. Hill is an important figure in Canada for his early challenge to school segregation.[23] The "et al." here is significant, for it represents three important partners: James Whipper Purnell, Absalom Shadd, and William Goodrich. James Whipper Purnell was a descendant of Benjamin Whipper, William's brother.[24] Absalom Shadd was a half-brother to Abraham Shadd, father of Mary Ann Shadd Cary. Members of the Shadd family were prominent abolitionists in Pennsylvania, and Mary Ann was the publisher of the *Provincial Freeman* in Toronto and, later, Chatham.[25] William Goodrich owned railcars that operated in York, Pennsylvania, up the line from Whipper's Columbia location. Goodrich, like Whipper, may have been involved in transporting escaped slaves via railcar.[26]

Some of these partners relinquished their Survey 128 lots through J.B. Hollensworth, who was Whipper's brother-in-law and who often acted as his land agent. In 1872, Whipper signed over a large portion of his Survey 128 lands in a quit claim to Julia A. Purnell and Adelaide Wormley (daughters of Absalom Shadd). Julia retained ownership of some Dresden properties until 1877.[27] Some lots owned by J.B. Hollensworth remained in the family's possession until 1903.[28]

Survey 127 did not see similar mass purchases of lots such as the ones made by Hill et al. and Whipper. However, this survey provides an interesting glimpse into a larger community of African Americans who made land purchases in Dresden. In some cases, unlike Whipper and Goodrich, they chose to live on their lots or develop property there.

Whipper began acquiring land in Survey 127 around the same time Hill et al. began doing so in Survey 128. His purchases were staggered and seem to have followed a plan. He purchased three lots in May 1854; another (Lot 35) in 1855; and another three (Lots 14, 64, and 65) in 1859, around the time when he is believed to have been seriously contemplating moving to Canada.

A puzzling discovery in the land records is a deed from 1859 for Lots 14, 64, and 65 that seems to contradict the story that Whipper did not take up residence in Canada, as he claimed he had done in his letter to William Still published in *History of the Underground Railway*. The deed to Lots 12, 64, and 65 indicates clearly that Whipper was residing in Dresden at the time of the purchase in 1859. Could this be an error by the land office clerk? Or did Whipper in fact stay in Dresden briefly before the Civil War? The Camden census of 1861 tells us that his wife Harriet was living alone in Dresden at that time.

Survey 127 was the more developed of the two, being outside the flood zone. All of Whipper's purchases in this survey were on Metcalfe Street, the town's main street, near the two principal town docks.[29] They included developed lots, one of which was the site of an inn built shortly before he purchased the property.[30] Inns at this time were important to land development, for people could stay in them while looking for land to purchase. As such, this was a very shrewd buy for a man whose close associates had just bought large mounts of land in the area and were probably looking to resell.

We also know from accounts in the *Provincial Freeman* that Whipper and his associates founded some significant early industries at Dresden. These included the Charitys' highly successful corn mill and shops in Survey 128, Hollensworth's white pine lumber mill, and Whipper's warehouse and "flouring mill."[31] None of these structures survive, and to date we have found no early photographs of them. However, property records for what would later be the Dominion Milling Company tell us that Whipper was working cooperatively with White businesspeople in the community and that his investments and loans – and possibly, in one case, his partnership with a White entrepreneur – may have helped the community prosper economically. In fact, some industries founded by Whipper may have survived into later decades under the ownership of White businesspeople who purchased these properties after Whipper and his associates, and other Black pioneers, had left the area. The Dominion Mill may have been the site of an earlier flour mill that Whipper established in Dresden. In the early 1870s, it was owned by William Cragg, a White entrepreneur who had purchased the property from Whipper, who held its mortgage until 1872. Also, fragmented oral accounts later written down in Victor Lauriston's *Romantic Kent* and Robert Brandon's *History of Dresden* (1950) suggest that before his death, Whipper had begun building a brick structure on Main Street. This was said to have been the Shaw (or Tiffin) Hotel. It is curious that Cragg also owned the hotel property, at the opposite end of Main Street from the flour mill. The hotel was an impressive three-storey brick building at the town's main intersection. Although land records fail to link it to Whipper, Cragg and Whipper's joint involvement in the mill site raises interesting questions about the extent of their business relationship. Even if Whipper had not been involved directly in building the Shaw Hotel, could Whipper's loans to Cragg have spurred the latter's business success?[32]

The Cragg mill is not the only example of Whipper providing mortgage money to White businessmen in Dresden. And Whipper was not the only Black lending money to Whites.[33] The Watson and Weston families, who would soon rise to prominence in Dresden's rapidly growing shipping industry, also benefited from Whipper's willingness to be an "equal opportunity lender." The White population's apparent willingness to accept his loans demonstrates what can perhaps be viewed as an early example of interracial cooperation in economic development.[34] This is all the more remarkable considering the frequent references by the Reverend Thomas Hughes, a missionary in Dresden and a staunch proponent of desegregation, to the rising prejudice and discrimination in the community in the late 1850s.[35]

These loans challenge the long-accepted notion that Black pioneers depended financially on Whites when they came to Canada. They also call for us to re-examine the assumption that African Americans in the Dawn Settlement were passive recipients of aid from the BAI and other missions. Instead, people of African descent in Dresden contributed actively to community development by establishing businesses and industries, lending money, and building infrastructure.

Quite possibly, Whipper's "flouring mill" was one early "Black" industry that laid the foundation for a later White business. The land records support this. There is less concrete evidence regarding other Whipper properties sold in 1874. Ongoing research into lots on former BAI property owned by Whipper, and into other sites, may draw connections between what may have been early mill sites owned by Whipper or the BAI and successful White businesses later operating on these same sites. Too much information about industries developed by African American investors has been lost for us to be sure about this. This is merely one indication of how impoverished our local history – and, by default, our Canadian history – has become as a result of Black history being undervalued and unrecorded. The lack of interest in the history of our Black pioneers is all the more disappointing given that Whipper's last property in Dresden was not sold until 1885, a period that is especially rich in documentation of early White businesses. We know what many of the early White businesses looked like from surviving photographs; significantly, there are no photographs of Black-owned businesses and precious few written accounts of them in the public record. We continue to hope these might yet be unearthed through private family collections.

There are artefact houses from the years 1850 to 1884 that may be connected to the Whipper family.[36] But so many properties were recorded under the same set of names – Purnell, Hill, Hollensworth, Whipper – that it is impossible to state definitively which of them were family residences. One house, built around 1860 on former Whipper land, is particularly intriguing. Its architectural details, the fact that Whipper owned the lot, and the additional fact that Harriet Whipper held on to the Georgian-style cottage all suggest that it may at one time have served as a Whipper residence. We know that Harriet lived in Dresden briefly around the time of the Civil War: her name appears not only in the 1861 census but also as a witness to marriages at the Christ Church mission for family members after 1858 – an indication she lived here alone for at least four years. Whipper said he did not live in Canada, and he did not mention Harriet having resided here, but clearly she did. The timing of the purchase of the Georgian cottage lot and Harriet's reluctance to relinquish the property for several years after her husband's death together suggest that the property could have been

Figure 4.4. The Reverend Thomas Hughes's Christ Church circa 1880. Still exists today.

her residence. Because references to the cottage are absent from the historical record, we will likely never have conclusive proof that this was "the Whipper Cottage." The Georgian cottage on Metcalfe Street and a neighbouring one owned by Francis and Sarah (Whipper) Turner continue to raise intriguing questions about the Whipper family's relationship to the community, particularly in the post–Civil War era.

The attic of the Turner property has yielded one important artefact: a steamer trunk bearing the name F.M. Turner. Its inside is covered by the British newspaper *The Tribune*, edited by John Thilwell, dated 1796. Its exterior has a brass plaque bearing the name "Stewart" and the location "Boston." The trunk is noted as having been shipped via "Black and Young" of Detroit.[37] These associations hint at the richness of the stories we may yet uncover through further research.

In Survey 127, identifying Black-owned properties has been more difficult than in Survey 128, because determining "ethnicity" requires cross-checking with censuses, genealogies, and newspaper and other accounts. Not all of those who settled in Dresden were as prominent as the Whipper family, so determining whether they were of African descent and what their professions were, and so on, is not as easy as with well-documented families such as the Whippers and their associates.[38]

Only one of the Survey 127 lots was owned by the partners Dennis Hill et al., who are so prominent in Survey 128. Still, we have compiled to this point a nearly complete picture of Dresden's earliest landowners, and it shows that most owners of the Survey 127 lots were of African descent. A significant number of them were professionals, skilled tradespeople, or shopkeepers. This holds out the promise that more interesting "lost stories" will one day be told about the early community, provided that we can decipher the records and learn more about these people and their relationships.

Survey 127 was a much more diverse neighbourhood, home to a number of Scots-Irish and Germans, including the infamous Edwin Larwill, whose presence in particular hints at the complexities of race relations in this small community as well as some of the challenges people faced despite having "equal rights" under British Law.[39] Moreover, biographies of the first property owners there reveal that "Dawn" in its early years was a very complex community that defies historical portrayals of it as peopled exclusively by "escaped slaves" who lacked education and resources and thus relied on the BAI or the Dawn Institute for their survival. The names recorded in Surveys 127 and 128 between 1850 and 1870 include three ministers of the gospel, two grocery store owners, two dry goods store owners, a barber, two innkeepers, an ashery operator, and Dresden's first medical doctor – all of them of African descent. Some were purely African, but many were of mixed race (i.e., some mix of European, Native, and African).[40] One resident, William Whipper's estate executor Don Juan E. Barbero, was listed in the 1871 census as a South American who identified himself as "Spanish." He was married to an American-born woman who identified herself as "African." The couple claimed "Catholic" as their religion, so they would have turned to the mainly Irish church for the baptism of their children, who were born in Canada. Barbero's case illustrates the tremendous diversity (and mobility) of the people of Dresden and hints at the complexities of racial and cultural identity and interpersonal relationships as well as the remarkable "trajectories" and travels of early peoples of African descent.[41]

Dresden in the 1850s was a fully functioning community with a mixed population that included a large percentage of professionals and service providers of African descent, who were able to generate considerable economic and social activity. This community developed infrastructure that included at least two rental housing units.[42] They also created a variety of social and other institutions, including at least three churches. These included Christ Church (the Anglican Mission), founded by Thomas Hughes. His church was closely associated with the Whipper family and other Black abolitionists.[43] It seems natural to find the Hollensworths, Whippers, and Shadds all involved in the life of Christ Church from its founding in 1857, since many of them were affiliated with the Episcopal Church in their home communities.[44]

The baptism and marriage records of Christ Church refer to visitors from Detroit. One example is George DeBaptiste, who is recorded as the godfather at a christening of his namesake George de Baptiste Shadd.[45] Such details provide tantalizing clues about relationships between the abolitionists turned investors in Dresden and prominent abolitionists from Michigan and elsewhere, which in turn raises questions about the impact of these relationships on Underground Railroad activity in Dresden. For instance, was it significant that in 1854, the *City of Detroit*, owned by the Charities, docked in Dresden? Could there have been a link between Dresden and Detroit that was part of the Great Lakes marine route of the Underground Railroad?

Whipper and his contemporaries in Dresden provide us with a new lens that brings into sharp focus a far richer and more diverse picture of the people and their activities along the Sydenham River, on the border of the BAI, often referred to as the Dawn Settlement.[46]

NOTES

1 The Trillium Trail Historical Walk was a $50,000 Trillium Grant–funded project that created a 5-kilometre walking trail with historical plaques along its route depicting local founders of industries; the plaques were situated on the properties where their industries had existed. The project includes a kiosk with eight storyboards, a trail guide, twenty plaques, and a companion book by Carter and Carter, *Stepping Back in Time*. The project was initiated by the Dresden Horticultural Society and supported by other local service clubs, including the Catherine McVean Chapter of the IODE and Dresden Rotary. The project was completed between January 2002 and January 2003. Researchers for the historical walk project were the Carters.
2 Abstracts and deeds to Surveys 127 and 128, Chatham-Kent Land Records Office, Chatham, Ontario.
3 Still, *The Underground Rail Road*, 739.
4 Zimmerman, "William Whipper in the Black Abolitionist Tradition"; Hopkins, "Black Eldorado on the Susquehana."

5 Gaude, "Pragmatism and Black Identity."
6 Genealogical files of Lisa Finch, descendant of James Whipper Purnell; files from the Chatham-Kent Black Historical Society; marriage announcement of William Whipper, *Columbia Spy* (n.d.).
7 Zimmerman, "William Whipper."
8 Delany, *Condition, Elevation, Emigration and Destiny.*
9 Still, *The Underground Rail Road*, 735–40.
10 Ripley, *BAP* II:484 re: the steamship the *T. Whitney*; interview with John Palasek, Detroit Great Lakes marine historian, 2006.
11 Still, *The Underground Rail Road*, 735–40.
12 Alfred also taught at the Colonial Church and School Society's "Mission to Fugitive Slaves" in Dresden; see *BAP* II:332. He is noted in the mission's Christ Church records as having been married in the community by the rector, Rev. Thomas Hughes. Session records, Christ (Anglican) Church, Huron College Archives, London.
13 Hollensworth family listing, Camden Township Census, 1861, Dresden branch, Chatham-Kent Public Library; death notice for Mary Ann Hollensworth, *Provincial Freeman*, 31 July 1863; grave marker, Dresden Cemetery; archaeologist's notes, Dresden Cemetery Relocation Project.
14 Death registration for James Burns Hollensworth, Fox County Geneological Society, Appleton, Wisconsin; grave marker inscription from Appleton cemetery provided by Marj Crane, Fox County Genealogical Society; various newspaper articles supplied by Marj Crane (collection of the author).
15 Camden Township Census, 1861, 1871, 1881, Dresden Branch of the Chatham-Kent Library; Dresden Census, 1871, 1881, 1891, Dresden Branch of the Chatham-Kent Library; Lauriston, *Romantic Kent*, 381.
16 For more information and a map on shifting geopolitical boundaries and changing geographic names, see Carter, "Reimagining the Dawn Settlement," in this book.
17 Letter from William Whipper to Messrs A. Highgate, J. Hollensworth, H. Damrell, Wm Crosby, and David Smith, 25 July 1857, reprinted in the *Provincial Freeman*, 28 March 1857.
18 Carter and Carter, *Stepping Back in Time*, 23.
19 Numbers were tabulated by searching abstracts for all lots in Survey 128, cross-referencing names with available censuses, genealogies, and secondary accounts, and consulting with Gwen Robinson of the Chatham-Kent Black Historical Society, a leading expert on Black genealogy and history for the Chatham-Kent area, to determine the racial identification of those named on the abstracts.
20 Lauriston, *Romantic Kent*, 381.

21 Robinson and Robinson, *Seek the Truth*; interview with Gwen Robinson, Chatham-Kent Black Historical Society, 2006; land abstracts and deeds to Charity Properties for Survey 128, and for Charity holdings at Chatham, Chatham-Kent Land Registry Office; "Still ONWARD!, – Our beautiful little village, Dresden, is still ...," *Provincial Freeman*, 24 November 1855.

22 *BAP* II:263–4.

23 *BAP* II:484.

24 This relationship is not certain. He may have been a great-nephew. There are discrepancies between the genealogies supplied by descendants in Indiana and the Chatham-Kent Black Historical Society genealogy records supplied by the Dorothy Binga family of Chicago (indirect Whipper family descendants).

25 Shadd family files from the Chatham-Kent Black Historical Society.

26 Delany, *Condition, Elevation, Emigration and Destiny*.

27 Quitclaim documents, Chatham Kent Land Registry Office, Chatham.

28 Quitclaim documents, Chatham Kent Land Registry Office, Chatham.

29 The assertion that this is the more developed survey is based on an examination of local history that shows that most of the developments by White entrepreneurs were carried out in Survey 127, which was established nine years sooner than Survey 128. St Clair Conversation Authority Flood Maps indicate that this area is largely safe from the flooding that happens regularly on the Survey 128 lands, making it the more stable area for development. Most of the town's main docks are believed to have existed in this survey area (off St John, Metcalfe, and Main Streets), according to information found in various local histories, including Brandon's *History of Dresden* and based on evidence in survey maps.

30 Helen Burns papers, collection of the Dresden Branch, Chatham-Kent Public Library.

31 "Still ONWARD!"

32 Spearman, *Landmarks of the Past*; Brandon, *History of Dresden*.

33 Comprehensive list of mortgages for the former British American Institute grounds, compiled by the author from abstracts for Survey 133, 134, and 135; Chatham-Kent Land Records Office microfilm files, Chatham. This survey of properties shows that the Wilberforce Institute held a large number of mortgages on former British American Institute properties on their sale after 1872. A number of these mortgages were provided to White businessmen, who became the majority property holders of those surveys; they included Mayor Alex Trerice, Alexander Watson, Henry Weston, James Clancy, and Jacob Killiam. Chatham-Kent Land Records Office, Chatham.

34 C.P. Watson was an early ship owner and builder in partnership with various other members of his family and the Westons. Henry Weston was a prominent ship's captain who travelled the Great Lakes waterways. Curiously, a Henry Weston, Jr, would be involved with the Whipper family in later years regarding a lawsuit in Pennsylvania. More research is needed to determine whether this was Capt. Henry Weston's son and what his relationship was to the Whipper family in the United States.

35 Diary of the Rev. Thomas Hughes, Huron University College Archives, London, Ontario.

36 Carter, *Building Heritage.*

37 The Turner trunk is last known to have been owned by a Chatham-Kent antique dealer, who acquired it in an auction sale at the former Turner home.

38 This map, in fact, is a conservative estimate of this ownership. Genealogies on some names are in progress, and more of the lots may yet prove to have been owned by African Americans.

39 Edwin Larwill owned two lots on Metcalfe Street facing the Sydenham River, adjacent to property owned by Dennis Hill and J.B. Hollensworth. Larwill is best known for his opposition to the Reverend William King, founder of the Elgin Settlement at Buxton, and for a near-riot he inspired at Chatham in opposition to Black settlement. Larwill was also active in politics, and his signature appears as clerk on several land documents of the time, including those of the "freedom seekers" settling at Dresden.

40 Marie Carter, "The Dawn Settlement: Black Utopian Colony or Early Experiment in Multiculturalism?," presented at Claiming the Promise: 2012 Promised Land Symposium, Chatham.

41 Comparison of land records and census and genealogical files with the assistance of Gwen Robinson, Chatham-Kent Black Historical Society; land record for Harriet L. Whipper, document no. 3186, Lot 22, Chatham-Kent Land Records Office; Dresden Census, Dresden branch of the Chatham-Kent Public Library; Camden Census, 1861, 1871; Dresden branch of the Chatham-Kent Public Library; Kent County Census, 1851, Dresden branch of the Chatham-Kent Public Library.

42 According to later photographs, a home and a duplex in "Black architectural style," both dating to circa 1860, existed on properties owned by Dennis Hill and by the Charity brothers along Metcalfe Street. At the time they owned these residences, the Charity brothers and the Hills also owned several other properties, including a brick business block in Chatham. The modest frame structures in Dresden would seem to be unlikely principal dwellings for these "elite" families. Local historical accounts by Don

Spearman and others indicate that the duplex had a long history as a rental property. Other land record evidence suggests it is unlikely the buildings were ever occupied by the owners, so they must have been constructed as rental units. See Carter, *Building Heritage*.

43 On Christ Church and Thomas Hughes, see Nina Reid-Maroney, "'A Contented Mind Is a Continual Feast': Tracing Intellectual Migrations through the Promised Land," in this book.

44 Session records, Christ Church (Anglican), 1857 to 1880; typescript copy of the Diary of the Rev. Thomas Hughes, Diocese of Huron Archives, Huron University College, London; Winch, *Philadelphia's Black Elite*, 133.

45 Baptism record for George DeBaptiste Shadd, Christ Church baptismal records; Diocese of Huron session records for Christ Church (Anglican), Dresden, 1857–80.

46 See Marie Carter, "Reimagining the Dawn Settlement," in this book, for further discussion.

5 Nina Mae Alexander: Daughter of Promise

CLAUDINE BONNER

Throughout the nineteenth and well into the twentieth century, Black teachers in what was supposed to be the Promised Land of Canadian freedom had few opportunities for employment other than in "coloured" schools. In fact, prior to the 1940s very few Black women were employed outside of farmwork and domestic service. In both Canada and the United States, a race barrier prevented Blacks, especially women, from entering the professions, including teaching.[1] But there were exceptions, and this chapter examines a diary kept by Nina Mae Alexander, an African Canadian[2] woman who entered the teaching profession in Ontario in the early twentieth century. Through her own words, we can learn about her daily life, her values, her dreams, and her relationships with family, friends, and colleagues. This chapter explores these experiences and takes a close look at some of the prominent themes in her writing: the importance of education and the role of family in supporting educational aspirations; familial and other relationships as seen through her correspondence; the ebb and flow of her social life and, with that, society's expectations regarding how a young lady should comport herself in that era; the dreariness of winter; and the pervading theme of religion. Nina Mae's diary, a rare find, allows us to explore the lives and roles of people of African descent in Canada in the early 1900s, thus helping fill a gap in this country's history.

On 1 January 1907, twenty-one-year-old Miss Nina Mae Alexander of Amherstburg, Ontario, set out for her teaching position in Rondeau, Ontario. She was entering her second year at this post, prior to which she had taught for seven months in Merritton, a village on the Niagara Peninsula. As the new year began, she wrote: "[I] have decided to keep a diary in which to keep track of my moods, daily movements and acquaintances." With these words, the reader is introduced to Nina Mae, who then managed to write every day for the next four months, thus allowing us a brief look at her life. I do not know whether Nina Mae wrote beyond this period, as no other diaries or other reminiscences have so far been found in the Alexander family papers.[3]

Nina Mae's diary is in many ways unremarkable. It tells a story that has been told a number of times – that of a young woman called to teach in a small community somewhere in Canada in the early twentieth century. Recent decades have seen the publication of several Canadian studies exploring the lives of these ordinary teachers.[4] However, many perspectives on them remain to be told, as Bristow and her colleagues have noted: "the history of Black people in Canada and of Black women in particular is missing from the pages of mainstream Canadian history. Black people in Canada have a past that has been hidden or eradicated, just as racism has been deliberately denied as an organizing element in how Canada is constituted."[5]

Contributing to this invisibility and absence is the limited acknowledgment of the men and women of colour who have served in the ranks of Canadian teachers.[6] One of the few exceptions is the chapter in *"We're Rooted Here"* on Mary Bibb, a Black teacher,[7] in which Afua Cooper shows that in mid-nineteenth-century Ontario, several young Black women served as teachers, be they certified (i.e., having completed studies at "Normal School")[8] or not.

Nina Mae's diary extends our understanding of the lives of African Canadian teachers in Ontario beyond the mid-nineteenth century. Her voice helps us make greater sense of the sociohistorical text by centring the voice of a single Black woman in the process of making sense and meaning of her life. While she is just one Black teacher, her narrative offers us insights into her experiences as a young, visible-minority, female teacher in 1907 Ontario. As well, the interconnectedness of her life and story with those of others casts some light on the lives of African Canadians at that time, besides providing a snapshot of life in a small Ontario town in the early twentieth century. Her diary is a window onto the experiences of a successful[9] descendant of the nineteenth-century "freedom seekers" who came to Upper Canada seeking sanctuary and who chose to remain rather than return to the American South, as many others did after arriving here in similar circumstances.

To understand Nina Mae's diary, it is helpful to situate her in her familial and social context and to explain how her family came to Canada. According to her great-nephew Spencer Alexander, Nina Mae's paternal grandfather Thomas Alexander was born a slave in Kentucky. He escaped from slavery[10] and settled in Anderdon Township near Amherstburg. On his way there, Alexander met the woman he would marry, Catherine Harding Alexander. Catherine was born in Buckinghamshire, England, and came to America with her parents when she was nine years old. Marriage records[11] show that Thomas and Catherine were married on 5 June 1848 in Maumee, Ohio. The next time their names appear in the documentary evidence is in the 1861 Ontario census for Essex County, which shows them as married and residing in Anderdon Township. For Thomas, the census notes forty-two as his age, "coloured" as his race, labourer as his occupation, and Baptist as his religion. Catherine is listed as thirty-five and Caucasian. Thomas and Catherine have five children: Thomas, twelve years old; Philip, ten; James, eight; Martha, six; and John Henry, two. The youngest child, John Henry, is the "Papa" in Nina Mae's tale. All of these children were born in Canada and are listed as coloured. The fact that the oldest child, Thomas, was born in Canada and was twelve years old in 1861 suggests that Thomas and Catherine were in Canada by at least 1849.

I have learned a great deal about Nina Mae's paternal history; details of her mother, Annie Louise Crawford, remain scant. The oral history suggests that Annie Louise's father was Cherokee and her mother Black – possibly a former slave. So I begin this tale knowing that Nina Mae was a member of the second generation of her family to be born in Canada (taking the understanding of nationality here to be based on being listed as "Canadian" in the census documents) and the descendant of at least one and perhaps two former slaves: Thomas Alexander and the presumed former-slave mother of Annie Louise Crawford. The lack of information about Annie Louse Crawford and her origins is not surprising, given the treatment of women's histories and stories, as previously mentioned.

Nina Mae was the second of six children born to John Henry and Annie Louise. At least five of these six children would go on to hold jobs in the professions, with Arthur, Ethel, and Nina Mae becoming teachers, Marjorie becoming a nurse's aide, and J. Harold becoming a doctor. I have not yet been able to ascertain the employment history of the sixth child, Annie Louise, nor have I found any record of Nina Mae's mother having worked outside the home. Her father, John Henry, became a schoolteacher, having gained his teacher certification in Ontario in December 1883. He taught at the King Street School in Amherstburg and at a school in the community of North Buxton. From this information we can deduce that this family not only valued education but also had the financial means (or made the necessary sacrifices) to provide their children with access to it. This tradition of education and the Alexanders' ability to position themselves among the ranks of Blacks employed outside of domestic and farming jobs is something that drew me to learn more about Nina Mae and her family. I wondered how much this represented the values and actions of the "typical" Black family during this period, and what might have driven them to make the most of the opportunities they were afforded.

Education and the Family

The value of an education and the influence of the family in guiding and directing Nina Mae's education and career are overriding themes in her diary entries. In July 1899, before beginning her teaching career, Nina Mae passed the entrance examination that allowed her to attend a collegiate institute or high school. The certificate of successful completion of this exam was issued in Windsor; beyond that, I have not yet found information about the collegiate institute or high school she attended. I have been able to establish from her diary that when she was teaching in her first post at Merritton, and when she was at her 1907 position at Rondeau, she had not yet received her teaching certification and was contemplating her future in terms of furthering her studies and settling into a career. Clearly, she wanted or was expected to continue her studies, and the concerns her friends and family were expressing with regard to her education often appear in her diary entries. In her 6 January entry, she mentions nursing as a possible career when writing of an old schoolmate, Garrett Smith, then attending medical school in Detroit: "[He] urges me to give up the idea of being a nurse." That profession was apparently in transition in 1907, for another friend, Maude, told her in a letter that "the hospital doctors say nursing is improving slowly." There was no need for her friends to express concern about her entering this field, however; two months later Nina Mae writes in her diary she has applied to Normal School, with no mention of her earlier interest in nursing.

We find further evidence of the opportunities for study for members of this family when Nina Mae points out: "Received a nice long letter from Brother John. He wants me to attend Normal School at Toronto instead of London as he is thinking of attending the medical college in Toronto." The idea of having a daughter at Normal School at the same time as another child is attending medical school re-emphasizes this family's commitment to education, but it also raises questions about how these academic pursuits were to be funded. The diary never addresses this; instead, there is simply the understanding that whatever educational choices the young Alexanders make, the expenses will not impede them. Nina Mae chose to apply to the Toronto Normal School and was admitted for September 1907. Later, in her diary, she is ambivalent about the choices she faces: one of the local trustees has told her to "put off [her] Normal School term until 1908 and remain there [Rondeau] until then." She has consulted her father, who has advised her to wait a year before returning to school. He has suggested that she ask the trustees to hold her teaching position by having her younger brother Arthur serve as her replacement while she is away at Normal School. This plan suggests prudence on the part of her father, who is trying to ensure that Nina Mae's professional future is secure. She is steadfast in her aspirations, however, and makes it clear that she knows a successful career is in her future and that little will deter her. She writes: "The story 'when men come in' in the Diary was finished; I wonder if it is so that women who have careers are not satisfied. I will not draw back from mine."

With one brother soon to enter medical school and another able to take over her teaching position in Rondeau, Nina Mae obviously has role models to follow, as well as support she can rely on in order to accomplish her goals. That the grandchildren of former slaves can aspire to reach as high as they are is astonishing. Cooper and Shaw both point to the notion of "racial uplift" that drove many young Black men and women to seek upward social mobility and self-improvement, and that instilled in them an overarching sense of social responsibility in the decades after slavery. According to Shaw, it was not uncommon for these young people to travel great distances both socially and geographically in order to achieve their goals.

Nina Mae writes to her loved ones almost daily. I have no access to any of her actual correspondence, but her diary provides incredible detail, in that she notes to whom she has written, the page length of most of her letters, and the mail she received each day. For example, she writes on 5 January: "Wrote a long letter to Ena. Got the letter that I had written to Tot back; I had addressed it incorrectly. Sent a souvenir post card of Erieau to Maude." And on 16 March: "Received a nice long letter from Maude Foster full of the revival news of Amherstburg … I wrote an eight page letter to Glenn Patterson."

In the short five months of her diary, Nina Mae sent and received letters from her parents and siblings and from her Aunt Mattie, as well as from more than fifteen friends, who shared the events in their lives back in Amherstburg and elsewhere. Almost every day she received was word from someone new.

Besides chronicling whom she hears from, she indicates the days she received no mail. In her 27 April entry, she states: "No mail today. Somehow or other I am always disappointed if I don't get any mail on Saturdays." A few days later, she still has not received mail: "No mail again today. I will be getting lonesome pretty soon." It stands to reason that a young girl working away from home would exhibit loneliness, echoing the experiences of other young teachers in rural schools, who worked far from their loved ones.[12]

Nina Mae also receives various magazines in the mail, which provide further insight into this young woman. She receives regular issues of the *Toronto Weekly Globe*,[13] the *Detroit Informer*,[14] the *Amherstburg Echo*, and the *Weekly Star*,[15] which tells us she is a regular reader of the news and stays well informed in current affairs, be it national and transnational (Canadian and American), local (Amherstburg), or relating to the Black community. She also receives many magazines, to some of which she holds subscriptions. Examples include *Canadian Teacher* and *Teacher's World*, both of course relating to her professional practice, as well as popular women's magazines and journals, which points to an interest in fashion and women's issues. Another thing we learn about Nina Mae from her reading material is that she is also a writer. On 30 January she mentions letters she has had published in "The Circle of Young Canada," the *Globe's* children's page:[16] "[the] Weekly Globe came and in the Circle of Young Canada, two of the Circleites mentioned the last letter I wrote." On 20 February, she mentions a letter-writing competition she is entering:

> I finished my letter to enter the competition with letters advertising the Eaton Hurlbut Company's hot-pressed velum paper. Nine prizes, the first one $15.00. I wouldn't be satisfied with any but that and my letter was so poor that it won't be considered for a minute. I have written many nicer letters than the one I sent in yet I was a month writing it.

An ambition, a competitive streak, is evident here. Nina Mae acknowledges a desire to win this competition and speaks of the quality of work that she knows she can produce. She returns to this two months later, on receipt of a copy of *Collier's* magazine: "I saw in it where the Circle

Magazine is offering prizes for short stories, First prize $1,000. Nothing beats a trial but a failure so if I can concoct a plot I will frame a story around it."

A Full Social Calendar

The occasional loneliness experienced by Nina Mae is not to suggest she does not have a vibrant and active social life. This is clear from entries such as the one on 14 February: "Received two valentines, very pretty, one from Waring and the other a semi-comic one from Jared Bentham. Dan Scott, Milburt Hartford and Ross were over and we spent the evening playing cards." And there is this earlier entry, from 5 February: "Don Scott and Wilburt Hartford called. Mr. and Mrs. Wilfrid Lewis, Mrs. Fields, Irving and I spent the evening over at Will Lewis' mother; we had music and singing and the time passed very pleasantly." Week after week Nina Mae talks of evenings with friends, parties, church socials, and talks, in addition to other social gatherings. Her social life is integral to her narrative and provides insights into one side of the young teacher.

While reading her diary I found myself asking a number of questions, some in part because her entries do not clarify her living arrangements. I wondered, for example, what exactly she meant by "callers." Many entries mention single men staying until ten or eleven at night. Just how "normal" was it for a young woman to be entertaining men at her home at night in 1907? Undoubtedly, several of these men had romantic aspirations and expressed as much by bringing her gifts, taking her for drives into the country, and accompanying her on visits to the homes of mutual friends. Sometimes she makes multiple engagements with these gentlemen. For example, on 1 February she writes:

> Made an engagement to go for a cutter ride to Blenheim with Ross tomorrow evening. Made an engagement to go to church with Irving next Thursday night to hear Rev. Penick who will be there. Mrs. Fields, Ross, Mr. & Mrs. Tot Lewis, Irving and I spent the evening down to Blaney's, had a good time.

This active social life is consistent with Coulter's findings in her study of young female teachers in Ontario in the early twentieth century:

> Whether in Europe or in Canada, young teachers led the hectic social lives we associate with contemporary adolescence. Their diaries,

autobiographies, memoirs and letters recount a mad and merry circle of crokinole, euchre, skating parties, dances, sailing and canoeing, cottage life, visits hither and yon for dinner and tea, trips to town, snowshoeing, hiking.[17]

Nina Mae mentions several times receiving small gifts, such as one from Irving on 6 March: "Mrs. Fields, Ross, Will Lewis, Irving and I spent the evening over at Parkers. Irving gave me a bag of candy." For professional African American women during the Jim Crow era, accepting gifts from young men was a dangerous step towards explicit expression of their sexuality.[18] Parents who worried that their daughters were complicit in or open to such relationships would do all they could to prevent "inappropriate encounters" that could ruin their child's reputation and place her respectability in question. I see evidence of this kind of parental vigilance when Nina Mae writes to her mother about receiving letters from Garrett Smith, the Detroit medical student, who according to Nina Mae "already has four wives and all living." Her mother tells her to "let Garry slide." A gentle maternal nudge away.

Other studies of young African American teachers point to a great deal of concern over dating and sexuality.[19] Shaw notes that most of these young women would have been raised by parents who recognized that their children needed to maintain a semblance of propriety and respectability if they were to make the most of any opportunities available to them, especially in the professions:

Cognizant of racist and sexist slurs, parents emphasized the importance of disproving the sexual myths and stereotypes and insisted on sexual self-control and, thus again, the demonstration of respectability. Adhering to this code of morality would, however, do more than protect the individual, family and race from embarrassment. A breach of these practices, whether or not it resulted in a premarital or early pregnancy, could easily eliminate the professional opportunities for which the parents were preparing their daughters.[20]

The maintenance of the respectability of these young women was often not only the work of their parents, but also the responsibility of members of the community, who imposed strict expectations regarding standards of personal and professional behaviour. Rev. Penick, whom Nina Mae mentions in her diary, and who possibly knew her parents, seems to have gone out of his way to point out what he deemed inappropriate behaviour on her part, as indicated in the diary entry for 7 February: "The sermon from the Ten Virgins was I believe preached especially for me and after the services were over he called me to him and gave me a private sermon. Why can't they leave me alone." Nina Mae's final comment suggests that Penick was not the only one who noticed her behaviour, and she appears very troubled by this fact, as evidenced by her post on the following day: "Rev. Penick's talk bothered me more than I thought it would."

Penick's presence in Nina Mae's life is problematic. On the one hand, he seems to be a caring bystander, but on the other, his motives seem questionable and he appears to make Nina Mae uncomfortable. "Eva and I went to church at night to hear Rev. Penick, not many out. He didn't give me another sermon after church this time but said he would call at the house to see me. Oh! Me oh my!" Nina Mae's comment can be taken to suggest she recognizes Penick may have ulterior motives with respect to her. Or perhaps she is simply acknowledging that she is going to get another lecture about preserving her reputation. Her concerns about his inappropriate behaviour arise again in her entry for Wednesday, 10 April: "Rev. Penick preached a sermon I didn't much care for on men who seduce girls. I never had a sermon on that topic before." So, whatever his motives, Rev. Penick's behaviour is obviously very different from what Nina Mae has grown to expect from ministers, and she is deeply ambivalent where he is concerned.

In addition to all this, on 25 January, a gentleman named Mr Parker, whose home Nina Mae and her friends often visit, "warned me not to take candy from any of the young men here [in Rondeau] for fear of love powders." She laughs off his warning, which is likely the kind of teasing often directed towards young people. However, it seems that not all of the concern shown her is misplaced. She later writes of an unsavoury situation that has arisen between her and Mr Anderson, the husband of a friend, who has sent her an unsigned postcard on which the following words have been written: "I would leave my happy home for you." She isn't sure who wrote the card until he escorts her home one evening after she has paid a visit to his home. During their walk,

> he asked me if I would go for a drive with him some day. I told him I did not know whether I would or not. He then proceeded to get after me somewhat roughly about not answering his letter. We had a few words on the subject and he spoke about the driving again. I told him I might go with him sometimes if someone else went too and I know that settled him.

Nina Mae's diary often records the implied dangers of sexual exploita-tion. Several studies[21] refer to situations where vulnerable young fe-male teachers find themselves at the mercy of unscrupulous men. Nina Mae describes men she encounters who seem to think she will be sus-ceptible to their charms and wooing. Instead of sounding victimized, she scoffs at these attentions and shows herself more than prepared to guard her independence. Poor Irving seems to be the most smit-ten with her, showering her with visits, bags of candy, excursions to church, and drives in the country, yet she states: "People seem to think that by going to church with Glen 'I threw Irving down.' I did not in-tend to keep steady company with Irving or anyone else and I want others to know it." Obviously, Nina Mae knows what she wants at this stage in her life (relative to career and dating at least) and is not afraid to let people know.

Her confidence and convictions are also evident in the way she al-lows White gentlemen to call on her even though she well knows this is not acceptable to everyone around her. This provides us with an inter-esting insight into race issues in this community in the early 1900s. On her return to Rondeau after Christmas, Nina Mae writes: "Heard that some of my colored beaux objected to the White ones coming to see me. I am hired by both White and colored in the section and intend to treat all alike."[22] She is adamant about this, and when she refuses to change her behaviour, the issue is soon raised again:

> Mrs. Fields and I spent the evening down at Mr. G. Lewis.' Mr. Blaney was
> there and we had several stiff arguments; at least they did and I didn't
> join in although he tried to lecture me about entertaining White boys who
> came to pass the evening but the rest all took my part so I did not need to
> reply to him.

Presumably, there were those in the community who took issue with inter-racial dating. Clearly, however, there were others who felt differently. The racial identities of the people present during this conversation are unknown, so it is impossible to tell whether these were the sentiments of Blacks or Whites. Nina Mae, meanwhile, continues to allow White call-ers: "Messers Thompson and Colter, two young White men from the 4th line were over and we played cards until ten." Her refusal to change based on the sentiments of others is not surprising when one considers the diary's overall tone. As previously noted, Nina Mae seems to have known what she wanted at this stage in her life and was not shy about letting people know. She also seems to have been a woman who did not conform and instead acted on her own convictions.

The Weather and One's Mood

In Nina Mae's diary, the weather seems to weigh on her at times, perhaps because of her occasional loneliness and isolation. Fair days brighten her mood, while miserable weather seems to depress her, and those around her as well: "Jan. 4th, Another dreary day. Roads in an awful condition. Hard work to concentrate my mind on my work consequently pupils restless." She begins each day's entry with a weather report: What is the world like today? Her descriptions of the weather's ebbs and flows bring us closer to her, for they offer us insight into her changing moods. The "crankiness" and "crossness" she attributes to the weather make her seem all the more human.

Nina Mae and Religion

From the letters Nina Mae received from Amherstburg, some kind of religious revival was taking place in 1907, led by Rev. Nickerson, a Baptist minister who was converting people there, including many people Nina Mae knew. She recorded the conversions of various friends and family members as she heard of them by mail. In her diary, there is a subtext of questioning around her own religious convictions and those of her siblings. For example, she writes:

> Much to my surprise, Tot told me that she had become a Christian and Art was at the mourner's bench. I need not have been surprised either as so many in the Burg have been converted during Rev. Nickerson's revival meetings.

In another entry she writes: "Received a letter from Papa. All were well at home and as I expected, Art is now a Christian. I was somewhat surprised to hear that Waring Foster was also a Christian and that he was baptized Sunday." She is open about her own ambivalence to religiosity or at least these moves towards conversion: "Received a letter from Mama – Rev. Nicherson has stopped his meetings and I don't know whether to be glad or sorry that they won't be going on when I am home." The role of the Black church has always been central to any understanding of the Black experience. Historians who wish to gain a sense of the people and their culture, including their mores, music, and lifestyles, must take that role into account.[23] Many of the social activities Nina Mae records in her diary relate to her membership in the church community. While she expresses some ambivalence about the religious revival, there is no question that she accepts this aspect of her life as taken for granted. Life in Rondeau during her time there seems to centre on the church.

It is interesting that in her diary, Nina Mae rarely mentions her professional life. She seems concerned about the quality of her lessons, but the only references she makes to her actual practice relate to her Sunday School teaching. For example: "Feb. 10th, went to Sunday School and taught my class as usual; not many present. I taught a poor lesson." And again: "Feb. 24th, I went to Sunday School and succeeded in presenting a pretty good lesson to my class; the lesson was on Abram's covenant with god." Clearly, she is proud of the recognition she has received as a teacher, and she sees herself furthering her career: "visit from inspector Colles. He praised me very highly and said I was one of his best teachers … I am glad he was satisfied." But at this point in time, she has not positioned teaching as the central thing in her life. At best, she seems ambivalent about her teaching, sometimes seeing it as routine ("Day after tomorrow I must return to Rondeau and the daily routine of school duties again") or tiresome ("It is quite a task to superintend a lot of children in such work and I had a bad head-ache at night").

Nina Mae's diary suggests that she was following a path very similar to that of many of her African American counterparts, both personally and professionally.[24] In many ways, her diary presents her as a modern, independent woman who does not allow the societal constraints of race, gender, and status to prevent her from doing the things she wants to do. But this story also speaks to a very different context, that of early-twentieth-century rural Ontario, where Blacks made up a very small percentage of the population. Unlike the women in Shaw's studies, Nina Mae did not have access to the vast social network of the sort enjoyed by many professional African American women of that time. In Toronto, and perhaps also in Windsor, the African Canadian community was relatively large, and supportive; rural communities were unlikely to offer the same kinds of support.[25] This suggests a different and perhaps more difficult path for women like Nina Mae, as well as a reliance on different kinds of support than those discussed by Shaw. Like women in other Canadian rural communities,[26] Nina Mae seems to have forged a number of relationships beyond her family that were vital to her emotional well-being. Most of these relationships seem to have been with other young African Canadians,[27] but some crossed social groupings, as evidenced by her White gentleman callers. In no way does she resemble someone beaten down by oppression or struggling to survive from one day to the next. She has chosen to remain single (in fact, she would never marry) and to pursue a career in teaching (which she did in Ontario until her retirement). Shaw suggests that women like Nina Mae, who were only a generation or two from bondage, were raised to be independent, and that this independence is what shaped them more than anything else. Their families had succeeded in surmounting so many barriers that they did not see new ones as deterrents, but simply as obstacles they would have to work to overcome. Shaw refers to them as having "boundless world views."[28] This description sounds like the Nina Mae revealed in her diary, the Nina Mae of evenings passed with music and dancing, of competitive card games where she is annoyed to be beaten by her male colleagues. This is the Nina Mae who is unswayed by male suitors and free to date as many or as few men as she chooses. She enjoys the freedom afforded her by earning her own money, and she exercises that freedom by purchasing fashionable clothing and small gifts such as the novels she sends to her sister. How much or how little the realities of race affect her daily life is not evident from her writings, but as noted earlier, it is important to recognize that the context in which she was living would not have afforded her freedom from systemic constraints. In spite of this, she appears to be a woman with agency and promise who seems to be well on her way to truly knowing who she is and what she wants out of life. This woman is in keeping with Coulter's young women, who struggled through the difficulties that came with teaching during this period but who also found ways to build deep friendships, to splurge sometimes on nice things, to ponder issues of equity (not necessarily having named it as such), and most importantly, to live like the young women they really were.[29] Nina Mae lived at a time when someone like her was only just beginning to have opportunities afforded her, and at a time when the uplift of her race was of the utmost importance. She worked hard and strove to establish a fulfilling career in teaching, supported by her family and all those around her.

The people of African descent who crossed the border into Canada seeking sanctuary from slavery and racism experienced a multitude of outcomes. The story of Nina Mae Alexander and her family is likely atypical and should be looked upon as one of many trajectories these stories followed. Many individuals and families, facing racism and lack of opportunity, chose to return to the United States after the Civil War and well into the twentieth century. Of these, many retained their ties to Canada; others simply treated it as a "stop" on the Underground Railroad, albeit a long one. However these stories are viewed, they should all be seen as representing threads in a tapestry woven from the enduring myth that both slave and free people of colour used to survive: Canada was a place where Black men and women were free in the eyes of the law, and the fulfilment of this promise allowed many individuals and families to survive and provide a better future for their descendants.

NOTES

1 See Brand, "'We Weren't Allowed'"; and Carty, "African Canadian Women and the State."
2 It is difficult to determine the "correct" terminology for describing refugee slaves and other people of African descent in Canada and America. For the purpose of this chapter I utilize the terms "Black" and "African-Canadian" synonymously to denote this group of people, while recognizing that race is socially constructed and acknowledging that the people labelled as such are not homogenous.
3 Some Alexander family documents (including Nina Mae's diary) are housed at the Buxton National Historic Site and Museum, but the majority are in the private collection of great-nephew Spencer Alexander. Because the diary's last entry is made at the end of the small spiral notebook in which it was being kept, it is possible to conclude that it continues beyond what I have managed to locate.
4 See Coulter and Harper, *History Is Hers*; and Sheehan et al., *Schools in the West*.
5 Bristow, *"We're Rooted Here,"* 3.
6 Bristow, *"We're Rooted Here,"* 3.
7 Afua Cooper, "Black Women and Work," 143.
8 In the late 1800s and early 1900s, the term for schools that trained teachers for the public school system. The program length was two years, expanding to four years when the BEd degree was introduced.
9 In this chapter, I define "success" in terms of family and community persistence – that is, in reference to those who remained in Canada after the Civil War and made a life here.

10 According to Spencer Alexander, this story has been passed down through family oral history.

11 Amherstburg marriage record.

12 Varpalotai, "Rural Teacher/Farm Wife," in Coulter and Harper, *History is Hers*, 33–54.

13 A newspaper based in Toronto but circulated throughout Canada.

14 A Negro newspaper based in Detroit, Michigan.

15 Local Amherstburg newspapers.

16 This publication "gave many young Canadian writers their first taste of publication." Lang, *Women Who Made the News*, 53.

17 Coulter, "'Girls Just Want to Have Fun," in Coulter and Harper, *History Is Hers*, 220.

18 Shaw, *What a Woman Ought to Be and Do*.

19 See further discussion in Wilson, "'I Am Ready to Be of Assistance When I Can'"; Shaw, *What a Woman Ought to Be and Do*; and Patterson, "Voices from the Past."

20 Shaw, *What a Woman Ought to Be and Do*, 24.

21 See again Wilson, "'I Am Ready to Be of Assistance When I Can'"; Shaw, *What a Woman Ought to Be and Do*; and Patterson, "Voices from the Past."

22 By 1907, segregation in the school system, which had been entrenched since 1850, had almost completely ceased, although it remained in legislation in Ontario until 1964. Although the school in Rondeau was funded by both White and Black residents (taxpayers), it is difficult to ascertain whether it was integrated in practice. For more on race relations and schooling in Ontario, see Winks, "Negro School Segregation."

23 For more on the role of the church in African-Canadian life, see Higginbotham, *Righteous Discontent*; and Shadd-Shreve, *The Africanadian Church*.

24 Shaw, *What a Woman Ought to Be and Do*.

25 According to Walker and Thorvaldson, segregationist American society allowed for a separate Black society within which ambitious young Blacks could work hard to rise to the top of that society. In Canada, where discrimination was more covert and there was no legislated segregation, it was "more difficult to break out of the social role the White majority had assigned to Blacks." See Walker and Thorvaldson, *Identity*, 31.

26 Varpalotai, "Rural Teacher/Farm Wife."

27 The documentary evidence does not state explicitly that her social group was all of the same age, but the tone of their exchanges leads me to believe this.

28 Shaw, *What a Woman Ought to Be and Do*.

29 Coulter, "Girls Just Want to Have Fun."

6 "A Contented Mind Is a Continual Feast": Tracing Intellectual Migrations through the Promised Land

NINA REID-MARONEY

The story of Parker Theophilus Smith in the "Promised Land" is a short one. It begins in the summer of 1861, when Smith, an established Philadelphia carpenter and shopkeeper, sold almost everything he owned and moved to the abolitionist community of Dresden, Canada West. Three days after arriving in Dresden, he reported to his friends in Philadelphia that the village was "as fine a little place as ever the sun shone upon." This favourable judgment extended to the weather ("the most pleasant climate we have ever been in"), to the water ("the nicest water here I ever drank"), and to his economic prospects. Using the capital from the sale of his Philadelphia drugstore, Smith set himself up as a partner in his father-in-law's carpentry business and did his best to settle into the cultural life of the place. He bought a cow and looked at farms. He went to church, sang in the choir, and when the winter came, took his children on sleigh rides – but despite his best efforts, he was unable to make himself over in the model of a Canadian pioneer. A few months after he arrived, he declared to his friends, "*in Canada I will not stay.*" By the summer of 1862, the Smith family had moved back to Philadelphia.[1] At first telling, Parker Smith's story might seem little more than a familiar account of migration and reverse migration (although oddly timed) across the "fluid frontier" between Canada and the United States.[2] He arrived late in the history of Black immigration to Canada West, and he was neither the first nor the last to return in the tumult of war. It is clear that he missed his friends and was, in his own words, homesick. But there is more to it than that. Why did a few months in Canada – time spent "under the beneficent sway of Victoria's sceptre" – fire in him a deep republican and abolitionist passion that could only be lived out in the home he had just abandoned?

Smith had the historically obliging habit of writing descriptive letters, of substantial length, and generated in a short period during his life in Canada. A series of these were intended for public readership and were printed in the *Christian Recorder,* the African Methodist Episcopal paper. Others were private, addressed to Smith's friend in Philadelphia, Jacob C. White, Jr. All of the letters offer interesting commentary on the political, social, and religious life of Black abolitionists in the village of Dresden. Together, they provide an account of Smith's efforts to find his place in a political world that was shifting under the pressures of civil war and allow us to approach the puzzle of his Canadian experience.

Precisely because it was brief, and because he wrote about it with intensity and candour, Smith's experience in Canada has much to tell us about the larger theme of intellectual migration through the Promised Land. I am using "intellectual migration" to draw attention to the neglected intellectual history of African Canadian communities, to the movement of ideas that changed as a result of that movement and in turn changed the world in which they were applied. It is a useful term to apply to a study of Black migration to Canada because that historical reality has been so often treated in terms that ascribe a causal power to broad historical forces, without much reference to individual decisions. In the nineteenth century, even sympathetic observers used aggregate terms to describe areas of Canada "thickly settled" by Black migration, or the passage of people forced out by the Fugitive Slave Act of 1850, as though the movement of so many people in the face of oppression could only be described on the sort of scale that made individuals all but disappear.[3] Nor does the contemporary invocation of the Underground Railroad necessarily help much, given the tendency to use that term as a shorthand that circumvents rather than provides historical explanation, particularly in the sense that it obscures the history of free people. My narrow focus on Parker Smith and the theme of intellectual migration is a purposeful if temporary device. I mean to dwell on the agency of individuals, who were convinced that even in the face of larger structures of power and sweeping historical forces they could not control, ideas mattered.

Parker Smith's intellectual migration, however, will ultimately draw us outward, towards an expansive vision of the world through which he moved. His letters show us particular and clearly delineated threads in a vast web of connections between Philadelphia's Black community and abolitionist enclaves across the southwestern counties of Canada West. A close reading of his work makes those connections plain.

By following Smith, and the experience of one family among thousands drawn to the Promised Land communities, we can begin to see patterns in the complex ideological landscape created by Black migration to Canada West.

Part of the key to understanding this ideological complexity lies in sorting out the way in which Canada West was both a metaphor for freedom (in any number of senses of the word) and the actual ground on which freedom might be constructed. The land itself was important. In a recent study of regional and national identity in eighteenth-century France, Graham Robb notes the hostility and resistance that often met government map-makers as they travelled through the countryside trying to bring bureaucratic order to the outer reaches of the French nation. For those on the margins, being "placed on the map" meant losing a separate identity. In nineteenth-century Black communities in Canada West, a different dynamic was at play. Creating a historical geography of freedom – finding a way *onto* the map – was an act of affirmation rather than denial. Throughout the history of Black settlement in Upper Canada / Canada West, the firm details of geography worked to bring the symbolic discussion of life in the Promised Land back down to earth.[4]

The abolitionist record of Canada West is filled with references that combine the elements of metaphoric language with a specific sense of place.[5] In such cases, biblical language signalled the way in which ordinary life in the Promised Land was never altogether ordinary. Even in its most mundane aspects, it was shot through with spiritual meaning. This was certainly true among visitors writing about Canada for the abolitionist press, who were quick to conflate the ordinary and symbolic meanings of the landscape through which they moved. With even greater power, this identification affected those who came to stay. It was one thing to observe, as the Black abolitionist Samuel Ringgold Ward did, that Canada was the "great moral lighthouse for Black people on this continent"; it was a different matter to make the Promised Land one's own – to feel, as Smith did, "more free here than in any other place I have lived."[6] For Smith, the move to Canada had a startling effect. It forcefully collapsed the ironic distance between the idealized and the ordinary; it also invited him to see himself stepping into the historical process whereby freedom might be secured. In Philadelphia, Smith understood that a historical consciousness formed the core of resistance against racial oppression; in Canada West, he suddenly found himself in a position to do something about it. Ideas about freedom mattered everywhere, but they mattered here because those ideas could be safely drawn down from the realm of abstraction. Smith came to understand the ways in which the language of liberty could be translated in terms most solid – in the ownership of land, in the political franchise, education, prosperity. There was racial prejudice here, too, but it did not entirely create the terms of reference for Black culture. The irony of his circumstance was not lost on Smith. Ten months in the "Promised Land" had transformed his hopes and was sending him back into the wilderness of the American republic, sure of the part he might play in its redemption.

In order to see something of what Parker Smith found in the Promised Land, we must go back to Philadelphia. Smith and his wife Margaret Mount Smith first appear in the historical record as new arrivals in the Quaker city in the 1840s. They had followed a well-travelled path leading from the politically active free Black community in the neighbouring slave state of Delaware to the broad cultural vistas of Philadelphia.[7] In the same period, other members of Margaret Mount's family, including her parents and younger sister Eliza, also left Delaware, continuing on to Canada West.[8] From the outset, then, Smith knew – and resisted – the emigrationist argument. For the moment, Philadelphia offered sufficient grounds for optimism.

In their new home, Smith worked as a carpenter and invested in a small drugstore. The family prospered. On the eve of his move to Canada, Smith appears in the federal census as a steady shopkeeper, thirty-eight years old, who owned six hundred dollars in real estate. The city's cultural opportunities, even more than its economic ones, appealed to Smith's imagination and sense of identity. Between 1855 and 1860, he secured a place in the Banneker Institute, a literary and debating society founded in 1855 by some of the leading sons of Philadelphia's Black community.[9]

On the crowded stage of literary clubs, religious societies, and voluntary associations that flourished in nineteenth-century Black Philadelphia, the Banneker Institute claimed a unique role. Its namesake, Benjamin Banneker, was an African American astronomer and mathematician as well as the publisher of an early-nineteenth-century scientific almanac. His correspondence with Thomas Jefferson during the latter's term as president had made Banneker's learning more widely known while at the same time exposing the uneasy combination of admiration and condescension that characterized Jefferson's dismissal of Banneker's scientific achievements. Following Banneker's model, the institute's members dedicated themselves to self-improvement and racial uplift. They took the Banneker legacy seriously and worked throughout the 1850s to recover original Banneker letters and artefacts (then in the keeping of the Pennsylvania Abolition Society), to create a proper monument to him, and to bring his remains to a burial site at Philadelphia's Olive Cemetery.[10] Nineteenth-century Philadelphians remembered Banneker's work but were most taken with his cultural persona. As a learned African, his very presence in the field of scientific inquiry had shaken the scaffolding of Jefferson's carefully articulated views on racial difference. Banneker's name evoked a powerful tradition of resistance against racial prejudice lodged in the highest places.

As an officer in the Banneker Institute, Parker Smith proved energetic and capable. He helped arrange the institute's lectures and debates, tended its library, and worked as its corresponding secretary, and in 1860 he became the institute's president. His colleagues there included the sons of the most prominent Philadelphia families – Octavius Catto, Jacob C. White, Jr, Isaac Wears – and the institute's early records reveal a good deal about their social and intellectual aspirations, particularly their emphasis on fostering scientific learning among Black men. This work had a dimension of outreach to a wider world – early on, for instance, the institute had extended membership to Solomon Brown, the first Black natural historian and clerk at the Smithsonian in Washington – although it focused intensely on the Philadelphia community. The Banneker Institute had close links with other groups, including the Philadelphia Library Company of Colored Persons (with which the institute shared meeting rooms) and the Institute for Colored Youth. The Banneker Institute, then, provided Smith with an avenue to the centre of Black Philadelphia's literary and cultural life.[11]

By a fortuitous twist, we know even more about Parker Smith's intellectual interests and reading habits. The institute kept a detailed record of his personal library, which he sold to the Banneker Institute in 1861. The 166 volumes in his collection ranged from classical works to modern physiology, from travel accounts to some unexpected books on Moravian theology. There was a particular emphasis on works dealing with African history, travel, and culture, and he had assembled an up-to-date collection of materials on the emerging science of ethnology. These latter works included Alexander Walker's treatise *Intermarriage*, the natural historian John Bachman's *The Doctrine of the Unity of the Human Race Examined on the Principles of Science*, and R.G. Lathman's *Man and His Migrations* (1851).[12] Ethnology was Smith's particular forte, and in a series of lectures sponsored by the Banneker Institute in 1860, he brought the latest scientific evidence on the unity of the human species to bear on a broader discussion of racial equality. No one in attendance at the lecture could have missed the highly charged political point noted in the Banneker Institute account of the talk: Smith's lecture "entirely swept away the monkey theory as applied to negroes" and demonstrated the scope and richness of ancient African civilizations.[13]

In the record of Smith's Banneker activities, we see an emerging portrait of a figure most at home in a scientific and cultural tradition that drew its greatest lessons from the study of history. When it came to human history, Smith turned to the conjectural model provided by the historians of the Scottish Enlightenment. David Hume's *History of England* and *Essay on Human Understanding* appeared in Smith's library, and judging by Smith's own work on the subject, it is clear that he recognized in the Scottish Enlightenment's appreciation for conjectural history a set of possibilities well suited to his own purposes. It was the conjectural historian's business, after all, to gather the available evidence from widely scattered sources, filling in the gaps in evidence by supplying causal connections based on the general principles of human nature. In the hands of Parker Smith, conjectural history provided a way back to an African and American past that had been obscured by slavery, denied by slaveholders, and all but erased by the constructs of racial prejudice. Conjectural history was a way of writing a history that reached beyond all of this. It was the sort of history meant to illuminate the problems of the present – in particular, the way in which any path towards human progress in the United States had been turned back at the abyss of slavery.

We find Smith from the summer of 1859 through the spring of 1861 engaged in editing a long treatise on African history by John H. Johnson: "Argumentative Observations on the Ancient Civilizations of the Ethiopian or African Race," a work that the Banneker Institute had acquired in manuscript form and hoped to publish. Promising an impartial gathering of the evidence rather than an impassioned plea for equality, Johnson set out to "prove the ancestral greatness of his despised race and to defend them from the imputation of natural inferiority." It was the sort of argument – free, as the author put it, from "all declamation or sickly sentimentalism" – that appealed to Smith's scientific and historical interests.[14]

Smith's work on the Johnson manuscript also illustrates the way in which the Banneker Institute focused not only on encouraging the intellectual life of its members but also, more generally, on gathering a historical record of the intellectual life of Black Americans. The institute's members propounded the idea that they were bearers of Black intellectual history. They gave this role formal expression later in the nineteenth century when the institute became the foundation for the American Negro Historical Society, founded in 1897 by Jacob C White, Jr, Parker Smith's closest friend. The bibliophile William C. Bolivar, who assembled the Historical Society's library, was also a friend of Smith as well as an early member of the Banneker Institute. As William C. Welburn reminds us in his account of Bolivar, such men saw an activist purpose in gathering the scattered materials of Black intellectual culture. Philadelphia had long been a place for the gathering of people as well as the gathering of fragments of Black historical memory – it was almost as though this sort of work was meant to offer some measure of counterbalance to the diaspora itself. It was an act of bearing witness. The work was never easy, nor was it especially safe, given the thread of racial violence that ran through Philadelphia and was woven into the fabric of everyday experience, but that made it all the more important. In his account of Philadelphia and the creating of historical memory, Gary Nash points out that Philadelphia was at the centre of African American efforts to harness historical consciousness to present-day political aspirations. This was, as John Ernest termed it, the creating of a "liberation historiography" – a tradition of nineteenth-century African American writing that enjoined readers to take an active part in tipping history itself towards racial justice.[15]

In the 1850s, Parker Smith was prepared to write liberation historiography, but was he prepared to live it? The question becomes even more interesting when we consider that the Banneker Institute had ambivalent relations with an earlier generation of Philadelphians who had long been engaged in abolition work. The members of this latter group, self-described by abolitionist Robert Purvis in an 1867 letter to Parker Smith as "composed of fossils," closely shared a history of political work through the convention movement and the Philadelphia Vigilance Committee.[16] William Still, Stephen Smith, William Whipper, and Jacob White, Sr, were all known to Parker Smith, and he to them – Still and Stephen Smith had both accepted honorary memberships in the Banneker Institute in 1858. But there was perhaps more than a generation gap dividing the older men from the Banneker Institute's members. In the 1850s, men like Smith, Still, and White, Sr, were hardly unfavourable to intellectual freedom and cultural advancement of the sort they too had been working towards since the 1830s. But they also believed in direct action.[17] The Banneker Institute had taken a clear public stand against slavery and racial prejudice, and Parker Smith himself had given an impassioned speech on this subject on the Fourth of July in 1859.[18] But while there may have been, as Tony Martin has argued, "a thin line between purely intellectual and more broadly-based activism" for the men of the Banneker Institute, it was nonetheless a line that Parker Smith seemed reluctant to cross.

A review of the Banneker Institute meetings from the winter of 1860 makes the point. In November, a few weeks after the election of Abraham Lincoln, Parker Smith gave a lecture at the institute on formal logic. In December, the members resolutely returned to a discussion of Smith's lecture, and Smith spent a good deal of time, we are told, clarifying the distinction between the philosophical categories of logic and metaphysics. It is almost as though such discussions were a means to impose order and reason on a world that seemed to be moving rapidly beyond both.[19] Then in January 1861, as a wave of secession votes swept the South, the institute's former president, J. Wesley Simpson, rocked the intellectual calm by suggesting that its members at least think about taking up arms in self-defence. "We are living in dangerous times," he said, "and we must be acquainted with military tactics." Asked by Parker Smith to explain himself, Simpson explained that the institute must be prepared to act:

> We are in the middle of a revolution. We must not stop to consider whether it is literary or not, if we are such we must be prepared to defend ourselves … If the question of slavery which is now threatening justice and ruin is settled without appeal to arms, we will be made offerings of sacrifice upon the altar so let us be prepared to know how and when we will be sacrificed.[20]

Parker Smith was not prepared to sacrifice himselfd. Within a month of this meeting, he had abandoned his editorial work on the Johnson manuscript. In June, he sold his library to the Library Committee of the Banneker Institute. Until the last possible moment before his departure, he held on to the post of president, resigning in a letter dated two days before he boarded the train for Canada. He left three days before the Fourth of July. The timing seemed to symbolize the departure, at least for a time, of his faith in the republic itself.

The question of immigrating to Canada had been part of Philadelphians' debates about reform and civil rights at home since the 1830s, and Parker Smith's move to Canada played out against this backdrop. The Banneker Institute had entertained many an academic discussion on the question, including a spirited and formal debate in 1855 between Isaac Wears and Mary Ann Shadd, whose 1852 *Plea for Emigration or Notes on Canada West in Its Moral, Social, and Political Aspect: Suggestions Respecting Mexico, W. Indies and Vancouver's Island For the Information of Coloured Emigrants* set out the most influential framework for immigrationist discussion.[21] Other Philadelphians, most notably William Whipper, William Still, and Stephen Smith, all made silent trips to Canada in this period as part of the Vigilance Committee's work. In the case of Smith and Whipper, supporting immigration to Canada also meant developing their own family connections to the small village where Parker Smith would settle. Whipper and Smith quietly invested a fortune in Dresden businesses and properties, even as they kept their options open and their homes in Philadelphia.[22]

In the case of William Whipper, the beginning of the war signalled a resurgent hope for social and political progress at home. He changed his immigration plans and stayed in Philadelphia. For others, though, the outbreak of the war was not cause for optimism. Another member of the Banneker Institute, William H. Parham, working in 1861 and 1862 as a teacher in Cincinnati, wrote to Jacob C. White that he, too, was considering immigration to Canada. For Parham, leaving Ohio was an attractive countermeasure against the rising sense of despair brought on by wartime racial violence in the "free" cities of the north:

> Each day brings in its train of events, which unceasingly admonish us to go hence, for this is not our abiding place. I know very little of Canada, but this much I do know, that there, men are not proscribed by law on account of complexion – color neither makes nor damns the man – the Black man may stand shoulder to shoulder with the White, and declare and maintain his manhood and equality.[23]

But while Parham talked of immigration, in the end he did not go. In Parker Smith's case, the move seems to have been undertaken as a permanent affair, guided by the same view that "without equality we are slaves still." It would be unfair and inaccurate, however, to ignore the context and view his leaving Philadelphia apart from the wider implications of immigration itself, which was always a political act. And although Smith may have intended the move to be an act of disengagement, this was not its effect. In Canada West, Smith found no respite at all from questions of political commitment.

It may not have appeared so at first. Three days by rail and Great Lakes steamer brought the Smiths and their two young daughters as far as Chatham. From there, a coach ride over what Frederick Douglass once described as "no velvet road" brought the Smiths to Dresden. His wife's parents were waiting to give welcome, and the family arrived in Dresden well and happy, as Smith reported promptly to his friends in Philadelphia. The only casualty of the journey was the family looking glass, which had been shattered on the journey. It was a prelude to the dramatic refashioning of identity required of the Smiths in their new home.

Once settled, Smith tried with goodwill to adjust to the odd habits of nineteenth-century Canadian farmers. His new neighbours, Smith noted, made a substitute for coffee using dried peas. They grazed cattle in the forests in winter, sending them out to browse for elm branches when the supply of hay ran out. The hardest thing for Smith to get used to was the way that Canadians blithely used the most beautiful "curled maple and splendid walnut stuff," the envy of Philadelphia cabinetmakers, to make a cheery fire in the family cook stove. Such peculiarities aside, Smith's initial reaction to Dresden brought out a kind of Franklinian hymn to the possibilities awaiting anyone who wanted to come. "The only requirement," he wrote triumphantly, "is INDUSTRY."[24]

One of Smith's first jobs in the partnership with his father-in-law was to build a house for Josiah Henson, the former slave and co-founder of the British American Institute best known for his association with the character of Uncle Tom in Harriet Beecher Stowe's novel. With his hand to the work of building this particular house for "old Father Henson," Smith moved into a world in which freedom was defined by things immediate and tangible. In part, this pleased him. But during his first weeks in Canada, he also wrote home to Jacob White, Jr, and to the *Christian Recorder*, asking for news, books, letters, cigars – anything that might help him re-create the atmosphere of intellectual debate and sociability that had sustained him at the Banneker Institute. These requests came with varying degrees of subtlety: "There are no papers here of any account. Do for gracious sakes send me some daily papers, so that I can see some of the news. When you see anything which you think will be of any interest to me in the papers ... put them in an envelope and direct them to me ... Tell all my intimate friends to do the same, as I cannot get any here." Sometimes he sounded desperate: "Pray what about the Banneker Institute? I have not forgotten it, but I suppose it still lives as it is immortal. The people here know all about it ... Long may it live. *Vive le Banneker Institute.*" Some of his letters published in the *Christian Recorder* put a brave face on the matter of homesickness. "There is something going on nearly every evening," he wrote in August, citing choir practice, the regular meetings of Odd Fellows lodge, a lecture series at church, Bible class, and a "reading circle among the elite of our village."[25] But the life of even the elite in the village was not sufficient. "I could easily accumulate property," he told White, yet "a contented mind is a continual feast you know, and unless a person is satisfied there is no use of talking about staying in a place."[26]

His cultural life having been attenuated, Smith turned his energies towards the institution in the settlement that seemed to show the most promise – the Episcopal mission church led by the English cleric Thomas Hughes. In 1856, Hughes had arrived in the Church of England's mission field in London (Canada West). There he joined the Colonial Church and School Society's "Mission to the Fugitive Slaves." In 1859, at the request of Black leaders and with the blessing of Benjamin Cronyn, he came to Dresden as Bishop of the new Diocese of Huron in order to establish a new church and school.[27]

By the time Smith arrived in Dresden, his mother and father-in-law were already communicants in Hughes's congregation. Other ties bound Hughes's mission church and school to Smith's social circle in Philadelphia. Alfred Whipper, the brother of William, was the schoolmaster at Hughes's mission school, and other members of the Whipper family lived in or near the village, in which they had invested heavily.[28] So it was quite natural for Parker Smith, a member of the African Methodist Episcopal Church in Philadelphia, to join in Hughes's services, to sing in the Anglican choir, and to see the church as a useful foundation for a literary and debating society. Shortly after his arrival, Smith persuaded Hughes to establish the Dresden Mutual Improvement Association. The topics the association chose for debate were reminiscent of those set by the Banneker Institute, and it is not hard to see Parker Smith's hand behind the programs on subjects such as the morality of capital punishment, and whether or not conscience was an innate principle. Through the association, the mission church became the focus of Smith's efforts to replicate some aspects of Philadelphia's literary culture.

At the Mutual Improvement Association's Thursday night meetings, Smith was clearly a long way from the Banneker meetings at Sixth and Walnut Streets on the doorstep of the Pennsylvania State House. Yet with regard to the intellectual companionship that developed between Smith and Hughes, the association did not always suffer by comparison. The Banneker Institute having recently been rejected by the Literary Congress in Philadelphia, which had voted against "any motion made to admit a coloured society," Parker Smith was gratified to find easy intellectual collaboration across the racial divide. He was taken with Hughes – "this gentleman is an untiring advocate of the equality of man, and knows no complexional distinctions" – and with the experience of interracial debate on broad philosophical issues, especially now that those issues need not be centred on slavery. The Dresden association was remarkable to Smith largely because it seemed to have carried all of its participants, at least for a time, beyond the boundaries of race.[29]

The novelty of this arrangement was evident to Hughes as well. During Smith's time in Dresden, Hughes wrote his first and only comment on the emerging class distinctions in the Black community. His remarks on the "trying position of the better class of colored persons" make an interesting contrast to the frequent accounts of his work among the poor (the latter were the sort of accounts more likely to produce donations from the network of English patrons who paid Hughes's salary). Thus, the passages in which Hughes addresses economic and social status are all the more striking. In his reports and letters to the Colonial Church and School Society between 1859 and 1872 (the year the mission school closed), Hughes mentioned the social standing of his parishioners in but a single report, written in February 1862, shortly after the Mutual Improvement Association was created. The difficulties faced by Parker Smith, the erudite and sophisticated Philadelphian trying his best to sustain the life of the mind far from the companionship of his friends and books, come through in Hughes's impassioned description:

We have several extremely well-conducted families here, not fugitives, whose habits and manners and general intelligence are far in advance of the majority of the Whites in the neighbourhood. These persons are entitled to as much, if not more, of our sympathy than even the fugitives. Spurned by the ignorant Whites on account of their color, and regarded with jealousy by the lower class of fugitives, who delight to drag all down to their own degraded level, their position is most painful. The obstacles that lie in the path of colored people, rising in the scale, are insuperable. Good conduct, education and even wealth avail them but little. Any, as a rule, I believe they are disliked worse on these counts. This, to my mind, is the worst feature of American society. What makes the matter more shocking is this, that all branches of the Christian Church give way to it! Ministers, both in the states and in Canada, being for the most part dependent on their congregations for support, are in no position to set themselves against the general feeling. While, therefore, numbers are to be found loud and eloquent enough in their advocacy of the abolition of slavery, and denouncing in the strongest terms the cruelty of the slave-owner; yet hardly a minister of the Gospel can be met with who will take the free-colored man by the hand and treat him as a friend and brother. When I think of these things I cannot help calling to mind the words of our Saviour in Matt. VII 5: "Thou hypocrite, first cast out the beam out of thine own eye; and then shalt thou see clearly to cast out the mote out of thy brother's eye."[30]

Hughes's willingness to expose the hypocrisy of the anti-slavery clergy constituted a risk for him, given his audience. Even more significant is *how* Hughes came round to the view that the abolition of slavery and the destruction of racial prejudice were separate problems. He worked this out not merely as a principle but through his interactions as "friend and brother" to men such as Parker Smith. In this example from the history of intellectual migrations, Smith was not the only one to have changed his mind. And in acknowledging the problem, Hughes offered his friend Parker Smith a measure of hope.

One further episode related by Hughes offers another glimpse of the new patterns of interaction and friendship. In the winter of 1862, Hughes received a gift from his parishioners – a parcel containing cloth for a new suit of clothes, a note to say that the tailoring expenses had been covered, and new dresses for his wife and niece.[31] Hughes accepted these gifts as a mark of confidence and an "indication of the gradual removal of mistrust." For those who made them, the gifts were more than that: they reversed what was by 1862 an iconic image of mission work among fugitive slaves – the distribution of clothing. By clothing the minister and his family, Hughes's benefactors were subverting the racial politics of the mission and expressing that Hughes was a friend and equal. In such relationships, worked and reworked in a fresh political setting, Hughes and Smith alike found new ways to think about how a long-imagined freedom might be made manifest.

Moreover, Smith's perspective on the Promised Land was changed by his realization that Canada West was intimately connected to Philadelphia – or rather, to the aspects of Philadelphia from which he had been insulated by the intellectual comforts of the Banneker Institute. Until he came to Canada West, Smith had little contact with refugees from slavery, and he knew little about the good accomplished through the labours of the Black abolitionist network centred in Philadelphia. In Dresden, reminders of these connections appeared everywhere, worked into the comings and goings of everyday life. An example close at hand was that of Mary Smith, who owned a grocery store in the main part of the village. When Thomas Hughes's initial attempts to find a building lot for his church and a room for his mission school met resistance from White villagers, Mary Smith offered the use of the room above her store. She was closely connected, though not directly related, to Stephen Smith, the wealthy lumber merchant and Philadelphian, who already had family and business connections in Dresden. A few years before Hughes came to Dresden, Mary Smith was quite likely in Philadelphia, where Whipper and Still and other honorary members of the Banneker Institute offered assistance through the Vigilance Committee.[32] As he worshipped in the upper room of the grocery store, praying the prayers he would have known at St Thomas's church in Philadelphia and listening to Hughes affirm the brotherhood of all men in Christ, Parker Smith would have heard a familiar message. But how different was the resonance and meaning of that message in this new setting?

In his growing restlessness over the winter of 1861, Smith was in good company. A restive spirit was moving through the community, focused not only on the American Civil War but also on other promises in other Canaan lands. In October of that year, he witnessed a lively debate over immigration to Haiti as it surfaced in a series of speeches given at the Dresden Baptist Church. He wrote to the readers of the *Christian Recorder*:

Some two or three weeks ago, *our dark minds* were enlightened by William Wells Brown. Brown appeared as the master spirit and Harris as an auxiliary; both being deeply interested for the welfare of the poor, benighted, Canada Negroes. Brown was advertised to speak on Haitian emigration, at the Baptist church in Dresden, and at the appointed time he appeared, armed with all the brazen effrontery that the mission and the occasion required. He stood up, Diotrephes-like, and took to himself all the pre-eminence of Haytien affairs.[33]

It was during his speaking tour of Canada West, which he undertook with James Harris in the autumn of 1861, that the abolitionist William Wells Brown wrote his letters on "The Colored People of Canada." These would be consulted by his contemporaries and by historians when they assessed the success of Canadian settlement. Brown's letters reminded readers that while the Black pioneers had done everything in their power to make Canada work, all was not as it should be – and more importantly, all was not as it *might* be elsewhere.[34] Parker Smith was skeptical; even as he entertained thoughts about leaving Dresden, he found nothing redemptive in the prospect of moving to Haiti.

Brown's insistence that the people of Dresden ought to "make trial in the land of the palm" drew the full force of Smith's intellectual disdain. More importantly, however, the appearance of the Haitian immigrationists in Dresden highlighted the community's importance to what was a transatlantic culture of abolition.[35] Smith understood that Canada West was part of a global movement of people of African descent and that the ideological questions raised by immigration from the United States to Canada West or Haiti – or anywhere – were far from resolved. He must surely have recognized that something strange was at work. By moving to Canada, he had not abandoned the political and social and historical preoccupations of abolitionist Philadelphia at all – if anything, he had moved closer to them.

This should not be surprising, given the context. Abolitionists of every persuasion had been churning through Dresden throughout the 1840s and 1850s. The resulting ideological admixture made for a potent draught and was even more concentrated in what Smith called "the diminutive ... village." In such close quarters, it was impossible to remove any contemplation of education, or for religious instruction to take place *without* reference to racial politics and emancipation.

One of the first events Smith attended in Canada drove this point home. The occasion was an end-of-year school picnic, held at the Hughes farm just outside the village. The jubilant tone of the spirited addresses from prominent Black abolitionists, including Revs. William P. Newman and Samuel Davis, all but evaporated when the White superintendent of schools, the Reverend John Gunne, took the stage. Smith recorded:

> The tenor of his remarks, in great measure, went to justify the prejudice now existing here. He said in substance, that the colored people came here as fugitive slaves; that it is the disposition of Englishmen to rule ... [that] the word of God teaches me, Servants obey your masters ... [He]

instanced the case of the Israelites, who waited until Jehovah sent them a deliverer, thus inferring that the colored people must wait until God sends them a deliverer.

In his response, Smith the historian spoke freely to expose the "unmitigated audacity" of Gunne's remarks: "I wonder what White people ever waited until God sent them a deliverer to rescue them from slavery. What did the Angles, the Saxons, the Danes, the Franks, and the Normans do when the Roman empire encroached upon their territories?" Then, in a well-placed barb to catch Gunne, Smith ventured out of the realm of history and into the moment: "I supposed he knows that the days of miracles have passed away, no more Moses are raised up in our days, their race being played out, and a race of men taking their examples from Onesimus having supplanted them." Standing in the grove at Hughes's farm, in the middle of what was supposed to be the Canadian Canaan, surrounded by abolitionists and the self-emancipated, there was simply no room to keep the discussion of freedom at the safe distance afforded by historical abstraction.[36]

Smith's letters contemplating a return to Philadelphia do not suggest that he had suddenly acquired what Mary Ann Shadd had wryly alluded to as a belief in some "powerful miracle for the overthrow of slavery" in the United States. The days of miracles, as Smith had said, were gone. When he left Dresden, there was not yet any sign of even the most preliminary of emancipation proclamations, and the war news offered little to inspire hope. Smith's letters tell us he was finding hope elsewhere: in education, ownership of land, economic prosperity, political participation, and freedom from racial violence, and in the example of goodwill as preached and practised by his friend Thomas Hughes. In one sense, this was, as Hughes put it, the "day of small things," not to be despised.[37] Smith seemed to realize that the "day of small things" sometimes blazed a path to things large – to abolition, civil rights, history, progress, and liberty. In Dresden, where "everybody is civil and polite and everybody knows everybody," the discontented Parker Smith found reason for good cheer and a growing sense of what might come to pass if the Promised Land turned out to be in Philadelphia after all.

A few months in this strange community – a distant outpost of the British Empire that was also a remarkably well-connected centre of transatlantic abolition – was enough. Gazing out over the placid waters of the Sydenham River, and reading copies of Forney's *War Press* kindly forwarded to him by Jacob White, Parker Smith recovered some of his old passion for the republic. In his last letter to White, the transformation was complete. Smith the man of letters now placed himself in other company. Abolition, he wrote – using that word in his letters for the first time – "is my desire. And as William Whipper said to me, I am satisfied to share with my brethren in bonds, and if the war leaves me with a shirt and a pair of pantaloons, if it abolishes slavery, I am satisfied."[38]

Parker Smith's sudden translation into the Promised Land in July 1861 had drawn him away from conjectural history as an intellectual pursuit and towards a lively historical consciousness that demanded some sort of intervention in history's course. His return to Philadelphia placed him squarely in the company of his Banneker friends once more, but now, his work would be directed towards the explicit goals of racial and political progress. In the space of a few months, Smith had gone from hosting choir practice for the Anglican mission church in Dresden to hosting the Hutchinson family singers – whose performances of the nineteenth-century equivalent of protest songs had made them celebrities in abolitionist circles – at a benefit in Philadelphia for the Social, Cultural and Statistical Association of Pennsylvania.[39] Smith turned his energies to this association, which was more activist than literary, and joined William Still, Octavius Catto, Jacob White, and other old friends as it led the state through civil rights work in wartime and through the years of radical Reconstruction.

Parker Smith's remaking of his political identity draws our attention to the world of abolition and racial community that straddled the border between the United States and Canada West. It also tells us much about how this interaction shaped the character of Promised Land communities. For some, the sense that everyday life was infused with political meaning gave every reason *not* to return to the United States, even though it was clear that the Promised Land could be a deeply disappointing place. This world's ideological sophistication does not really come through in descriptions of Canada as the "end of the Underground Railroad." Nor do we do that world justice by thinking only of the symbolic understanding of the emigrationist debate, as interesting as those symbolic associations are. Parker Smith's experience points to interesting things about his sojourn in Canada West, but it also opens new questions about the world in which his Canadian relatives and neighbours chose to stay.

Accordingly, Parker Smith's story becomes a starting point, and the most interesting questions it raises may turn out to be ones I have yet to address. There is little in Smith's letters about his wife and his children, although at times it seems that Smith's own identity was bound up in traditional ideas about masculinity as the measure of humanity – as in his remarks on the "manful exercise" of the vote in the election of 1860. Institutions like the Banneker Institute, which was open to the discussion of topics such as women in history (one of Smith's lectures) but not open to female participation, shaped concepts of class *and* gender identity and the ways in which those categories were tied to race and overall "improvement." Regarding Margaret Mount Smith's experience of freedom, her sense of identity in her Canadian home, and her views on whether the family ought to be uprooted for a second time in the space of a year, we know almost nothing. However, a singular reference in the diary of Thomas Hughes turns our attention towards the household of Smith's father-in-law, Albert Mount, and the actions of Smith's sister-in-law, Eliza. In January 1863, Hughes tried to bring about a reconciliation between Mount and his wife and daughter, who was a communicant member of his church. "It appears that her father and mother, neither of whom make any profession of religion," Hughes wrote, "quarreled about a week ago and she in taking her mother's part, gave way to ungovernable passion which was witnessed by the adjoining neighbours and of course soon got noised abroad."[40]

Although he claimed "nothing that has occurred since the opening of this mission has occurred that has been to me a heavier blow than this," Hughes disciplined Eliza Mount by suspending her from communion. The rebellious daughter, by engaging in a public quarrel with her father, had challenged the patriarchal authority that both Hughes and her father sought to maintain, even as she commanded an authority of her own on religious grounds. On the level of the personal, it was she, and not the father, whom Hughes respected. In a world in which the sacred and mundane, the personal and political, the redemptive and practical all ran together, at what point did it become possible for women of the Promised Land to escape traditional expectations regarding how and where their spiritual authority might be exercised? The evidence for this draws us into a discussion of the next generation, of the daughters who pushed the theology of freedom towards its logical consequences for women.[41]

There are deep and resonant ironies in the relationship between African American and African Canadian cultures of resistance, and there are good reasons for us to listen for them now with particular care. John Ernest has argued that nineteenth-century African American historiography was meant to dwell in the land of paradox. African American historians, including Smith's friends in Philadelphia, fashioned new historical narratives even as they challenged the sufficiency of the *idea* of historical narrative itself. Could any narrative structure contain or cope with the incomprehensible enormity of slavery's evil? In his reading of African American historians, Ernest posits something approaching a postmodern awareness of the way in which historical understanding breaks down. It is appropriate, then, that even in our own time, Smith's account of the Promised Land still carries with it the edge of "liberation historiography," cutting across the grain of prevailing narratives in African Canadian history and in Canadian history more generally. Smith alerts us to the dangers of easy and sentimental interpretations of his past. He shows us that the movement of people and of ideas defined the Promised Land, and his intellectual migration through the Promised Land reveals that it was complicated terrain indeed. It could contain hope and disappointment, loyalty and disaffection, divine intervention and worldly ambition. Such complexities bring us back to Smith's use of the aphorism that "a contented mind is a continual feast," to describe precisely what he was not. The Promised Land did not provide contentment, or complacency, or a feast of any kind – but it did supply in abundance a new kind of hunger.

A coda: In the autumn of 1871, Parker Smith's friend, Thomas Hughes, was preparing for the consecration of the new church in Dresden – the crowning achievement of his life's work. But on the eve of the visit from his Bishop, we find Hughes in anything but a triumphal mood. "Felt very much depressed in spirit," he confided to his journal. "Sometimes think that my work is done in this mission. The change brought about by the great influence of the Whites has made my work much more trying and difficult than formerly. The unchristian prejudice against color seems to be ineradicable." At the same time, Parker Smith in Philadelphia had his own reasons for despair over ineradicable prejudice. His old friend from the Banneker Institute, Octavius Catto, had been murdered in Philadelphia in the midst of election-day violence that targeted Black political leaders in the wake of the Fifteenth Amendment. Both Smith and Hughes were in mourning. Their shared sense of loss can be used to measure the distance, and the common ground, between Smith's Philadelphia and the Promised Land he had left behind.

NOTES

1 Parker Smith's letters first came to my attention through the introduction to Ripley, *Black Abolitionist Papers* (*BAP*), vol. II. Parker Smith to Jacob C. White, Jr, 27 July 1861, Jacob C. White Papers, Moorland Spingarn Research Center, Howard University.

2 The term "fluid frontier" is Afua Cooper's. See his "The Fluid Frontier."

3 For an insightful historiographical approach to the quantitative study of African American migration and historical agency, see Blocker, *A Little More Freedom*.

4 Robb, *The Discovery of France*.

5 For one striking example, see Lucretia Mott to Edmund Quincy, 24 August 1848, printed in Palmer, ed., *Selected Letters of Lucretia Coffin Mott*, 165–6. The point is discussed in further detail in Reid-Maroney, "Millennialism and the Church of England's Mission."

6 Samuel Ringgold Ward to Henry Bibb and James Theodore Holly, October 1852, in Ripley, *BAP* II, 224–8. The discussion of the fragile nature of freedom in the "Canadian Canaan" still begins with Winks, *The Blacks in Canada*, and the work's general orientation, which was to shatter the resilient myth of Canadian moral superiority and complacency on matters of race. "Canadian Negro Hate," to borrow Ward's term, is the subject of Silverman's *Unwelcome Guests*. On the history of race and the Canadian legal system, see Backhouse, *Colour-Coded*; and James Walker, *"Race," Rights, and the Law*. For further discussion of Ward, see Reid-Maroney, "History, Historiography, and the Promised Land Project," in this book.

7 See Dalleo, "African-American Abolitionist and Kinship Connections in Nineteenth-Century Delaware, Canada West, and Liberia," in this book.

8 Federal Census, Philadelphia 1860; Camden Township Census, 1861; Dresden Village, 1881.

9 On the Banneker Institute's history and influence, see Lapsansky, "'Discipline to the Mind'"; Tony Martin, "The Banneker Literary Institute of Philadelphia"; and Banneker Institute Minute Books, Microfilm of MS, American Negro Historical Society Collection, Historical Society of Pennsylvania.

10 Banneker Institute Minute Book, 14 December 1859.

11 On the wider literary and cultural world of free Black Philadelphia, see Winch, *Philadelphia's Black Elite*; Winch, *A Gentleman of Color*; and Winch, *The Elite of Our People*. On Jacob C. White, Jr, see Harry Silcox, "Philadelphia Negro Educator, Jacob C. White." On Octavius Catto, see Silcox, "Nineteenth-Century Black Militant: Octavius V. Catto"; and Biddle and Dubin, *Tasting Freedom*.

12 6 September 1861, List of Books from library of P.T. Smith, Banneker Institute Minute Books, ANHS Collection.

13 Notice of a lecture by Parker T. Smith, 4 March 1860; Roll book, 1854–65, Banneker Minute Books, ANHS Collection.

14 John H. Johnson, "Argumentative Observations on the Ancient Civilization of the Ethiopian or African Race," MS fragment, Banneker Institute Records, ANHS Collection.

15 Welburn, "To 'Keep the Past in Lively Memory'"; Nash, *First City*; Ernest, *Liberation Historiography*.

16 Robert Purvis to Parker Smith, 2 February 1867, Banneker Institute Letter Book, ANHS Collection.

17 Richard Allen, "Address to the Free Persons of Colour of these United States" (Philadelphia: 1830); see Bell, *Minutes of the Proceedings of the National Negro Conventions, 1830–1864*. There are many accounts of the Convention Movement and its place in African American political life, including the analyses offered in Winch, *Philadelphia's Black Elite*; and Bethel, *The Roots of African-American Identity*. McCormick cites the 1833 convention at which delegates, including Whipper, passed resolutions toning down the sense of urgency about Canadian emigration and turning up the pressure to address the problems of free Blacks in the United States; see McCormick, "William Whipper, Moral Reformer." See also Hopkins, "Black Eldorado on the Susquehanna."

18 "Celebration of the eighty-third anniversary of the Declaration of Independence, by the Banneker Institute, Philadelphia, July 4, 1859," Philadelphia, 1859.

19 Banneker Institute Minute Book, 28 November 1860; 5 December 1860; 2 January 1861.

20 6 January 1861, Banneker Institute Minute Book, ANHS Collection.

21 On the emigrationist movement in the Delaware Valley, see Dalleo, "African-American Abolitionist and Kinship Connections," in this book.

22 Whipper's account of his work giving safe passage to fugitives is found in Still, *The Underground Rail Road*, 735–40. See also Whipper to the First of August Committee, *Provincial Freeman*, Dresden, 22 August 1857. On the extensive investments that Whipper made in Dresden, see Carter, "William Whipper's *Lands along the Sydenham*," in this book.

23 William Parnham to Jacob C. White, 9 December 1861; October 1862, MS, Jacob C. White Correspondence, ANHS. See Parham to White, 7 September 1862, in Ripley, *BAP* I:148–9.

24 Smith to Jacob C. White, Jr, 27 July 1861; Jacob C. White Papers, Moorland Spingarn Research Center, Howard University; "Letter from Canada," *Christian Recorder*, 10 August 1861.

25 Smith to *Christian Recorder*, 2 August 1861.

26 Smith to White, November 1861; 27 December 1861; 17 January 1862.

27 Dillon, *Annual Report of the Colonial and Continental Church Society*; Diary of Thomas Hughes, 1859–1872, Diocese of Huron Archives, London;

"Account of the Ministration of the Reverend Thomas Hughes," MS, Diocese of Huron Archives, Huron University College, London.

28 On Alfred Whipper at the mission school, see Colonial Church and School Society, *Mission to the Fugitive Slaves in Canada*, 22; Parker Smith to Jacob C. White, November 1861; Records of the Correspondence Committee, Colonial Church and School Society, MS, Diocese of Huron Archives, Huron University College, London.

29 Report of Delegates to the Literary Congress, 20 May 1858, MS, Banneker Record Books, ANHS Collection; Smith to Jacob White, November 1861.

30 Thomas Hughes to the Colonial Church and School Society, 3 February 1862, in *Mission to the Fugitive Slaves in Canada*, 33.

31 Ibid., 31.

32 1850 Census Records, Lancaster County, PA; Carter and Carter, *Stepping Back in Time*; Account Book of the Philadelphia Vigilance Committee, HSP. On the difficulty in securing a site for integrated worship, see Hughes, *Mission to the Fugitive Slaves*, 20–1.

33 *Christian Recorder*, 26 October 1861.

34 As the editors of the *Black Abolitionist Papers* point out in their introduction to Brown's notes, for all he intended to convince Canadians that the future was in Haiti, parts of his account carry a degree of optimism regarding the life that Black Canadians had made for themselves. *BAP* II:461. It was Brown who wrote these now well-known words about the Dawn settlement: "No place in the Western Province has excited more interest, or received a greater share of substantial aid, than this association, and no place has proved itself less deserving" ("The Colored People of Canada," *BAP* II:477). In his letter to Redpath reporting on his tour, Brown does not mention his address to the people of Dresden (*BAP* II: 458–9).

35 The connections between the village and transatlantic abolition are complex, but to make the point with specific reference to Parker Smith, we need look no further than the Colonial Church and School Society Mission and that society's patron, Lord Shaftesbury, the leading anti-slavery reformer in Britain in the 1850s. *BAP* vol. V: *The British Isles*, contains ample and detailed evidence on the transatlantic connections.

36 Smith to the *Christian Recorder*, 7 September 1861. Hughes gave an account of the same event in his diary entry, 1 August 1861.

37 Hughes, *Mission*, 12. The reference is to Zechariah 4:10.

38 Smith to White, 5 April 1862, in White Papers, Moorland-Spingarn Research Center, Howard University.

39 On the Hutchinson family, see Gac, *Singing for Freedom*.

40 Diary of Thomas Hughes, 5 January 1863, Diocese of Huron Archives, London.

41 See, for example, the life of Rev. Jennie Johnson (1868–1967), baptized by
    Thomas Hughes. Johnson grew up in Chatham Township on a farm a few
    miles from Dresden village and attended the Eleventh Concession school
    in which Hughes preached. She became the first ordained woman called
    to full-time ministry in Canada. See Reid-Maroney, *The Reverend Jennie
    Johnson*.

PART III

Transgeographical Trajectories
and Identity Formation beyond
the Underground Railroad

7 Resisting Imperial Governance in Canada: From Trade and Religious Kinship to Black Narrative Pedagogy in Ontario

OLIVETTE OTELE

In the sixteenth century, England entered a lucrative commerce that up to that point had been dominated by the Portuguese and the Spanish. It was in 1555 that London trader John Lok introduced his fellow countrymen to what would later be referred to as the transatlantic slave trade. Britain spent the next two centuries building up her naval fleet and establishing commercial ties with African traders and American partners before taking the lead in that trade. Meanwhile, opposing ideas about how the British Empire should be managed were emerging. According to the philosopher Edmund Burke, Britain as the world's most powerful kingdom had to protect her reputation and wealth by closely guarding profitable territories – that is, her colonies in the Caribbean. The economist Adam Smith worried about Britain's too close relationship with plantation owners in the West Indies, noting that the entire country was paying the costs to maintain the heavy colonial apparatus. While some quarrelled over colonial profits, the debate over abolishing the trade in slaves mobilized the efforts not of only writers and historians but also of Members of Parliament and religious leaders.

Abolition of the slave trade had not been an issue in the eighteenth century, except when American traders impinged on British networks in Africa. It was in the nineteenth century that the bone of contention between the two became the emancipation of slaves. Indeed, that century came to be known as a century of abolitions, marked by debates over the abolition of the slave trade and by discussions about emancipating slaves in the British colonies and other European settlements. Britain became determined to promote abolition all over the world, with North America as the locus of what many British considered unfinished business. That business was a pressing matter because of political and economic measures taken by the new republic after the American War of Independence.

Canada was to serve as a strategic base from which Britain would work to contain rampant expansionism and dangerous ideas about republicanism. Key questions remained: How could the British government connect with its North American counterparts without aggravating them as it had done when it tried to impose its views on colonial rule before 1783? And how could Britain develop links with North American Black abolitionists? There were Black abolitionists in Britain such as Ottobah Cuguano, Olaudha Equiano, and the group called Sons of Africa, and these people were playing a crucial role in the debate over abolition. Would it not be more appropriate to send Black British abolitionists to Canada to establish a solid base for transatlantic anti-slavery work? Doing so, however, might weaken British influence over the issue, especially among conservative royalists. Clearly, the great question was whether British and North American abolitionists would be able to establish long-lasting transatlantic connections.

Examining the relations between Britain, the United States, and Upper Canada in the nineteenth century will shed light on how old trading partnerships, and military and diplomatic conflict between Britain and the young republic, served as a backdrop against which closer transatlantic exchanges between Britain and Upper Canada would have to be fostered. It is possible that the interplay of race and class heightened tensions between North American and British abolitionists in the nineteenth century. Paradoxically, these tensions may have nourished an already established practice of Black Narrative pedagogy.

The Europeans' appetite for new territories led them to North America. By the sixteenth century, French and English claims over these territories were well established. In the eighteenth century, Canada was still attracting traders and other immigrants. The Canadas, Upper and Lower, were seen by both the British government and runaway slaves as lands of opportunity. The British Colonial Office, established in 1801, encouraged immigration, and newspapers relayed that there was a shortage of labour in these northern territories.[1] Upper Canada needed Britain, or so the British government contended. Economic self-interest and spiritual guidance would be vital to promoting British migration. In this context, it was not unusual for Black abolitionists to tour Britain in order to gather support and raise funds. Yet the relations between British, North American, and Black abolitionists were not always free of tensions.

We contend that the religious praxes and theological discourses of abolitionists in North America – in particular, those of the Black preacher Josiah Henson, a founder of the Dawn Settlement in southern Ontario – were among many examples of Black Narrative pedagogy.

Canada and Britain: Economy, Diplomacy, and Legislation

In 1783, the Treaty of Paris settled the American War of Independence, leaving Britain bereft of thirteen of its North American colonies. American independence and the threat of revolution in France led Britain to enact conservative measures relating to the administration of her remaining colonies. From the British perspective, Quebec would have to have a conservative constitution, and language would be the means to establish British dominance there. In 1791, Quebec was divided into two provinces. At the same time, Canadians would be permitted a form of autonomy that would not jeopardize the principles of empire. The Governor General and assembly would deal with local matters; Westminster would retain its authority to pass laws that protected British interests. As an example, the Church of England was designated the established church in Canada and was provided with lands ("clergy reserves") aimed at helping Protestants gain a solid foothold.

After the American War of Independence, around 40,000 United Empire Loyalists who had sided with Britain during the conflict fled to Britain's remaining North American colonies.[2] Some of them were Black. These British territories had also engaged in slavery, yet they did not wait for the British Parliament to end the practice. At this time, Canada's links with Britain were maintained through men such as John Graves Simcoe, a naval officer appointed Lieutenant Governor of Upper Canada in 1791. A 1793 bill introduced by Simcoe was aimed at gradually abolishing slavery in Upper Canada. In 1803, Chief Justice Osgoode pointed out the obvious: as a result of the 1793 bill, slavery was no longer profitable in British North America. Slaveholders there, after all, had to supply clothing, food, and shelter for slaves all year round even though requiring their labour only for planting and harvesting.[3] After the new legislation was passed, significant numbers of Black people migrated from the United States to Upper and Lower Canada. They often arrived in closely knit communities, where they were employed by the militia to protect British North American borders against ongoing threats from the neighbouring republic.

Around this time, commerce was also at stake, with Britain striving to achieve commercial dominance. In these efforts, it infringed on what the United States considered to be its trading zones. The Chesapeake Incident of 1807, tensions in Ohio between the United States and Native Americans aided by Britain, and the Royal Navy's habit of "press-ganging" American sailors all led to a declaration of war in 1812. Britain had been seeking a reason to spread the Napoleonic Wars to North America, and after Napoleon's troops were defeated, some British forces were sent to Canada. Opinion between Upper and Lower Canada was divided over what would later be called the War of 1812. The British authorities signed a peace treaty more quickly than expected.

By the mid-1840s, relations between Canada, the United States, and Britain were defined essentially by trade. Slavery was now a peripheral issue in those relations; however, each party was struggling individually to come to terms with it. Sigrid Nicole Gallant has suggested that slaves were encouraged to flee and join the Canadian forces. Those who did found opportunities to settle in Canada. Free Black men already living in Upper Canada were offered land if they signed up to be soldiers. From 1783 until the end of the American Civil War in 1865, there was a constant flow of Black people to Canada. In British North America there seems to have been a mutual understanding between White and Black communities regarding the fight against slavery. One could argue that this common ground sometimes contributed to social cohesion. In fact, though, social cohesion in 1830s Upper Canada rested on a careful stratification of society. At the bottom rung of the social ladder were the free Blacks, who were determined to gain voting rights as well as social mobility through land reform and other legislation. Many Black people succeeded in this. According to the historian Frank H. Underhill, Ontario's population was comprised of "ambitious, dynamic, speculative and entrepreneurial business groups who aimed to make money out of the new business community or to install themselves in the strategic positions of power within it – the railway promoters, banks, manufacturers, land companies, contractors."[4]

Immigrants from the mother country also played a key role in Canadian society. A few abolitionists left Britain for Upper Canada, in part for a better life. Belonging to a religious denomination or, better yet, being a trained minister could open the doors to a valuable position. As Allen P. Stouffer has noted, "ministers arriving from the mother country were in great demand, for generally they had better credentials than those trained in the limited facilities of the province; they were quickly put into positions of leadership in the churches and elsewhere, and their status was secure."[5] Rising to a place of prominence was slightly more difficult for those holding clerical positions and for merchants. Stouffer has contended that because they were in professions that did not have direct links with churches, and because they were newcomers, these people were in general "outside the circle of power."[6]

Other newcomers such as runaway slaves struggled to find their place in communities. The response of Whites to the arrival of Blacks in British North America varied according to location. Winks has remarked that "on the whole the Negroes who came to British North America on their own, without the assistance of the British government, were well received into 1830s. By the end of the decade, voices of protest could be heard in various quarters of White Canada against an unchecked Negro immigration, and in the 1840s and 1850s the Negro found himself distinctively unwelcome in many areas of the provinces."[7]

The Fugitive Slave Act of 1850 brought about another wave of Black migration from the United States. In addition, Black people living near the border migrated farther north, where their arrival generated mixed reactions. Stouffer has noted that "the earlier expression of racism was relatively muted, for to have voiced it openly would have risked being branded as a defender of slavery, which mostly people wanted to avoid ... Some British North Americans remained on the sidelines because their racial beliefs told them that emancipation in the long run would be largely a futile pursuit."[8] There were several causes of this shift in public opinion. During the 1820s and 1830s, Blacks had laboured mainly in road construction, in the timber industry, and on tobacco farms.[9] In the 1840s, Irish newcomers were often willing to take on jobs that until then had been the province of Black workers and to accept equally low wages. The shrinking number of jobs in rural areas forced Black workers into cities, where they encountered segregation. Winks notes that there were large Black populations in Canada West and Nova Scotia. By the 1850s, these places had established separate schools, the justification for this being that Negroes and Whites needed to be educated with their own people.

The Howe Commission benefited from the contributions of key figures such as the Reverend Hiram Wilson, a co-founder of the British American Institute, and other prominent people from Toronto, Buxton, Hamilton, London, and Chatham.[10] Its report, published in the United States in 1864, revealed that the place of the Negro in Canadian society needed to be understood in order to avoid any possible uprising

and prepare for their emancipation, which was inevitable. In the report's conclusion, the author, S.G. Howe, contended that emancipation
was necessary but would have to be carried out within a particular
framework. This report raised several points worth mentioning. "With
freedom and equality before the law, they [the Negroes of Canada]
are, upon the whole, sober, industrious, and thrifty, and have proved
themselves to be capable of self-guidance and self-support."[11] Yet even
though Canada was the Promised Land for Black people who succeeded
in crossing the border, life in the British colony was a challenge: "When
they congregate in large numbers in one locality, and establish separate
churches and schools, they not only excite prejudices of race in others,
but develop a spirit of caste among themselves, and make less progress
than where they form a small part of local population."[12] Howe made
no reference to the economic hardship facing Blacks in the larger cities
and towns, who were met with resentment. However much lip service
they paid to freedom and rights, White communities in Canada barely
differed from their American counterparts in their opinion of free Black
people. Howe noted in his conclusion:

> 7th: That prejudice against them among the Whites (including the English)
> is engendered by the same circumstances, and manifested with the same
> intensity, as in the United States. 8th: That they have not taken firm root in
> Canada, and that they earnestly desire to go to the southern region of the
> United States, partly from love of warmth, but more from love of *home*.[13]

Even so, the report's final words emphasized that the labour of free
Blacks benefited Canada: "upon the whole, they promote the industrial
and material interests of the country, and are valuable citizens."[14] This
highlighted the importance of trade.

According to Cain and Hopkins, it is through trade that one can understand the relationship between Britain and her North American colonies in the nineteenth century. Commerce with the United States was
unavoidable – indeed, it was crucial if Canada was to remain under
British rule. Britain's apparently loose grip on the colony's domestic
affairs was in fact what allowed Britain to protect her interests in North
America. In the first half of the century, Lower Canada was thriving
thanks to its agriculture. That prosperity, however, depended on the
St Lawrence waterway. To increase trade with the US Midwest, canals
would have to be built, and those would require financing. In 1841,
Britain offered to help by lending money on the condition that Canada

West and Lower Canada unite under one name, Canada. This condition was intended to reassure London's financial institutions that investing in Canada was worthwhile and to subordinate the rebellious French part of the colony. As a goodwill gesture, the British government extended favoured status to wheat shipped from Canadian ports. However, this preferential treatment ended in 1846, with devastating consequences for the Maritime colonies. Meanwhile, US power was growing, and Britain faced a heavy bill to defend Canada. Public opinion favoured an end to this dependency, with some radicals calling for Britain to leave Canada entirely. Money and reputation were at stake; as British Prime Minister John Russell put it at the time: "The loss of any great portion of our colonies would diminish our importance in the world, and the vultures would soon gather to despoil us of other parts of our empire, or to offer insults to us which we could not bear."[15] Lord Grey, the Colonial Secretary, and Governor General Lord Elgin signed the Reciprocity Treaty with the United States in 1854. The idea was that in order to be independent from the United States and safe from republican ideas, British North America needed to be economically strong. A unified and economically strong Canada would be well rated in London, thus encouraging British businesses to invest in the region. This scheme worked until the 1860s. Cain and Hopkins point to two principal phases in nineteenth-century Canadian history, shaped by particular versions of "Britain's indirect imperialism" that created a "distinctive" North America:

> The first was the attempt between the late 1840s and the early 1860s to achieve growth through closer economic ties with the United States; the second included the emergence of a united Canada from the British North America Act of 1867 and the acceptance of the reality of Confederation by the United States in the Treaty of Washington signed in 1871.[16]

Cain and Hopkins also suggest that Britain was exercising power over the region. Phillip Buckner has argued that this power was negotiated and shared with rather than held by British colonial institutions such as the Colonial Office, noting that "Canadians frequently disliked specific Imperial policies and even more frequently complained that their concerns were not adequately understood in London, but they participated in the Empire voluntarily and for the most part enthusiastically."[17] Drawing on Doug McCalla's work,[18] Buckner continues that "the role of Imperial policies in the economic development of Canada has probably been overemphasized both by Imperial and by Canadian historians."[19] He contends that Canada benefited from an economic, political, and military framework provided by the Empire as a whole, which helped it "develop and evolve into an increasingly self-conscious and mature nation."[20] This brings to light once again the interactions that inevitably existed between the British North Americans and the British themselves. One embodiment of this interaction (among many) was the British Foreign and Anti-Slavery Society.

The British and Foreign Anti-Slavery Society, the Anti-Slavery Society in Canada, and Other Abolitionists in Southern Ontario: From Religious Kinship to Black Narrative Pedagogy

The founding of evangelical churches and the Quaker initiative to speak out against slavery in the eighteenth century culminated in the birth of the British and Foreign Anti-Slavery Society (BFASS).[21] Evangelicals believed strongly in prayer and in the power of the Bible. According to them, one had to experience revelation in order to convert. From that moment on, the individual had to lead a life free of sin. Among the evangelical denominations were Methodism, founded by John Wesley, and the Baptist Church. Evangelical Quakerism appeared in the seventeenth century.

As early as 1657, George Fox, the founder of the Religious Society of Friends, also known as the Quakers, was advising his fellow Christians to treat slaves with care and to free them after thirty years of bondage. According to historian David Brion Davis, the Quaker initiative to end slavery in the eighteenth century came at a time when ideas about natural rights and political freedoms were also being developed.[22] Davis suggests that some American Quakers favoured the slave system in the eighteenth century. In 1730, for example, Quaker merchants in Philadelphia were buying and selling enslaved West Indians. Then in 1750, a key figure emerged among the Quakers: Anthony Benezet, an American who was unknown to British Quakers, published pamphlets against slavery and urged American Quakers to unite against its practice. Benezet's tracts and pamphlets were read in Britain by the abolitionists Granville Sharp and John Wesley, among others.

Benezet's work shaped the abolitionist activities of Thomas Clarkson, whose defence in 1767 of two fugitives, Jonathan Strong and James Somerset, provided him with further arguments in his campaign against slavery. By the 1770s, most Quakers involved in the slave trade or who owned slaves had been excluded from the Society of Friends. American Quakers against slavery suggested to their British counterparts that they create an abolitionist committee, and in 1783, the Committee on the Slave Trade was born, with Clarkson a member. This committee admitted non-Quaker members. Funds raised from members and donors were used to print letters that informed people about the group's meetings and the progress it was making and that asked for more money. These letters were sent to donors all over the world. Also, members' individual skills were recruited: for example, Josiah Wood, a pottery designer and manufacturer, helped design and produce the committee's wax seal, which bore the image of a kneeling African in chains encircled by the words "Am I not a Man and a Brother?"

According to Brycchan Carey,[23] the committee brought attention to the debate through popular journals such as *The Gentleman's Magazine*. It also looked for first-hand accounts of the trade, and to that end, Clarkson travelled throughout Britain talking to people involved in the slave trade, be they sailors, surgeons, carpenters, captains, or whomever. During those travels he met William Wilberforce, a Member of Parliament from the north, who had read his essay on slavery. Clarkson wanted Wilberforce to raise the issue in Parliament; so did Prime Minister William Pitt, a close friend, who knew that the issue could raise Wilberforce's profile both inside and outside the political arena. Shortly before his encounter with Clarkson, Wilberforce had become an evangelical. Although fighting sin was his priority, he agreed to consider taking up the abolitionist cause. On 22 May 1787, the Committee for the Abolition of the Slave Trade was founded, and as one of its first acts, it launched a petition. Clarkson finished his tour in November 1787 and provided Wilberforce with the details he needed to launch the debate in Parliament. Quakers still dominated the committee, but donors and supporters came from all congregations. The fight for abolition did not go as smoothly as expected by Clarkson and Wilberforce. The former had to face the opposition of pro-slavery campaigners who used the same religious arguments as he did; the latter became increasingly isolated among his colleagues in Parliament.

In 1807, Parliament abolished the slave trade in the British colonies. At this point, the committee changed its name as well as its purpose: it now dedicated itself to promoting free trade with Africa. Wilberforce, Clarkson, and others used their connections to convince the government to establish a naval squadron in Africa. Meanwhile, the lives of slaves in the British colonies were still miserable. With the help of the

Quakers, the Society for the Mitigation and Gradual Abolition of Slavery throughout the British Dominions, also known as the Anti-Slavery Society, was founded in 1823. Between then and 1833, it campaigned as before. In August 1833, Parliament passed a bill that abolished slavery in the colonies as of 1 August 1834. Only Antigua and Bermuda freed their slaves immediately. Plantation owners received the equivalent of C$40 million as compensation. The act was worded so as to call for total abolition; but it included an eight-year apprenticeship system that required slaves to work for their former masters in return for food and clothing. This apprenticeship proved to be just another form of slavery. The Anti-Slavery Society accepted that emancipation would come in 1840. However, the Agency Committee, a separate group led by Joseph Sturge, a Quaker from Birmingham, thought it urgent to respond. Under pressure from the public and the government, and facing resistance from apprentices, slaveowners abolished apprenticeship in August 1838.

The Agency Committee now decided that slavery was to be eradicated from the world. Thus, in April 1839, the BFASS was founded. This group, which attracted members from Quaker, Baptist, Methodist, Moravian, and Nonconformist churches, sent missionaries to most British colonies. These missionaries were encouraged to focus on the story of Moses leading his people to the Promised Land. Their first aim was to convert slaves by following rituals that were specific to those populations. The ritual of baptism, for instance, was performed in a river. Church sermons were marked by songs and prayers as well as by direct participation of the congregation. Having been converted, slaves were provided with a membership card indicating they belonged to a religious group. Missionaries also provided slaves with education.

The BFASS organized the first anti-slavery convention in 1840. It collected an impressive number of documents relating to conditions in the colonies and brought them to the Colonial Office in London. The society also provided missionaries with funds to buy settlements for families in need and to free them from the planters' grip. In need of labour, planters turned to Indian labourers in 1837. This would prove to be yet another system of slavery – one that according to the BFASS secretary John Scoble was characterized by high mortality, poor housing, and poverty. By the 1850s, the society had turned its attention to the United States, which, however, had its own anti-slavery movements so that the BFASS was just another fish in the pond. In fact, the position taken by the BFASS during the American Civil War was detrimental to the cause, for it urged people not to fight, being against all wars in principle. In some circles this was perceived as a pro-slavery attitude. Another anti-slavery convention, held in 1867, focused on slavery in the Muslim world and the Indian Ocean region. Around this time, the BFASS decided to reinforce its links with North America by joining forces with Canadian abolitionists.

To that purpose, the BFASS sent representatives to North America. John Scoble was one of them. Born and educated in England, Scoble became a member and then a minister of a Congregational Church. A characteristic of Congregational churches was that they advocated self-government. From the start, members were encouraged to strengthen their congregations by raising funds for them. This practical approach would be crucial to establishing links with abolitionists in Chatham and the Dawn Settlement. After the Emancipation Act of 1833, and the debate over the conditions of slaves in the British colonies, Scoble travelled with Joseph Sturge in the West Indies and South America. He later published a number of books about what he saw, and also lectured against apprenticeship. When apprenticeship came to an end, the London-funded Central Negro Emancipation Committee sent him to the United States. He arrived in North America at a time when anti-slavery groups had opposing views on how slavery could be ended. William Lloyd Garrison was against political action and in favour of women's rights; Lewis Tappan and James Birney favoured the former but were against the latter. It has been suggested, perhaps unfairly, that Scoble, as a member of the Anti-Slavery Society and a witness to the quarrel, prompted the BFASS to exclude women as delegates from the first world anti-slavery convention, held in 1840. Scoble was appointed secretary of the Anti-Slavery Society in 1842, serving until 1852, when his disagreement with Garrison compelled him to resign.

Scoble's links with the Dawn Settlement were forged through his encounter with Josiah Henson while he was touring settlements in Canada. Scoble praised the British American Institute of Science and Industry, a vocational school opened by Henson, Hiram Wilson, and James Fuller at the Dawn Settlement in 1842. In 1851, Henson went to England to raise funds for the school. Around that time, Hiram Wilson and Samuel May, trustees of the institute, challenged Henson's management of it. In London, a committee of anti-slavery philanthropists sent Scoble back to the Dawn Settlement to investigate the matter and to find a means of supporting Henson's school. The board of trustees was to be transferred to the philanthropists' committee once it had settled the school's debts. This was achieved in 1853, at which time Scoble became a trustee of the school. Disagreements with the American Baptist Free Mission Society and then with Henson would lead to costly lawsuits. Scoble's links with the Dawn Settlement were based on practical matters such as the management of the school; however, one important aspect of that collaboration has generally been ignored: the importance of religion in binding the Canadians to the British. They believed they were working for a higher purpose – not just the education of communities, but religious instruction as well.

The discourse of North American abolitionists in some ways resembled that of the British anti-slavery movement. This was because many Canadian abolitionists had been involved in the British anti-slavery campaign before immigrating to Canada.[24] Stouffer has noted that some of these people, including John Roaf and Robert Burns, became leaders of their local anti-slavery societies, while others, such as Charles Stuart, became national figures. Interestingly, out of the 96 Canadian anti-slavery leaders who came from Britain in the 1830s, 77 were Scottish. In this regard, "the London-based British and Foreign Anti-Slavery Society did not emerge until the late 1830s, and only 20 of the Canadian leaders came from England."[25] This is not to say that British North Americans waited for abolitionists from overseas before involving themselves in the emancipation movement. The North American abolitionist movement was well under way by the time Scoble and many of his peers arrived in Canada.

The short-lived Upper Canada Anti-Slavery Society arose in the 1830s. Unable to respond adequately to several high-profile cases and overshadowed by demands for broader reforms that culminated with the Mackenzie Rebellion in 1837, the movement slowly lost momentum. The Fugitive Slave Act and the subsequent wave of migration of Black fugitives prompted Canadian abolitionists to found the Anti-Slavery Society of Canada (ASC). This society's membership included Scottish anti-abolitionists as well as Canadian farmers and labourers, some of whom were Black. Stouffer notes that in the Elgin Association in Ontario,[26] one-quarter of the members were Black. This society focused on two areas. The first was the urgent need to help newly arrived fugitives; the second was the raising of awareness. According to Stouffer, the ASC was more successful at the first of these. By the mid-1850s, public meetings had become fewer and the movement was beset with internal divisions.[27] The society was suffering from a lack of support. Major religious denominations such as the Anglicans, the Roman Catholics, the Wesleyan Methodist Church, and the Presbyterians either ignored the movement or blatantly disapproved of what they saw as meddling in American domestic affairs. This was coupled with serious doubts that Black people would be able to integrate into Canadian society. "This undercurrent of prejudice," Stouffer writes, "retarded the germination of anti-slavery in the province and inhibited the campaign for public opinion."[28] These setbacks did not prevent Black abolitionists from playing a key role in informing public opinion and in educating both Black and White communities in British North America.

Let us examine more closely the praxes and the theological discourse of the North American abolitionists. Yolanda Pierce has established that by the 1830s it was well known that most British and American religious denominations had been involved in the slave trade. Supporters of slavery who had become abolitionists turned to revivalistic evangelicalism to underscore that they had moved away from their former lives and had been born again through conversion. So-called Evangelical Perfectionism allowed them to take possession of the theological discourse and transpose it onto their daily lives. One example of this related to politics and slavery. Political action of the sort advocated by, for instance, Lewis Tappan was thought by some of the newly converted to be the key to ending slavery. Newly converted evangelicals were torn between that political stance and the belief that if God condemned the institution that made slavery possible, he would have made it known; in other words, North America's social organization could not exist outside God's will. Ecclesiastical abolitionists believed that a common ground could be found between what they viewed as these two extremes. They believed that mankind was weak and therefore needed to be supported by institutions such as churches, legal systems, and political parties. Ontario came to be known as one among many "burned over" regions – that is, places where religious revival was regularly experienced. The church reform convention in Syracuse in December 1843 did not lead to unity in terms of how abolition was to be achieved. Yet the various groups involved, such as the Presbyterians, the Congregationalists, the Lutherans, and the Baptists, all had common principles. According to Douglas Strong,

> they were drawn together by a shared ethical interpretation of entire sanctification as a theological justification for innovative activities such as the reorganizing of churches and outright political campaigning ... The

anti-slavery religious groups shared facilities, practiced open communion, and promoted the mutual recognition of members and ministers.[29]

Other Nonconformist churches involved in anti-slavery movements in burned-over regions included the Methodists, the Congregational Friends, and the anti-slavery Baptists. Wesleyan Methodists were also part of that group. They derived their name from the founder of Methodism, John Wesley. Wesley had considered slavery an evil institution that Methodists should have nothing to do with. Yet American Wesleyan churches accepted pro-slavery members because they wanted to grow the church in the American South. In the nineteenth century, condemnation in principle was no longer enough. Methodists adopted the ecclesiastical abolitionists' methods previously cited. The Methodist Church had established itself in Chatham as early as 1786. As for the Baptist Church, it was directly involved in the Dawn Settlement through the work of Edward Matthews, a trustee of the British American Institute. There seems to have been a shift in the ways in which Black groups in Canada viewed White leadership in Black communities. Indeed, although they shared in the battle against slavery, Black Methodists and Baptists were looked down upon. The African Methodist Episcopal Church and the Black Baptist Church accepted them. By 1840, the former had organized a general conference in Upper Canada. In that context, it appears that the figure of the Black preacher was instrumental in empowering Black communities.

Let us examine Josiah Henson's life as he recounted it in his autobiography.[30] That narrative has three main parts: his life as a non-Christian slave; his conversion, and his decision to free his family from bondage; and his life in Canada. In her study of slave narratives, Yolanda Pierce suggests that telling one's story over and over again was one of the many results of the revelation experienced by the slave or former slave. Renewing one's mind, being born anew, was so powerful an experience that it needed to be told over and over again in order to inspire others. In Henson's case, the revelation came when he heard an anti-slavery White settler preach:

> The divine character of Jesus Christ, his life and teachings, his sacrifice of himself for others, his death and resurrection were all alluded to, and some of the points were dwelt upon with great power, great, at least, to me, who heard of these things for the first time in my life. I was wonderfully impressed, too with the use which the preacher made of the last words of the text, "for every man."[31]

The revelation that Henson experienced is called a conversion. In the Bible, conversion can be the result of steady personal growth, or it can be a sudden impulse that has a lasting impact. The individual is inspired to reject old ways and accept Christ as saviour. Conversion is not the result of human deeds; rather, it is the work of the Holy Spirit (as with the conversion of Saul in Acts 9:1–31). Conversion is a three-step process. After the revelation, one must repent and then be baptized. Baptism brings the converted into the sphere of specific social codes. Conversion introduced Henson to the sphere of collective recognition and drew him into social activism. He became a leader of the mind, a preacher, but also – in the context of slavery – a freedom fighter. One does not need to be converted to be passionate about rights and equality, but in Henson's case the association of religion and oppression was reminiscent of the flight of the Jews in the Bible. Examples of conversions in the Bible, from the Samarians to the Corinthians, testify that converted Christians no longer rely on their own determination to pursue potentially life-threatening goals. Why is conversion so important for the oppressed? It is because they learn to humble themselves by looking at God, who according to the New Testament now lives within them. Conversion is therefore a process in which the converted needs Godly guidance. Psalm 37:3 and Micah 7:5–7 tell the believer what lies ahead when one places trust in God. In his narrative, Henson presented one of the many benefits that flowed from his choice to rely on God. Being a member of a recognized religious group gave him a sense of worth and generated the momentum he needed to take action. His first step was to learn more about Jesus Christ, and about preaching, although at the time, he could not read. His conversion introduced him to a sphere that had been denied him up to that point. As a result of the Christian revelation, he was no longer just a slave; he was also a being who had been created by God and who was loved by Jesus Christ:

> He said the death of Christ was not designed for the benefit of a select few only, but for the salvation of the world ... I was in a state of the greatest excitement at the thought that such a being as Jesus Christ had been described should have died for me – for me among the rest, a poor, despised, abused slave, who was thought by his fellow creatures fit for nothing but unrequited toil, and ignorance, for mental and bodily degradation.[32]

Henson, having been converted, had to abandon his old ways. In his narrative, he placed great emphasis on trust, or faith, which was tested through tragic events that would either destroy or strengthen him. During his forced journey to New Orleans, he had the opportunity to kill his young master to gain his freedom. But during his spiritual journey, he had learned to abandon his anger and to trust even when he did not understand why he was being subjugated or why trials came so often during the journey. Asked to lead slaves in Kentucky, he had the opportunity to let his companions go and be free from slavery. He decided not to because his master had put his trust in him. That episode would haunt him for the rest of his life; paradoxically, though, it would also reinforce his belief that one cannot serve two masters and that – as Proverbs 3:5–6 teaches the believer – one should not lean on one's own understanding but instead trust the Lord. In his autobiography, Henson refers several times to the difficulty he experienced at first in allowing God to work in every area of his life. But he finally surrendered to divine advice: he remembered it as the moment he understood he had been tricked by a master to whom he had been obedient and faithful (the man had stolen the money Henson had been saving to buy his own freedom).

Henson's journey to Canada was also a journey of faith. His narrative was similar to the story of Moses leading his people to the Promised Land. It also bore similarities to the story of Saul, who, once converted, became Paul and set about spreading the gospel. Henson's voyage to Britain to seek funding for the institute was another spiritual journey that compelled him to leave his community and its comforts. His story had an impact on British Christians when he went to England in 1849–51 and 1851–52 not only because of Harriet Beecher Stowe's use of his life in *Uncle Tom's Cabin* but also because of its resemblance to the lives of Old Testament prophets and New Testament apostles. From those books, we learn mainly through the stories and parables related to people's lives. It is what we call the Narrative Pedagogy, meaning both teaching *through* narrative and preaching *the* narrative. His journey reminded British abolitionists of the lives of iconic figures such as Ramsay, Clarkson, and Wesley. For instance, there were similarities between Henson's journey north and Clarkson's touring the unknown and sometimes hostile environment of British ports, towns, and cities. There was also Henson's quest for viable funding for the school, which was similar to Wesley's battle to provide education to the forgotten collier communities on the outskirts of Bristol. Finally and perhaps most importantly, Henson's physical and spiritual journey had required a leap of faith that turned him towards his fellow human beings, for mutual help and bonding was the ultimate result of a conversion. As Paul said to the Ephesians (4:16): "The whole body is joined and knitted together by what every joint supplies, according to the effective working by which every part does its share, causes growth of the body for the edifying of itself in love." The narrative testifies that Henson's story did not stay in the spiritual realm. To borrow Pierce's words: "The callings force us to examine not only personal journeys of faith but the impact of religious conversions on the families and communities of these converted believers."[33] Henson's reappropriation of the story of the New Jerusalem would therefore be "a new interpretation of scriptural language, specifically rooted in slave experience."[34]

In this chapter, we have analysed how the anti-slavery movement was organized in Britain and how it operated in the nineteenth century in a context dominated by British imperial ambition and paternalistic views on overseas territories. We have examined the ways in which economics, diplomacy, and legislation were intertwined, and we have debated the principles and the limitations of the BFASS. As a leading player in raising awareness about slavery, the society tried to connect with American settlers and with the newly independent American republic. We examined the nature of the bond between the BFASS and abolitionists in Canada – more specifically, Chatham and the Dawn Settlement. We suggested that a common conception of Christianity (i.e., religious kinship) united the two groups even though the tie proved to be confrontational at times.

NOTES

1 "Gold in Canada," *Staffordshire Adviser*, 15 January 1853; "Demand for Labour in Canada," *Walsall Free Press*, 31 January 1857, 3.
2 Landon, "The Anti-Slavery Society of Canada," 40.
3 Gallant, "Perspectives on the Motives."
4 Quoted in Cain and Hopkins, *British Imperialism*, 234.
5 Stouffer, *The Light of Nature*, 188.
6 Stouffer, *The Light of Nature*, 188.
7 Winks, *The Blacks in Canada*, 142.
8 Stouffer, *The Light of Nature*, 214.
9 Winks, *The Blacks in Canada*, 144.
10 Howe, *The Refugees From Slavery*.
11 Howe, *The Refugees From Slavery*, 101.
12 Howe, *The Refugees From Slavery*, 102.

13 Howe, *The Refugees From Slavery*, 102.

14 Howe, *The Refugees From Slavery*, 104.

15 Cain and Hopkins, *British Imperialism*, 230.

16 Cain and Hopkins, *British Imperialism*, 231.

17 Buckner, *Canada and the British Empire*, ix–x.

18 McCalla, "Economy and Empire," in Buckner, ed., *Canada and the British Empire*, 240–58.

19 McCalla, "Economy and Empire."

20 McCalla, "Economy and Empire."

21 The English Reformation was characterized by the separation between the Pope and King Henry VIII, primarily over King Henry's divorce. This split led to the creation of the Anglican Church. The new Church of England was to be the established church. Clement at first with Roman Catholics, the king rapidly decided on a hard line. Roman Catholic monasteries were dismantled and monastic lands sold to rich noblemen favoured by the king; a hard campaign of repression followed, leading to the tragic episode of the Pilgrimage of Grace in 1556. Non-Anglican believers such as the Jews and other Protestants enjoyed few civil rights, while many Anglican clerics benefited from the Church of England's privileges. Corruption became rampant among the Anglican clergy. Protestant rebellions and religious fervour also became widespread. The Evangelical movement was on its way.

22 Davis, *The Problem of Slavery in the Age of Revolution*, 221–3.

23 Carey, *British Abolitionism*, 119–27.

24 Stouffer, *The Light of Nature*, 40.

25 Stouffer, *The Light of Nature*, 172–5.

26 One of the many groups that supported the Anti-Slavery Society of Canada.

27 Stouffer, *The Light of Nature*, 218.

28 Stouffer, *The Light of Nature*, 219.

29 Strong, *Perfectionist Politics*, 93.

30 Henson, *The Life*.

31 Henson, *The Life*, 15–16.

32 Henson, *The Life*, 18.

33 Pierce, *Hell without Fires*, 11.

34 Pierce, *Hell without Fires*, 129.

8 African American Abolitionist and Kinship Connections in Nineteenth-Century Delaware, Canada West, and Liberia

PETER T. DALLEO

Throughout the nineteenth century, descendants of Africans in the slave state of Delaware persistently advocated the abolition of slavery and the Atlantic slave trade. Influential transnational events such Emancipation in the British West Indies (1 August 1834) were extremely important to the Delawarean message and methodology. Resistance fit into the broader struggle against racial discrimination as well as into the promotion of equality, especially in the city of Wilmington. The migration of Delawareans, some free, some recently freed, and some self-emancipated, to Canada West and Liberia extended the geographical scope of the agitation for reform. Much like their counterparts at home, emigrants abroad lobbied against the Atlantic slave trade and enslavement and racial discrimination in the United States. Although international in their outlook, they remained linked to developments and kin in the First State. Once freed by the violence of civil war, Delaware's African Americans shifted their efforts to achieving full equality by propounding goals such as the passage of the 15th Amendment, which protected the right to vote.

This chapter focuses on the cross-generational public actions and the record of protest in the Shadd and Anderson families and on individuals such as Solomon and Thamar Bayley, Joseph G. Walker, David Gustus, and Peter S. Blake. These were among the Delawareans who interacted with abolitionists, White and Black, on the local and national level to oppose the Atlantic slave trade and enslavement in America and other parts of the world. These Delawareans remained divided over colonization in Liberia, but they were ready to settle, at least temporarily, in Canada West. They valued self-reliance through educational and economic opportunity. To draw attention to their multiple goals, African

Americans organized festive events, issued statements and placed items in the abolitionist and Black press, and signed petitions for increased educational opportunities and civil and political rights.

It is important to remember that Delaware was, and remained until 1865, a slave state and a border state, as did Kentucky, Maryland, and Missouri. The importance of enslavement to each of these places varied. In Delaware the numbers of enslaved had diminished considerably before 1860. Delaware's free Black community was considerably greater by percentage of the total Black population than in any of the other border states. Nonetheless, the enslavers who controlled Delaware's political structure and its economy remained a serious obstacle to abolition.

Border states' free Black population as percentage of total Black population, 1790–1860 (%)

	1790	1810	1840	1860
Delaware	30.5	75.9	86.7	91.7
Kentucky	1.0	2.1	3.9	4.5
Maryland	7.2	23.3	40.9	49.1
Missouri	–	16.8	2.6	3.0

Source: Derived from Kolchin, *American Slavery, 1639–1865*, 241. For a concise description of the border state issue, see Patricia Faust, ed., *Historical Encyclopedia of the Civil War*, http://www.civilwarhome.com/borderstate.htm. For Delaware laws related to enslavement, see http:/www.slaveryinamerica.org/geography/slave_laws_DE.htm.

The first descendant of Africa in what would become Delaware was brought there by the Swedes in 1639. It is unclear whether Antoni Swart, or "Black Anthony," was enslaved or indentured, but he was known to be free man at a later date. During the 1650s and 1660s, Governor Johan Printz employed Anthony to cut hay and sail his sloop. The Dutch supplanted the Swedes, brought more enslaved people, and were in turn displaced by the English, who were also enslavers.[1] By 1790, now a part of the United States, Delaware held 9,887 enslaved persons and 3,999 freemen. By the time of Delaware's initial August First celebration, the enslaved population had declined to 2,605 and the number of free Blacks had increased to 16,919.

Manumission, self-emancipation, and kidnapping accounted for the decline in the numbers of enslaved, and that trend would continue into

Population of Delaware, 1790–1860

Year	Enslaved	Free Black Population	Total Population
1790	8,887	3,899	59,096
1800	6,153	8,268	64,273
1810	4,177	13,136	72,674
1820	4,500	12,958	72,749
1830	3,202	15,855	76,748
1840	2,605	16,919	78,085
1850	2,290	18,073	91,532
1860	1,798	19,829	112,216

Sources: Williams, *Slavery and Freedom in Delaware*, 249–50; Kolchin, *American Slavery*, 241.

the early 1860s. Being a free Black in Delaware, however, did not mean full liberty or equality. Delayed manumission and discriminatory practices had created what William Yates in 1837 described as "a mere mock freedom."[2] White Delawareans devised laws to protect the political and property rights of the majority, and these disadvantaged the free Black community. In January 1808, following the lead of Great Britain, the United States outlawed the external slave trade, but legal and illegal internal traffic continued. Laws intended to limit the flow of enslaved persons in and out of the state were easily evaded. Yet another threat to the security and well-being of the free and unfree Black population on the Delmarva Peninsula was the widespread practice of kidnapping. Delaware's location and easily passable landscape and waterways facilitated travel from and back to other slave states, especially Maryland and Virginia. Organized gangs operated with the sole purpose of grabbing Blacks. Their victims were sold to networks that carried them deeper into slave territory, sometimes even to the West Indies. Ironically, this situation undercut local enslavers, many of whom lost their "property" to kidnappers.[3] Daniel B. Anderson has painted a troubled picture of the First State's tainted past:

We cannot well understand the value of our present position without taking a retrospective view, and contrasting the past with the present condition of the colored people in this country. In the days of slavery, under the State law, we were forbidden to leave our homes and go into a distant State and there continue for a short period and return. Some of us, who, being denied the advantages of education here for our children, were compelled to send them to other States for an education. On the passage of a law forbidding them to leave the State sixty days after the passage of the law, the children had to be brought home. We were denied the right to keep a fowling piece at our houses. Even the church followed suit and oppressed us. The State forbid us testifying on our behalf. If one of the White race used us roughly, and one of them was present and observed the treatment, our lips were sealed; our testimony was of no value. The church followed the same regulation as the State.[4]

This writer might have added that the few laws that protected free Blacks were unevenly enforced. Some White and Black Delawareans actively challenged enslavement but made little headway.

The Delaware legislature rejected numerous abolition petitions between 1792 and 1849. In 1849 it voted against the extension of slavery in the United States, but its directive to the Congressional delegation to follow its lead in Washington was ignored. It was the Civil War that brought about federal legislation to end racial discrimination. Yet not until 1901 did Delaware officially abolish slavery.[5] Prior to 1865, White abolitionists organized a series of anti-slavery societies. These organizations' ranks were filled with members of the Society of Friends, as well as Methodists, Presbyterians, and Catholics. Throughout the period under study, these societies invited abolitionists, some prominent, some less so, to speak in Delaware. A few meetings were integrated, but most were not. These visitors, some of whom were African American, undoubtedly served as conduits for information and ideas to and from the broader abolitionist world.[6]

In 1813, Peter Spencer and William Anderson, spurred by discrimination, created the independent African Union Methodist Church. That institution spread throughout the state and eventually into Pennsylvania and beyond. The mother church and its branches became focal points for discussions about and protests against enslavement and the inequality faced by free Blacks. The inhabitants of free Black communities were active participants in the UGR. In 1845, Wilmington was home to 1,215 free Blacks; by 1853, their numbers had grown to 2,187, or about 15 per cent of the city's population. By 1850, 4.4 per cent of the minority population owned real estate worth between $100 and $6,000.[7] "Fugitives from labor" came primarily from Maryland and Virginia but also from as far away as Louisiana. Meanwhile, an undetermined number of Delawareans were rejecting their enslaved status. Some fled to the neighbouring free states such as Pennsylvania and New Jersey. Canada attracted the self-emancipated, especially after the Fugitive Slave Act was passed in 1850.

This trend continued throughout the mid-1860s. For example, the recruitment in Delaware of Blacks for the US Coloured Troop regiments (USCTs) encouraged the enslaved to leave. In 1864, a newspaper reported on one Delawarean's successful flight to freedom. His "pretend master" had kept him handcuffed in an outhouse while recruiters from the 8th Regiment were in the area. This determined freedom seeker managed to escape to Philadelphia with his handcuffs still attached. When his enslaver followed him to the camp, the commandant refused to surrender the man because he was now a Union soldier. The same reporter claimed that the escapee was one of fifty men recently arrived from Delaware and that "nearly all" had left their owners.[8]

With the above in mind, a review of the anti-slavery involvement of the Shadd family in Delaware, Pennsylvania, and Canada, of the Bayley and Anderson families in Delaware and Liberia, and of individuals in Wilmington such as David Gustus, Joseph G. Walker, and Peter S. Blake demonstrates their commitment to the cause and fleshes out the transnational and cross-generational nature of abolitionist and kinship connections, which characterized Delaware's participation in the movement to end slavery.

The Canadian Connection

The breadth and depth of Delaware's abolitionist and kinship connections are revealed by the Shadd family's activism and that of its close associates, such as the Williams and Williamsons in Delaware, Pennsylvania, and Canada West. Those connections stretched across time, place, generation, and gender and were also evident in the post–Civil War dispersion of many African Americans from Canada. While he lived in Delaware, Abraham Doras Shadd was involved in abolition and anti-slavery activities, which he aggressively continued when he moved first to Pennsylvania and later to Canada. His children, Mary Ann, Isaac D., and Amelia Cisco Shadd, were also reformers. The Shadds were descended from a German, Jeremiah Schad, who had fought in the American Revolution, and two African American women he had married, one of whom was from the French West Indies.[9]

Abraham D. Shadd earned his living as a shoemaker and farm owner. He was named for a local barber, Abraham Doras, who had come from Haiti with his enslaver before gaining liberty in Delaware. Doras and a fellow Haitian owned a barbershop on French Street in Wilmington. When he died, Doras donated $100 to the Abolition Society of Delaware, but we do not know what abolitionist activities he engaged in, if any. It is possible that Jeremiah Shadd's second wife, Amelia Cisco, was Doras's sister, but that is not yet determined. Except for trade and an influx of Haitian émigrés and their slaves, Delaware's links to French territories in the West Indies were minimal. About fifteen years after Haiti became independent, however, a few of the state's free Blacks saw that country as a possible area of settlement.[10] Apparently there were no Shadds among those who immigrated to Haiti.

As a young man, Abraham devoted himself to bettering the lot of other free Blacks. For example, he signed the 1820 petition to form the African Benevolent Society of Wilmington. The petitioners explained why they had approached the state legislature:

> Sensible of the ignorance, and consequent moral degradation of their Brethren the people of Colour; and being sincerely desirous of improvement to lead them to cultivate virtuous principles and so to make them good, and useful Citizens of the State, your petitioners in ... 1820 did ... associate themselves together for the purpose of affording to their brethren the people of Colour, relief in sickness, want and distress, and did form a Constitution and laws for the good government of the Association.[11]

The petitioners sought an act of incorporation as well as the right to receive, take, and hold any lands, rents, goods, and chattels and to sell and dispose of the same. In a separate petition, the free Blacks in the town of New Castle included the right to sue and be sued in courts of law and equity and to purchase and sell goods, chattels, and every description of property. Both requests were rejected.

Ten years later, Shadd joined other prominent Delawareans and non-Delawareans in the fight against the American Colonization Society (ACS) resettlement plans for Liberia. He served with the Reverend Peter Spencer, Thomas Dorsey, Junius C. Morell, Benjamin Pascal, and John P. Thompson. On 12 July 1831, at the African Union Church in Wilmington, in what was characterized in the press as a large and respectable meeting of people of colour, Spencer and the others considered the subject of colonization on the coast of Africa. The following resolutions were unanimously adopted:

> *Resolved*, That this meeting with deep regret the attempt now making to colonize the free people of color on the western coast of Africa; believing as we do that it is inimical to the best interests of the people of color, and at variance with the principles of civil and religious liberty, and wholly incompatible with the spirit of the Constitution and Declaration of Independence of these United States.
>
> *Resolved*, That we disclaim all connexion with Africa, and although the descendants of that much afflicted country, we cannot consent to remove to any tropical climate, and thus aid in a design having for its object the total extirpation of our race from this country, professions to the contrary notwithstanding.[12]

A three-man committee was appointed to develop a report, a part of which stated:

> Africa is neither our nation or home ... That our degraded condition ... cannot be bettered by removing the most exemplary individuals of color amongst us ... Our highest moral ambition should be to acquire for our children a liberal education, give them mechanical trades, and thus fit and prepare them for useful and responsible citizens.[13]

At this time, Shadd remained firm in his belief that Black Americans should not be sent to Liberia or elsewhere out of the country. Instead they should be free to pursue their livelihood as equals in the United States. This approach remained central to his thinking until the mid-nineteenth century. It is significant that this report first appeared in a local newspaper, the *Delaware Free Press*, before William Lloyd Garrison published excerpts in the *Liberator* and then in his *Thoughts on Colonization*. As late as 1839, extracts were being printed in other anti-slavery publications. This serves as an example of Delaware's influence on abolitionist thinking outside the state.

By the early 1830s, Abraham had strengthened his ties to like-minded reformers from other parts of the United States. By 1830 or 1831, he had purchased farmland in Pennsylvania near West Chester in Chester County. The new locale offered his family opportunities unavailable in the slave state of Delaware, such as education for his children. Abraham supported them with sales from his bootmaking shop, which was attached to the main house on the farm. Departing from Delaware allowed him to expand his abolitionist activities in a free state.

Shadd's participation during the 1830s in national abolitionist and anti-slavery meetings brought him a reputation as one of the "old convention men."[14] He was present in Philadelphia at three different sessions of the National Convention for the Improvement of Free People of Color. At these sessions, he served as an officer and took an active role in crafting resolutions. He was among the fifteen African Americans who attended the first gathering in Philadelphia, which attracted delegates from Delaware, New York, Pennsylvania, and Maryland. By 1832 the number of African American delegates had increased to twenty-nine, from the aforementioned five states as well as Connecticut, Massachusetts, New Jersey, and Rhode Island. These delegates, augmented by prominent White participants such as William Lloyd Garrison and Benjamin Lundy, focused on abolition, colonization, education, and moral reform as well as on whether African Americans should relinquish claims to being US citizens or emigrate to Canada. In 1831, the Delaware delegation included Peter Spencer and William S. Thomas, with whom Spencer had worked on the colonization study, as well as Jacob Morgan and the Reverend Peter Gardiner.

At these assemblies, Shadd was exposed to abolitionists not only from other states but also from abroad. For example, Rev. Harrison, who had lived on St Kitts, Nevis, and Tortola for twenty years, spoke to the condition of the enslaved there. This cleric praised their acquisition of skills such as reading and viewed them as redeemable. He noted that many of the wealthiest and most influential people on St Kitts were free Blacks. Rev. Harrison named a number of minority women whose Christian deeds and philanthropy distinguished them. Shadd was concerned about the methods being used to market the abolitionist message. When he presided over the Third Annual Convention of People of Colour ("with a firmness and dignity"), he criticized one aspect of his colleagues' plans. He worried that the discussion of parades with their "processions and pomp ... old ... hats and uniform, and rusty swords followed by a rabble," would distract the members from more serious matters.[15]

In 1833, Shadd increased his involvement in the Garrisonian movement, which was transnational in character. He was one of the few Blacks to attend the first Annual Meeting of the American Anti-Slavery Society. Although few in number, these Black delegates moved Garrison away from his pro-emigration view. Now a representative of

Chester County, Pennsylvania, Shadd took an active part in the 1835 and 1836 annual meetings. He also served as a subscription agent for Garrison's *Liberator* and promoted fellow abolitionist and then-Delawarean Charles Denison's prospectus for a new book, *The History of the People of Color in the United States*. In the early 1840s, Shadd accepted a leadership role in the planning of the Salem, New Jersey, regional temperance convention. When the planning group met in Wilmington, representatives from Pennsylvania, New Jersey, Maryland, Delaware, and the District of Columbia attended. The former Delawarean also collaborated with Philadelphia's Robert Purvis and William Whipper in an unsuccessful effort to repeal a portion of the Pennsylvania constitution that limited the franchise to White males. In 1850, at a meeting in Phoenixville, Pennsylvania, Shadd joined others in protesting the Fugitive Slave Act.[16] Shadd had long been an ardent proponent of staying in the United States and fighting for equal rights, but the passage of that act encouraged him to move his family to the protection of Canada West. Perhaps his vulnerability as a known UGR agent forced him to leave, or perhaps he simply felt there was more opportunity for his family outside the country.[17]

In Canada West, the actions of Abraham's adult children showed that they had adopted his sense of justice, his drive for equality, and his desire for opportunity that would lead to economic self-sufficiency. Like their father, they willingly sacrificed their personal needs to achieve racial equality, which included the abolition of slavery. The eldest child, Mary Ann, proved to be an ardent feminist and a tenacious opponent of segregation. Once in Canada, she moved from Windsor to Toronto to Chatham. As she had in Wilmington and West Chester, she supported herself as a teacher, which allowed her the flexibility to publish the *Provincial Freeman*. She filled that paper with articles and editorials in support of abolition, emigration to Canada (but not Liberia), temperance, and women's rights. The newspaper's masthead included a sentence with which August First celebrants would identify: "Self-Reliance Is the Fine Road to Independence."[18] To obtain financial support for the *Freeman*, she toured the United States, sometimes with her father, and sometimes visiting Wilmington. She communicated regularly with Wilmingtonians such as her aunt Elizabeth J. Williams, other abolitionists, and UGR agents such as the Quaker Thomas Garrett. Meanwhile, in Canada, she married Thomas Cary, a barber.[19]

In 1855, Mary Ann's brother Isaac D. Shadd took over the management of the *Freeman*. He continued Mary Ann's thematic approach to the news. Shortly afterwards, Canadian authorities arrested Isaac for assisting a suspected runaway. In the end, he was only fined for disrupting the peace and released. In 1858, Isaac and his father supported Martin R. Delany's Niger River Valley expedition. That same year, Isaac attended John Brown's Chatham Convention along with his brother-in-law Thomas Cary and John Whipper Purnell, who had married yet another Shadd cousin, Julia. While Brown was in Canada, he roomed in Isaac's home, which was where Osborne Anderson, who would accompany him to Virginia, boarded. When the Civil War erupted, Mary Ann and her brother Isaac recruited for the Union army, and their brother, Abraham W., enlisted in a USCT regiment.[20]

Another sister, Amelia C. Shadd, one of the youngest of Abraham's children, helped publish the *Provincial Freeman*. She, too, had taught refugee children; now, she took over the paper's daily operations while Isaac tried to increase circulation. Earlier, Amelia had gained teaching experience at the Quaker-supported African School in Wilmington, which had attracted an unusually high proportion of UGR activists. Among them were Thomas Garrett, his wife Rachel and their son Ellwood, Isaac and Edith Flint, and free Blacks such as Henry Craige, Comegys Munson, and J.C. Bustill.[21] The younger Shadds' aunt, Elizabeth J. Williams, also taught at that school and had direct ties to the UGR. Elizabeth and her husband made available at their grocery store copies of Mary Ann's *Notes on Canada West*. That pamphlet was a recruitment tool meant to draw free and self-emancipated Blacks to Canada. In 1858, Elizabeth attended an American Anti-Slavery Society annual meeting and spoke against enslavement and racial discrimination. Her comments mirrored statements made at the August First meetings. After her husband's death, Elizabeth joined the other members of her family in Canada. She probably died there, as did her brothers Abraham D. and Absalom. At least one of Abraham D.'s sons remained in Canada. In the 1890s, Garrison Shadd involved himself in a campaign to desegregate Chatham's public schools.[22]

It is not surprising that the thoughts and language expressed by Abraham D. Shadd at the 1840 August First celebration in Delaware continued to appear in accounts about his children. For example, William "Box" Brown asked William Still to craft a sketch of Shadd Cary for his project about notable African Americans. The profile that eventually emerged may have used Mary Ann's own words. It praised her for her strength, determination, and ability to manoeuvre in a man's world. It viewed her as a formidable woman active "in the service for the moral, social and political elevation of the colored race."[23]

Clearly, the Shadds' anti-slavery activism was of greater duration, and more widespread and multifold, than that of the few Delawareans who went to Liberia or even of most of those who remained in the First State. The Shadds' extensive interactions with abolitionists in Canada, the United States, and England exemplified the transnational character of the diaspora. The family's dispersion after the war created a network of relatives in Canada and in many states. No no matter where they lived, members of the Shadd family continued to organize and agitate for equal rights for the descendants of Africa.

The African Connection in Liberia

The handful of Delawareans who immigrated to Liberia helped end the Atlantic slave trade and its pernicious effects, but they did not have as great or as long an impact in Africa as did the Shadds in Canada. Among those few adventurers in Liberia were Solomon and Thamar Bayley, Joseph Whittington, and members of the Anderson family. The Bayleys, from the Camden area in Delaware's Kent County, spent about a decade in Liberia in the 1830s while it was being administered by the ACS. Whittington, a contemporary of the Bayleys, ended up in Wilmington after a brief stay in Africa. In mid-century, nearly half a dozen Andersons, also from that city, settled outside Liberia's capital, Monrovia. From around 1853 to 1872, they worked and lived in an independent Liberia. They probably made a greater impact on Liberia than had the earlier Delawarean immigrants who were there when it was governed by the ACS.

Solomon Bayley was one of the first Americans of African descent to author a fugitive slave narrative and one of the few who produced a pamphlet on Liberia. In 1825 a London publisher printed two editions of his life story, which circulated in abolitionist circles in the United States and England. Solomon also corresponded with people in Delaware, Philadelphia, New York, and England. Solomon and Thamar's experiences also outlived them in compendia about notable African Americans, which included them as examples of strong moral character, religiosity, hard work, and economic self-reliance. Solomon and Thamar's experiences also outlived them in compendia about notable African Americans, which included them as examples of strong moral character, religiosity, hard work and economic self-reliance. In his story, Bayley wrote that around 1690, his maternal grandmother was enslaved and brought from Africa to Virginia. He described how after he was born in Delaware, he was taken out of that state and sold illegally in Virginia. He recounted the dramatic events that accompanied his escape back to Delaware in July 1799. After that his *Narrative* focuses on his successful efforts to buy his own freedom from his "pretend owner," and that of his wife and children from separate enslavers. Buried in the *Narrative* is a brief section about how he emancipated his mother from Virginia to Delaware before settling her in New Jersey. Eighteen years later he brought her back to the First State. Solomon also noted that Captain Paul Cuffe's experiment in settlement in Sierra Leone had inspired him to leave the United States.[24] In 1827, after his children and his mother died, he and Thamar headed for Liberia, where they hoped to find complete freedom and the opportunity to convert indigenous Africans to Christianity. As he stated: "The colored man in America, whether bond or free, is not likely while living among the Whites, to enjoy those civil rights and privileges, and opportunities of improvement, which the impartial justice and goodness of our common Father, 'with equal eyes as God of All' intended for his whole rational family."[25]

One of Bayley's contemporaries, the Reverend Joseph Whittington, lived briefly in Liberia before returning to America. Originally from Maryland, he settled in Delaware, where he became a well-respected preacher at Ezion Church. One of the prayer givers at the 1840 August First meeting, he also attended the Wilmington meeting at which the agent for *Colored American*, his brother-in-law W.P. Johnson, promoted that newspaper. Three years later, Whittington participated in the 1843 regional temperance convention, which focused on the evils of alcohol as an obstacle to good moral character. Among that convention's participants were abolitionists from other states, such as Alexander Crummel (who would later migrate to Liberia), Daniel Yates, A.D. Shadd, the Reverend Daniel A. Payne, and Delawareans Daniel B. Anderson, Thomas B. Walker, and the Reverend William Saunders.[26]

Before discussing the activities of the Andersons who went to Liberia, brief mention of their father, Daniel B. Anderson, is in order. Prior to the Civil War, Daniel was involved in all manner of anti-slavery events in Delaware. He was a major figure during the August First celebrations as a speaker and organizer and a signer of many petitions calling for equal rights. After the Civil War, he became heavily involved in the annual Emancipation Proclamation celebrations, which continued at least into the 1870s. He also helped establish and grow the Republican Party. More specific information about his contributions will be presented in the next section.

The Andersons manifested many of the same values that characterized the Shadd family: a strong sense of justice, a desire to rectify the
discrimination that beset their community, a willingness to speak about
what should be changed, and self-sacrifice. For example, one son, William Spencer Anderson, chose in the early 1850s to immigrate to Liberia, which had become an independent nation in 1847. According to
family memories, young William was disgusted with discrimination
in the United States, including economic discrimination. In Liberia, he
helped an older cousin from New York, J.M. Richardson, become a successful sugar planter outside Monrovia along the St Paul River. When
Richardson accidentally drowned, William took over and expanded the
plantation, which he now owned. Like many other recent settlers in
Monrovia, he differed from the earlier Americo-Liberians, who tended
to be light-skinned and American-oriented and to focus on trade. Upriver farmers tended to interact more with indigenous Africans, adopt-
ing their foods, utilizing their labour, and sometimes penetrating the
interior to trade with them. Besides growing sugar and coffee, Anderson produced rum. He implemented his cousin's plans to export products to Britain and the United States.[27] In 1857, Black journalist J.M.
Chester described the twenty-four-year-old Anderson as "a young man
of more than ordinary abilities and very assiduous habits; very modest
and affable, and enjoys a greater influence than any other young man
of his age in the Republic."[28] William also had political ambitions: he
served as a Justice of the Peace, and he ran, albeit unsuccessfully, for a
seat in the legislature.

Meanwhile, the new nation, which was recognized only by the United
States after the Civil War, continued to face the threat of the Atlantic
slave trade. The exportation of enslaved Africans abroad encouraged
internal warfare among indigenous Africans and attracted slavers
along the coast. In 1819, the Americans strengthened their anti-slavery
profile by assembling naval forces to police the African coast and
the Atlantic Ocean. Unfortunately, results were mixed because of
uneven enforcement by the African Squadron. For example, the self-
emancipated *Amistad* Africans originated in the Spanish-controlled
Gallinas enclave between Sierra Leone and Liberia, from which slavers
were not ousted until mid-century. Thus, resettled captives in Liberia during the pre-independence era numbered only in the hundreds.
During the late 1850s and late 1860s, however, that number rapidly increased. Recaptives were shipped to Liberia from as far away as Key
West, Florida. By 1870, around six thousand Africans had been resettled

in Liberia – a dramatic increase over the earlier period but not really that significant a number in the overall trade. Despite these efforts, slavers continued to infest the coast.[29]

Anderson's actions helped inhibit the growth of the trade in enslaved persons, but indirectly. That is, some would argue that the establishment of a stable political entity, the Republic of Liberia, accompanied by trade and commercial growth, led to a diminution of the Atlantic slave trade. Others would point out that Americo-Liberians such as Bayley, a missionary, and Anderson, a planter/businessman, were no different from their European counterparts during the period of imperialism, and that indeed, their actions destabilized indigenous institutions.[30]

August First festive events were not regular occurrences throughout the Republic; rather, they were held from time to time in some Liberian settlements. For example, the 1859 Monrovia festivities featured John W. Holmes and Edward Blyden, two Americo-Liberians who had been born in the West Indies on St Thomas, then a Danish colony. Holmes's businesslike speech provided statistics that refuted the accusation that the 1834 emancipation had caused the depression of 1847. Blyden spoke about the impact of Britain's Emancipation Act on the conditions facing Africans in the United States. And Martin R. Delany, a visitor from Canada, offered a brief comment about the significance of the pressure exerted by Blacks on the British Crown to emancipate the enslaved throughout the British West Indies.[31] It is not clear whether Anderson attended the 1859 event, although he figured prominently in the subsequent memorial.

Delawareans' contributions to the abolition of the slave trade in Liberia were tainted by the paternalism and sub-imperialism of the Americo-Liberians, who founded and developed the Republic of Liberia at the expense of indigenous Africans. The Bayleys, who spent about a decade in Liberia, drew attention to the instability of the new political entity during its early years but also to its potential. More than a decade later, members of the Anderson family became involved in Liberia. William S. Anderson's successful agricultural ventures and his establishment of sugar and coffee as exports to Britain and the United States strengthened the country's economic viability, and this in turn may have helped weaken the Atlantic slave trade. It is certain that Anderson's explorations of the near-interior kept government officials better informed about the illicit traffic in human beings. Finally, Anderson's willingness to hire recaptives offered a practical solution to the problem of what to do with formerly enslaved people who lacked a livelihood. Furthermore, the story of Anderson's hard work, ingenuity, and achievement as a planter/businessman was disseminated as a success story in Liberia, the United States, and England. Anderson's experience served as an important illustration of one of the August First celebrants' goals – economic self-sufficiency. His impact in Liberia, however, was diminished by his untimely death, especially since his relatives then left the country for the United States. Even so, the accounts of Delawareans in Liberia remind us that family and community ties reached across the Atlantic world. The Delaware example also points to the ways in which the Canadian and Liberian immigration movements were informed by each other.

The American Connection

Few Delawareans immigrated to Liberia. Some, however, left the Delmarva Peninsula to continue the struggle for equality in nearby states, such as Pennsylvania. And, of course, many others never left Delaware. Among those who moved to the Keystone State was Samuel Cornish, who became the co-editor of *Freedom's Journal* with John Russwurm, a Jamaican. The latter eventually went to Liberia; Cornish remained in Philadelphia before taking the editorship of *Colored American* in New York City. Both papers were highly critical of the slave trade and enslavement, not just in the British colonies but also in places such as Brazil. After Russwurm left *Freedom's Journal*, Cornish openly opposed colonization in its pages and in *Colored American*.[32] Each also carried anti-slavery news items related to progress or obstacles to its abolition in Delaware. The Reverends Richard Allen and Absalom Jones contributed to the anti-slavery cause in other ways. Allen was not originally from Delaware but spent many of his formative years enslaved in the First State. Together, Allen and Jones established an independent African Methodist Church in Philadelphia, which eventually developed branches in other towns. The first meeting of the National Convention for the Improvement of People of Color was held in the Bethel Church in Philadelphia with Rev. Allen presiding. The selection of his church for the convention reflected its reputation as an activist institution. Freedom seekers knew that Bethel churches served as havens and sources of employment for them on their journey northward.[33]

Daniel B. Anderson's family's activism stood out among those Delawareans who remained in the First State. Daniel was the son of William

Anderson, co-founder of Spencer Church. In his own right, Daniel became known as an anti-slavery man with superb organizational skills
and a gift for public speaking. His career as a brick maker, landlord,
and small businessman provided him with the economic security to
support his family and act on his abolitionist beliefs. He served as a
teacher at the Quaker African School and the Spencer Church Sunday
School, as the subscription agent for *Colored American*, and as a frequent
speaker at anti-slavery events such as the August First meetings and
even the 1843 regional temperance gathering. He also signed petitions
such as the one in 1846 that called for taxes paid by free Blacks in Wilmington to be applied to the improvement of education for their children:

> we the undersigned labour under great disadvantages for want of means
> to diffuse the general blessings of education among our children, & feeling
> ourselves called upon by the moral & natural obligations that we are under
> to our children to bring them up in the fear & admonition of the Lord, &
> to establish in them in every virtue, & thereby render them upright & hon-
> ourable members of this commonwealth.[34]

Anderson also contributed regularly to interracial gatherings such
as the annual 1863 Emancipation Proclamation meetings, the efforts
to promote the 1867 Equal Rights Convention in Baltimore, Maryland,
and the celebration of the passage of 15th Amendment. His appointment as bailiff by the US Marshal made him the first African American
directly hired by the US District Court. The subsequent hiring of his
son, Daniel B. Anderson, Jr., reflected the respect accorded the family
for its entrepreneurial success, political connections, and commitment
to the community.[35]

After William S. Anderson's death in Liberia, his brother James and
brother-in-law Gerald Rollins returned to the United States. What
happened to Harriet remains an open question. Like his father and
brother, James A. Anderson showed an interest in building opportunities for African Americans. In the 1870s and 1880s, J.A. Anderson and
Rollins organized Delaware's African American voters for upcoming
elections. They pressured the Republican Party for appointments to
government-controlled jobs. At a mass meeting in Wilmington, James
explained that many of the "colored voters" had not yet been assessed
by the Levy Court, and, therefore, ward committees needed to be created immediately. He argued that the Republicans would only reward

African Americans if they voted for the party. He called for improved turnout at the polls, which would translate into more positions for them on the police force and other municipal and state government posts. He explained further: "It is not so much what we expect to receive, but we want to lay the foundation and platform on which our posterity can walk."[36]

Joseph G. Walker was another postwar Republican with a long history of resisting the second-class status of the African-American community. He may have had a lower public profile than the Andersons, but he contributed to the anti-slavery movement in a number of ways. Like Anderson, Walker participated in the August First meetings in Wilmington. His parents purportedly came from the "West Indies," and he was known in Wilmington as a person of African and European descent. Perhaps his Caribbean connection had something to do with his commitment. In any case, the Wilmington directories usually list him as a labourer, and this is confirmed by census records. His role as a UGR operative has recently come to light, but his work as a Black activist has been obscured.[37] Besides contributing to the August First events, Walker signed the 1846 petition to Wilmington City Council seeking better schools for Black children. In the late 1860s, he joined the interracial meetings to establish an Equal Rights Convention. Although little else is known about him, it is significant that his son J.G. Walker, Jr, joined his father at postwar Emancipation Proclamation memorials and at political action meetings promoting the Republican Party.[38]

David Gustus's anti-slavery and equal rights activism started in the antebellum period and carried on into the 1870s. His commitment apparently did not spring from or involve other family members. Gustus was but one of the many barbers who signed documents calling for equal rights, such as the 1853 petition, which attacked as "grievously oppressive" the 1853 legislation passed by the Delaware General Assembly that limited the civil rights of free Blacks in the state.[39] Against the background of oppressive legislation at home in Delaware, he characterized immigration as a logical response.

Gustas resurfaced in the postwar period as a prominent organizer of and contributor to the Emancipation Proclamation annual celebrations. That proclamation, issued on 1 January 1863, at least symbolically freed all enslaved persons held in the rebel states. It brought together the prewar and postwar generations of activists and was annually commemorated into at least the 1870s and perhaps even beyond. Events for the day were planned and held in African churches, and the participants sometimes moved from one church to another for different functions. At these meetings, speakers addressed themes of discrimination and equality. They made speeches, gave readings, issued reports and proclamations appropriate to the occasion, and voted on resolutions.[40] Although these gatherings were dominated by local residents, occasionally a well-known former abolitionist such as Henry Highland Garnet was invited to address the crowd. One year, Rev. Brinckley, a White, referred to the ill-treatment of coloured men in the lower part of Delaware in times past. Other participants at these events would offer expressions of gratitude, sympathy, and praise for abolitionists, such as Thaddeus Stevens and Thomas Garrett, who had provided assistance during the prewar years.[41]

Speakers also raised unresolved issues such as the lack of education, problems related to voting rights, the ongoing desire for economic self-reliance. Daniel B. Anderson's 1873 address was especially pointed. In it he referenced a pending court trial in which Democrats argued that the federal government did not have the right to go into a state and prosecute officers of that state for failing to execute a federal provision of the law – specifically here, the 15th Amendment. He claimed that African American rights would not be preserved unless the US armed forces pledged to maintain them. He also suggested that the African American community should frame petitions to the legislature to strike out the word "White" from all laws, thereby putting African Americans on an equal footing with White people. In language and spirit similar to Shadd's 1840 August First presentation, Anderson pointed out once again that the Emancipation Proclamation of 1863 had transformed the status of men from shackled to liberated. He reiterated the need for self-reliance and industry and for continued pressure on state and local authorities: "Get your qualifications to take part in government affairs, as fast as you can. We must find men and qualify men to take positions under the political administration of the government and the State."[42] It is noteworthy that on occasion, a Delaware delegation went elsewhere to celebrate. In 1869, for example, William Howard Day, along with Wilmington's Mount Vernon Band, joined the memorial parade in Norristown, Pennsylvania.

Gustus also served as Grand Marshal for Wilmington's 1870 parade honouring the passage of the 15th Amendment. Although reminiscent in spirit of the earlier August First festivities, the 1870 celebration differed in that it attracted greater numbers of participants and watchers, many of whom travelled to Wilmington from throughout Delaware and from neighbouring states.

This special observance opened at dawn on April with a cannon salute, which was followed by a ten o'clock church service. One journalist reported: "In the colored quarters of the city, the houses were gaily covered with flags and though but a few were displayed from the White houses ... most of them had lent them to the colored people for use in the procession of freedom ... Never before was so great a collection of colored people in our streets."[43] By noon, country visitors had joined the city dwellers. Delegations from Delaware's Wilmington, New Castle, Christiana, Newark, Middletown, St Georges, Delaware City, Port Penn, Dover, Camden, Willow Grove, Frederica, Felton, Milford, and Hazlettville, as well as from places in Maryland and Pennsylvania, participated in the festivities. Hundreds of marchers, many of whom were descendants of enslaved Africans, wore badges and rosettes; women carried bouquets of flowers. They marched in bands, rode on floats, and carried slogans:

> Among the banners, was one with a picture representing the Emancipation Proclamation being shown to an old negro woman at her cabin door; one, with the words "constitution of the Fifteenth Amendment; in this sign we place our hope," and another with the title "Abraham Library Association" on a White banner representing the crucifixion and the words, "In God we trust." The parade stretched for over a mile as it moved down King Street. A Philadelphia reporter commented: "the streets were literally Black with people."[44]

Estimates of crowd ranged from 800 to 1,000 people. Many in the crowd were women who had contributed to the preparations for the parade. Among them were Mrs Susan Sharper, Mrs Frisby J. Cooper, Mrs E. Graves, and Mrs M.T. Williams.[45]

In his involvement in Delaware's equal rights movement, Peter Blake exemplified a new generation of activists who were not directly connected to the pre-war activist families. Peter was the son of Elijah Blake, a labourer from New Jersey who moved to Delaware and eventually became a barber/hairdresser. On 12 December 1862, at the age of twenty-three, Peter enlisted in the Union navy as a landsman. He served on the *Patapsco*, a monitor that had been built in Wilmington. The vessel was assigned to the South Atlantic Blockade Squadron, where it took part in bombardments of Savannah, Georgia, and Fort Sumter and Charleston, South Carolina. It also tested obstruction-clearing explosive devices.[46]

Blake was proud of his military service and that of his fellow African Americans. In a letter to the *Christian Recorder,* he dismissed lingering claims made at the outset of the war that Blacks could not fight or even act as servants or teamsters.[47] After his discharge from the Navy, he returned to his hometown, where he opened a barbershop on French Street, and dedicated himself to securing and maintaining voting rights. In 1866, for example, he joined reformer Thomas Garrett's proposal to proffer a legal challenge against those who continued to deny African Americans the right to vote. At a "principally colored" interracial meeting at the African Union Church, the attendees considered where to bring lawsuits in the New Jersey courts and in the Federal Court in Delaware to test the right of African Americans to vote. The newspaper described Blake as "a man of mixed blood" who had served in the Union navy during the Civil War and whose attempt to vote in the October election had been denied.[48] Nearly four years later, in the *National Standard,* Garrett wrote that "now that African Slavery is forever ended in this country ... there is much yet for philanthropists to do, for this people, before they can enjoy the great boon granted them by the Fifteenth Amendment. In this city on the 7th day last at an election for school directors, the colored peoples vote was taken at seven of the nine wards; at two wards with Democratic inspectors their votes were refused."[49] In 1876, Blake attended a meeting of forty fellow Wilmingtonians, among whom were Daniel B. Anderson and Joseph G. Walker. There, they discussed which candidates to support. At a mass meeting in 1884, Blake again spoke out against what the newspapers described as the "machinations of scheming White politicians," who were denying "colored voters" the representation they should have on the police force. He also devoted time to assessing the preparedness of ward committees for the upcoming election.[50] It is significant that Blake was one of the Delawareans who placed an advertisement for his shop in William Howard Day's newspaper, *Our National Progress.*

William Howard Day had returned from self-exile in England to join the forces of reform mobilized to help the newly freed bondmen. The Day family had long-standing connections with Delaware. His father was a Delawarean and during the War of 1812 had fought on the *Viper* against the British on Lake Champlain as part of Commodore Thomas McDonough's crew. William, however, had long been absent from the peninsula while building his abolitionist credentials in Ohio, Canada, England, and Scotland. These efforts ranged from organizing national conventions to working with fugitive slaves. A decade later, he supported John Brown in Chatham, interacted with the Shadds, and established ties with the abolitionist community in Dresden. From 1859 until his return, he supported himself in England and Scotland by giving speeches that condemned enslavement and promoted equal rights for African Americans.[51] He did not come to Delaware until the Civil War had ended.

Day spent part of the summer of 1867 on the Delmarva Peninsula on a lecture tour. While touring, he accepted the post of Inspector General of the Freedmen's Bureau in Delaware and Maryland. In that capacity, he applied his considerable organizational and promotional talents and well as his national and international contacts towards building the foundation for freedmen's schools in those states.[52] His activities included attending and speaking at meetings and conventions supportive of equal rights. Day marched in festive celebrations such as the Coloured Masons' parade in Wilmington, which boasted contingents from Delaware, New Jersey, California, New York, Pennsylvania, Virginia, and Maryland. He was present at the subsequent Negro Odd Fellows Parade, which included groups from New Jersey, Maryland, and Pennsylvania, and at a ceremony celebrating the passage of the 15th Amendment.[53] At that ceremony he offered a brief comment, the content of which Abraham D. Shadd would have applauded. Day pointed out that although African Americans had earned the franchise, which they were indeed celebrating that day, they needed to protect that achievement through "self-help, social and moral development, political elevation [and] full enfranchisement."[54]

In an approach similar to Shadd's in the 1830s, Day led the Delaware delegation to the National Colored Man's Convention in Washington, which brought together representatives from twenty-one states and two territories. He also took part in the Colored Men's Border Convention, which drew delegates from Delaware, Maryland, Virginia, Tennessee, Missouri, New York, New Jersey, and Pennsylvania.[55] At these functions, he interacted with other Delawareans such as David Gustus and Daniel B. Anderson. Day also took it upon himself to make symbolic announcements, such as the appointment of Anderson as bailiff for the US District Court for the District of Delaware.[56] Also while in Delaware, he produced the newspaper *Our National Progress*, which was published simultaneously in Wilmington, Camden, Harrisburg, Philadelphia, and New York City. Although it was geared to the middle and border states, it was viewed by some as the only national Black paper in the corridor between Washington and New York.[57]

Perhaps Day's most difficult work in Delaware was tied to voting rights for African Americans. The local press pilloried him for what it portrayed as his radical behaviour. Only later was a deeper understanding of his contribution advanced: "In 1869 Professor Day went to Wilmington, where he risked his life in organizing the colored citizens as voters, and was successful at the end of a year in entirely changing the representation in the lower house of Congress, a change for the first time in twenty years."[58] Exactly when and how did Day risk his life? During the late 1860s, it was understood that the passage of the 15th Amendment would add approximately 4,500 African Americans to Delaware's voting rolls. The expectation was that the new voters would vote Republican. It was also known that it would be more difficult to discriminate against potential voters on the basis of race. Therefore, opponents of equality became creative obstructionists. For example, the Board of Education would not allow African Americans to pay city school taxes, an abuse of the tax laws that in effect prohibited them from voting. Also, tax collectors listed thousands of Blacks as "dead" or "having left the state." As the November 1870 election day approached, tensions over the voter registry heightened. On election day in Smyrna, Odessa, and Wilmington, open confrontations developed between White supremacists and Blacks who had been denied the vote or who feared they were going to be denied it. The local newspaper accused Day of mustering a gang of African Americans in Wilmington and inciting violence by arming them with muskets in order to intimidate officials. Day, not surprisingly, was viewed as the ringleader.[59] There is no question that violence broke out in Wilmington that day and that physical force was employed and bullets were fired. Certainly, would-be Black voters and their White opponents were endangered. And undoubtedly, Day's courage in holding his ground emboldened his men. But prior to these events he had actually warned Wilmington's African American citizens *not* to confront their White opponents. Fortunately, no one was killed. Unfortunately for the Republicans, the Democrats carried the election. Their margin of victory, however, had been reduced to only two thousand votes.

Wilmington's African American community contributed greatly to the fight to abolish slavery in Delaware, in other American states, and abroad. That city's free Black community did not operate in an intellectual vacuum. Its members were tied into regional and national conventions, international events, and the abolitionist press, both Black and White. Abolitionists who visited Delaware served as conduits, carrying ideas and information to the First State and in turn transmitting what they had learned about the thoughts and deeds of Delaware's African American activists. Delawareans used time-tested methods to keep their anti-slavery beliefs alive over a considerable period of time; such methods included local gatherings, speeches, petitions, festive events such as August First, newspaper reports, regional and national conventions, and even immigration to countries such as Canada and Liberia. Some Delawareans moved away, to places like Philadelphia, Canada West, and Liberia, thus broadening the geographical scope of their challenge to injustice. And once abolition had been achieved in the United States, African Americans turned to securing and maintaining equality at home and the end of enslavement elsewhere. They sought an equality based on opportunity and self-reliance through improved education, greater economic opportunity, and political rights, especially the franchise. They believed that their success would disprove the negative myths that had plagued their community for so long. And this perseverance for freedom, for opportunity, and for equality was passed on from one generation to the next. In nineteenth-century Delaware, the Anderson and Shadd families offer the best examples of that transfer of ideas and goals, which in turn inspired younger people, especially in their own families. David Gustus and Peter S. Blake serve as examples of how these families inspired a new generation of activists. Their lives, and those of others such as William Howard Day, who lived in Canada West and Delaware for a time, and Martin R. Delany, who lived in Canada and visited Delaware and Liberia, contributed to a transatlantic discussion and efforts to achieve equality.

APPENDIX: A SELECT LIST OF ABOLITIONISTS WHO VISITED DELAWARE IN THE NINETEENTH CENTURY

Abolitionist	Initial Visit
Arnold Buffum	1833
Charles C. Burleigh	1837
Cyrus C. Burleigh	1839
Cassius Clay	1846

(Continued)

APPENDIX (*Continued*)

Abolitionist	Initial Visit
Paul Cuffe	1797
Martin R. Delany	1849
Frederick Douglass	1857
Robert Edmond	1850
Rev. Calvin Fairbanks	1865
James Fulton, Jr.	1839
Henry Highland Garnet	1866
William Lloyd Garrison	1865
Mary Grew	1847
Frances E. Watkins Harper	1856
Jane E. Hitchcock	1845
Sally Holley	1852
Erasmus Hudson	1845
Robert Hunard	1821
Hutchinson Family	1855
William P. Johnson	1840
Abby Kelly	1845
J. Miller McKim	1850
James Mott	1847
Lucretia Mott	1841
Daniel Neall	1841
Theodore Parker	1855
Robert Purvis	1840
Charles Bennett Ray	1839
Dr. John Snodgrass	1848
George Thompson	1852
Sojourner Truth	unknown
Samuel Van Brackle	1841
William Yates	1837

NOTES

1 Hoffecker, *Delaware*, 90; Essah, *A House Divided*, 9–35.
2 *Colored American (CA)*, 12 and 19 August 1837.
3 Dalleo, *Researching the Underground Railroad*; Wilson, *Freedom at Risk*.
4 *Every Evening (EE)*, 2 January 1873.
5 In 1901 it ratified the 13th, 14th, and 15th Amendments. Essah, *A House Divided*, 36–74.
6 For a select list abolitionist visitors, see the appendix to this chapter.
7 Dalleo, "'Thrifty and Intelligent.'" By 1870 the city supported three thousand African Americans. Hoffecker, "The Politics of Exclusion," 60.
8 *Delaware Republican (DR)*, 25 April 1864.
9 Shadd Genealogical Folder, Delaware Historical Society, Wilmington (DHS).
10 For information about French émigrés and their bondsmen from Haiti, see Williams, *Slavery and Freedom*, 199 and 233–4. For Bayley and Haiti, see Dalleo, "'Persecuted but Not Forsaken,'" 152–3.
11 Legislative Petitions, RG 1111, Delaware State Archives, Dover (DSA).
12 *Liberator*, 17 September 1831.
13 *Delaware Free Press*, 6 August 1831; Garrison, *Thoughts on African Colonization*, 36–40; *Sixth Annual Report of the Executive Committee of the American Anti-Slavery Society* (New York: 1839), 17; *CA*, 9 December 1840.
14 *CA*, 27 July 1839.
15 *Minutes and Proceedings of the Third Annual Convention for the Improvement of Free People of Color in These United States, Held by Adjournments in the City of Philadelphia, From the 3d to the 13th of June Inclusive, 1833* (New York: 1833). See also *Liberator* (Boston), 15 and 22 June and 22 October 1833; and Ripley, *Black Abolitionist Papers (BAP)*, vol. III, 104–15.
16 Jane Rhodes, *The Black Press and Protest in the Nineteenth Century* (Bloomington: Indiana University Press, 1998), 14; Kashataus, *Just Over the Line*, 58–61; *Liberator*, 21 December 1833; *CA*, 12 December 1840; *Minutes of the Union Temperance Convention of the Colored Citizens of Pennsylvania, Delaware, Maryland, New Jersey and the District of Columbia* (Philadelphia: 1843); *Pennsylvania Freeman* (Philadelphia), 31 October 1850.
17 Smedley, *History of the Underground Railroad in Chester*, 243; Kashatus, *Just Over the Line*, 58.
18 Hancock, "Mary Ann Shadd."
19 MacDonald, "Mary Ann Cary in Canada."
20 Rollins, *Life*, 306–7. In 1861, many Blacks in Chatham announced their intention to join Delany's project to immigrate to Africa. Among them were Isaac and Amelia C. Shadd, Abraham S. Williamson, and Osborne P.

Anderson. See *BAP*, III:2, Bearden and Butler, *The Life and Times of Mary Shadd Cary*, 195–8, 219.

21 African School Society Minutes, DHS.

22 Dalleo, "Not a Straight Line: Historical Research on the Underground Railroad in Delaware," presented at *The Underground Railroad in Delaware: Understanding the Resources*, DHS, 21 February 2008.

23 Rhodes, *The Black Press*, 172–3, 180–1.

24 Dalleo, "'Persecuted but Not Forsaken.'"

25 Bayley, *A Brief Account of the Colony of Liberia*, 8.

26 Dalleo, "'Persecuted but Not Forsaken,'" 164–5. See also *Minutes of the Union Temperance Convention* (Philadelphia: 1843).

27 Daniel B. Anderson, William Spencer Anderson, typescripts, Eckman Collection, DHS.

28 New York Colonization Journal (*NYCJ*), September 1857.

29 For the destruction of the slave trade in this area, see Dr James Hall's 1850 report, Maryland Historical Society, Manuscripts Division, Baltimore.

30 Akpan, "Black Imperialism."

31 *Weekly Anglo-American*, 15 October 1859.

32 See http://wisconsinhistory.org/libraryarchives/aanp/freedom/volume1.asp for *Freedom's Journal* and http://liberalarts.udmercy.edu/history/ba_archives.html for excerpts from *The Colored American* and the *Provincial Freeman*.

33 Allen, *The Life, Experience, and Gospel Labours*. See also Dalleo, *Researching the Underground Railroad in Delaware*.

34 Administrative Records of the City Clerk, City of Wilmington, 1846, RG 5100.091, DSA.

35 Peter T. Dalleo and Daniel B. Anderson, "Presentation for Federal Bar Association Luncheon," July 2007, Wilmington, typescript, personal copy.

36 *New York Globe*, 1 March 1884.

37 The claim that Walker worked with Thomas Garrett apparently originated in Smedley, *History of the Underground Railroad*, 243.

38 Administrative Records of the City Clerk, City of Wilmington, 1846, RG 5100.091, DSA; undated broadside, "Equal Rights Convention," DHS and *Wilmington Daily Commercial* (*WDC*), October 1867, 4 January 1871, 5 May 1876.

39 "An act in relation to free negroes and slaves" and "An act concerning apprentices and servants," Legislative Papers, 1853, RG 1111, DSA. See also petitions signed by Gibbs and Brinkley family members, who were UGR agents in Kent County (Legislative Petitions, 1849, RG 1111, DSA).

40 *DR*, 1 January 1866; *WDC*, 6 January 1868 and 2 January 1869; *Christian Recorder* (*CR*), 10 October 1869; *EE*, 2 January 1873.

41 *WDC*, 6 January 1868, 2 January 1869.
42 *EE*, 2 January 1873.
43 Helen S. Garrett Scrapbook, DHS; *WDC*, 15 April 1870.
44 DG, 15 April 1870.
45 *WDC*, 22 February and 9 and 15 April 1870.
46 For Blake's naval record, visit http://www.civilwar.nps.gov/cwss
    in the Soldiers and Sailors database; for the *Patapsco*'s war record, visit
    http://www.numa.net/expeditions/patapsco. See Wilmington directory,
    1853, 1857, 1860; U.S. Bureau of the Census, Manuscript Returns for Dela-
    ware, 1850 and 1860.
47 *CR*, 26 March 1864.
48 *WDC*, 26 October and 11 November 1866.
49 Thomas Garrett to Aaron M. Powell, 5 April 1870, *National Anti-Slavery
    Standard* (New York), 4 April 1870. *DR*, 26 June 1862; Smedley, *History of
    the Underground Railroad*, 244–5; *WDC*, 4 and 5 April 1870, 26 October,
    11 November 1866.
50 *WDC*, 5 May 1876; *MN*, 21 and 28 February 1884.
51 Blackett, *Beating against the Barriers*, 286–386.
52 Simmons, *Men of Mark*, 978, 983–4; Blackett, *Beating against the Barriers*,
    328–30; *WDC*, 20 April 1870.
53 *WDC*, 25 June 1867, 15 April and 11 October 1870.
54 *WDC*, 1870, quoted in Blackett, *Beating against the Barriers*, 335.
55 *WDC*, 10 June 1868 and 5, 19, and 20 January 1869.
56 *CR*, 22 January 1870.
57 Blackett, *Beating against the Barriers*, 336–7. *Our National Progress*, 14 March
    1874 (this is the only extant copy of this newspaper) (New York Historical
    Society).
58 Simmons, *Men of Mark*, 983–4.
59 DG, 15 November, 11 and 12 October, 11 November, and 16 December
    1870. See also Blackett, *Beating against the Barriers*, 332–6; and Hiller, "The
    Disenfranchisement."

9 Reimagining the Dawn Settlement

MARIE CARTER

Dawn: "Amorphous and Conflicting" Descriptions

The Dawn Settlement is well represented in the many histories of the Underground Railroad. Later histories often portray it as a "planned colony" that grew up around a British American Institute school after 1841, with its principal founder being the Reverend Josiah Henson. Both contemporary and later historical accounts of the settlement tend to reflect what William H. and Jane Pease call "amorphous and conflicting" descriptions.[1] Particularly confused or indistinct are the lines many accounts draw (or fail to draw) between the Dawn Institute (more properly, the British American Institute Manual Labour School) and the Dawn Settlement and its various religious and educational institutions and missions.[2]

Readers of such accounts are often left with the impression that the Dawn Settlement was a geographically defined place. In some instances, the British American Institute (or BAI) is erroneously portrayed as being this place. However, it is possible that a tight-knit settlement growing up around the BAI school may have been more "imagined" than real. It seems that simple misunderstandings about the evolving political boundaries and the renaming of geographic features during the time of the BAI may have hopelessly confused terminology. This has created an enduring problem for researchers today when they attempt to track census and other documents. All of this challenges us to consider whether long-accepted "truths" about the Dawn Settlement may need to be re-examined and rethought.

In *A Northside View of Slavery,* under the heading "Dresden; Dawn," Benjamin Drew describes two separate entities: the Town of Dresden, and the British American Institute. Yet at the same time, he applies the popular assignation "Dawn Institute" and then evolves this terminology further into "Dawn Institute Farm,"[3] by which he means the three hundred acres around the BAI School. This property at least partly sustained the institute's students and staff during its early years.[4] Drew's description of this farm is not of a "settlement." He indicates, for example, that only "three or four coloured families support themselves on the Institute Farm."[5] At the same time, he quotes the first annual report of the Anti-Slavery Society of Canada, which indicates that sixty pupils attended the institute's school.[6]

Similarly, newspaper accounts of other US Black abolitionists, including Frederick Douglass, regularly use fluid and interchangeable terminology for the settlement area and its school. In an article about "Dawn Mills,[7] Canada West," dated January 1853, Douglass describes the evolution of "Dawn" and quips about "brighter days about to dawn upon the 'Dawn Settlement.'" Douglass's play on words highlights the romantic appeal of the term "Dawn."[8] Yet in April of that same year, Douglass reprints a *Toronto Globe* report on the anti-slavery convention at Toronto, in which "The British American Institute" is reported to be "in a transition state." Unlike the other accounts mentioned, there is no use in the report of "Dawn" as a terminology officially describing the area or the school or its property.

Earlier news items in the *Provincial Freeman*, dated 15 September 1855, report on the "Dawn Convention" conducted by "friends of the British American Institute," held at "the School" on 29 August 1855. Throughout the report of this meeting, "BAI" and "Dawn Institute" are used interchangeably. Local people such as Weldon Harris, who lived next door to the institute, identify themselves as living not at "Dawn" but at "Camden, C.W. (Canada West)." Other local residents, including John Myers, who lived half a mile southwest of the institute on the 3rd Concession, are similarly identified as residents of "Camden" rather than "Dawn." Similar examples can be noted in the *Anti-Slavery Reporter* (1 May 1856) and in other abolitionist papers of the era. All of these examples indicate that "Dawn" was not an official name of the institute or the surrounding area after 1850; rather, it was a popular term that seems to have supplanted more precise geographic names for the region as well as the official name of the school and its surrounding three hundred acres.

Drew takes pains to be accurate in situating Dresden, the nearest community to the institute. His account tells us that this emerging village is "at the head of navigation on the Big Bear Creek, just above the bend in the river which indents the lands of the Dawn Institute" and in the "gore of Camden, being part of the township of Camden." He is less accurate in his description of the "Dawn Institute Farm," as he erroneously calls it, which he says "lies partly in the gore of Camden and partly in the township of Dawn ... on the river Sydenham (the Big Bear Creek of maps)."[9] Maps of the time do not bear out this assertion regarding the institute.[10] However, Drew's is an accurate description of the Township of Dawn, which at the time of his visit was situated exactly as he described, partly in the Gore of Camden and partly in Lambton County. Most later historical and scholarly accounts of the Dawn Settlement make little, if any, reference to Dresden or the Gore or Township of Camden or the Sydenham River or Bear Creek. Indeed, such references are unlikely to have had much currency or relevance to the average reader of these accounts at the time, or later, since none of these geographic features had any prominence then and would be obscure even to later scholars who were not from the area. Dresden, for instance, remains a quiet farming village, present population 2,800; if known at all, it is as "the Home of Uncle Tom's Cabin."[11]

Scholars describe the Dawn Settlement as a planned utopian colony. Many add that it was a failed experiment in communal living. They blame this failure almost exclusively at the feet of the Reverend Josiah Henson (often better known as "Uncle Tom" for his association with Harriett Beecher Stowe's novel). Canadian historian Daniel Hill in *The Freedom Seekers* (1981) offers the standard account of the Dawn Settlement, one that has consistently been retold by most Dawn scholars:

> The idea of the Dawn Settlement took root in the mind of Josiah Henson when he saw the need of his fellow refugees for land of their own and an education. In Colchester Township, near Amherstburg, Henson ... came to know Hiram Wilson, a Congregational missionary, teacher and abolitionist from Boston. In 1844, Henson and Wilson began to plan a settlement and school for escaped slaves.[12]

Under the heading "The Canadian Canaan, 1842–1870" in *The Blacks in Canada: A History*, Robin Winks notes that "perhaps the most significant of the attempts to plant a Negro colony in Canada West was one initiated, in 1842, under the promising name of Dawn. This institution, formerly called The British American Institute, was more representative of both the successes and failures of such community experiments than ... Wilberforce."[13]

These accounts continue the long-standing pattern of using "Dawn," "Dawn Institute," "Dawn Settlement," and "British American Institute" more or less interchangeably when describing the school, and often both the school and the settlement. William H. and Jane Pease, in *Black Utopia*, use these terms in much the same manner, even though theirs is one of the more detailed and accurate accounts of the settlement at "Dawn." They write that "the Dawn community grew around the Institute, for the presence of the school drew large numbers of colored people to the area. Reversing the pattern of most other communities, at Dawn the community served the school. The geography of the settlement was that of the school and its environs."

Yet the region's exact geography is not a feature of scholarly accounts, and there is little evidence of attempts to understand the shifting geopolitical boundaries that were the immediate backdrop of the Dawn Settlement's development. The Pease account notably lacks any mention of the evolution of Dawn Township, the only municipality in the region that officially bears the name "Dawn," and the entity from which Dawn takes its name. This lack of background regarding Dawn's evolution as a township has likely added to the confusion.

Any account of the Dawn Settlement (such as our Promised Land Project), then, to be complete and accurate, should thoroughly examine the early political boundaries in the area of the BAI and how these evolved. This is particularly true since the most radical changes to these boundaries coincided with crucial challenges the BAI faced regarding its basic purpose and mandate, and its ownership and leadership, as well as with peak periods of Black migration to the region.[14]

Examining maps and guides from the period can clear up terminological ambiguities and help us glean the actual names of communities of that era. Researchers will then find it easier to locate materials such as census documents and land records, which have been displaced to what might otherwise seem unlikely filing locations as a result of changed municipal boundaries. All of this can open up new lines of inquiry and analysis regarding the true nature, scope, and purpose of the Dawn Settlement.

It is understandable that the real names of actual geographic features have been suppressed in favour of the more romantic terms "Dawn" and "Dawn Settlement." That said, from the evidence, the Dawn Settlement emerges more as an "imagined" community than an exact geographic place. As mentioned, the only official use of the term "Dawn" in the immediate area of the BAI is for the Township of Dawn, which pre-existed the BAI. The BAI existed within the boundaries of that township when a Black settlement was first noted there in guides to the region. By 1850, however, the boundaries of Dawn Township had changed, and from that time on there was no technical reason to identify the location of the settlement as "Dawn" or to believe there was an actual community whose name was the "Dawn Settlement." The terminology "Dawn Settlement" can be more accurately understood as referring to a general region of Black settlement around the BAI, as William H. and Jane Pease describe it. However accurate their understanding, the definition of the Dawn Settlement as a specific area remains very vague. One aim of local research connected to the PLP is to determine whether this vagueness can be addressed. Is there indeed an area we can definitively map as the Dawn Settlement? Or will that settlement continue to defy all attempts to define it, and remain more a place of our imagination than a clearly definable geographic region?

This chapter prepares the ground for further investigation regarding the Dawn Settlement by describing the geopolitical realities as well as the caprices of guidebooks and maps that describe this area.

The Evolution of Canada West

Southwestern Ontario, where the BAI was established in 1841, was largely unexplored until the early 1800s. After the American Revolution and the ensuing flood of United Empire Loyalists into the region, the Constitutional Act of 1791 created a distinct area known as Upper Canada. Upper Canada (which includes present-day southwestern Ontario) would attract about 10,000 Black settlers by the time of Benjamin Lundy's visit in 1832.[15] As James W. Walker describes it, Upper Canada

> had attracted "a considerable settlement of coloured people" at Chatham, several hundred around London, and distinct Black districts at Woolwich near Brantford and in Oro Township on Lake Simcoe. Other Blacks were living ... throughout the Southwestern parts of the province, with fairly large numbers in Hamilton and Fairport (the present Dresden). As increasing numbers of slave and free fugitives entered Canada after 1830, they too tended to settle in locations already inhabited by earlier Blacks.[16]

In 1840, a year prior to the founding of the BAI at Dawn, the Act of Union created Canada West (formerly Upper Canada) and Canada East (Formerly Lower Canada).

Maps from the late eighteenth century tell us that Europeans had little accurate knowledge of the region; even large geographic features such as the lands between the Great Lakes are nearly unrecognizable from the shapes in which they are drawn.[17] By 1802, maps had improved but were still decidedly rough and inaccurate. One map of the region from this period is missing important details such as Lake St Clair and Bear Creek.[18] At this time, Bear Creek, later known as the Sydenham River, lay in territory controlled by the First Nations alliance of the Council of the Three Fires (Chippewa, Odawa, Potawatomi) and would still have been known by its native name of Jonquakamik (Milky River).[19] After White settlers arrived in the area, the two branches of the river became known as Big Bear and Little Bear Creeks, coinciding with astronomical references in guides to the Underground Railroad. This curious parallel with the Ursa Major and Ursa Minor constellations, which include the North Star, may be purely serendipitous. Still, the significance of the reference could hardly have been lost on those abolitionists who knew anything about the area and who exhorted their UGR "passengers" to look to these constellations and follow the North Star to freedom. Regardless, the name Bear Creek persisted, appearing in accounts of the area into the 1850s, even though the official name had been changed to the Sydenham River as early as 1845.

The area where the BAI would eventually be established did not become British until it was sold by the Chippewa in 1823.[20] After this sale, early Black settlers and others bought land along the Sydenham near the future site of the BAI. After nearly twenty years of official development (and a much longer presence of lumber companies and other squatters in the region before its sale to the British), maps as late as 1855[21] continued to reflect a lack of detail and accuracy. The Sydenham River on the Canada West map just mentioned is not identified by any of its names. The Township of Dover East[22] and the settlement at Chatham are not accurately placed. Chatham does not appear, as it should, on the Thames River, but rather half a county north of its actual location.

By 1840, following the rebellions in Upper and Lower Canada and the introduction of responsible government, changes were being made to the region's political boundaries. By the time of the influx of new settlers after the American Revolution – principally United Empire Loyalists – the British had begun dividing the District of Hesse, comprising most of southwestern Ontario, into smaller administrative regions. One of these was the Western Region, which encompassed the area of our present study. That region was later further divided into counties under the Municipal Act of 1850. Those counties included the

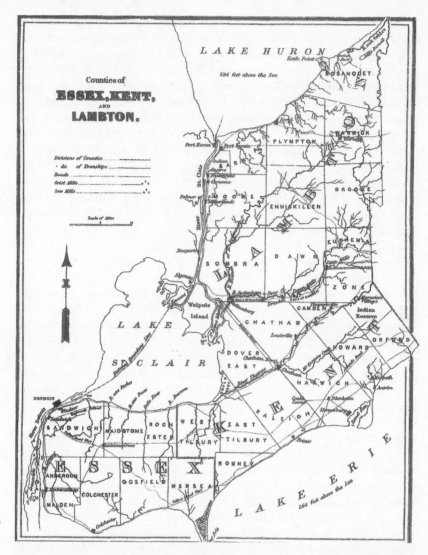

Figure 9.1. 1852 Map of the Counties of Essex, Kent, and Lambton showing the original boundaries of Kent and Lambton Counties, with Bear Creek (later named the Sydenham River) situated in the Township of Dawn in Lambton County. The map also shows major waterways and Dresden/Dawn's location relative to Chatham, the Thames River, Buxton, and Detroit.

From a map reproduction by Global Heritage Press, collection of the Kent Genealogical Society, used with permission of the publisher.

heaviest areas of Black settlement – Essex, Kent, and Lambton Counties. It was the county divisions that would have the strongest impact
on efforts to identify the Dawn Settlement's location.

Dawn was originally the name of a township in the south-central
part of what would become Lambton County. An early description of
Dawn (the township) appears in the 1846 *Smith's Canadian Gazetteer*.[23]
Inaccuracies in guides like Smith's may have played a role in confus-
ing the general public about the true geography of Canada West and
its emerging communities of the mid-1800s. It is difficult to say how
widely Smith's guide circulated, but if its accessibility did lead to its
frequent use as a reference, this could have contributed directly to
misunderstandings about the region. *Smith's Gazetteer* has often been
quoted in local histories, and this has tended to strengthen the connection of the name "Dawn" with the school and settlement area. The
gazetteer uses township names to head the brief write-ups. When this
is forgotten, the impression is left that "Dawn" is the actual name of a
Black settlement, instead of the settlement being but one component
of Dawn township.[24] Moreover, the guide's authors did not provide
a separate listing for Dresden or attempt to define which of the listed
businesses were in fact located in this emerging village. The omission
of Dresden as a separate heading may be explained by the fact that the
lots for this emerging community were surveyed only the year before
the guide was published, and the guide does in fact briefly mention this
development under the Dawn heading.

There are other inaccuracies even with respect to established communities. In the account under "Dawn," Smith confuses the "settlement of Dawn or Taylor's Mills" and further adds, "and there is also
a settlement of coloured persons on the river." It is easy to see how it
might be possible on a quick read to think that Dawn is the name of the
Black settlement on the river, when in fact there was never a settlement
of this name on the river. An examination of the area's history shows
that Dawn and Taylor's Mills were, most likely, alternative names for
"Dawn Mills," one of the earliest settlements on the Sydenham River
or Bear Creek, and established by a Colonel Taylor. Taylor also ran a
woollen and grist mill at this location, hence "Taylor's Mills." Dawn
Mills is given a separate listing immediately after the Dawn Township
listing, but Smith does not acknowledge that these three names are in
fact terms for one and the same community.

Dawn Mills, established upriver from Dresden and the BAI, was the
post office for the area prior to the establishment of a post office at

Dresden in 1856. Most early letters from people associated with the BAI and the surrounding area were posted from Dawn Mills. This further reinforced "Dawn" as the name associated with Black settlement in the area.

There is one further complication. After the severing of Kent and Lambton Counties, the settlement area's link to any geographical feature named "Dawn" disappeared when the area around the institute was taken out of Dawn Township altogether in an adjustment to the northern border of Kent. While Dawn (and Zone) Townships were originally to have fallen wholly inside the borders of Lambton, there were soon objections to this line of demarcation from people resident along the Sydenham and, in particular, at Dawn Mills. James Smith, an early representative on the County Council, argued that the county seat of Chatham in Kent County would be more accessible to residents than Sarnia, the seat for Lambton. Lambton's inaccessibility was felt to be an impediment to business. Consequently, residents petitioned to have the county border moved north so that the Sombra, Dawn, and Zone Township areas along the Sydenham would fall in Kent.[25] Before these objections were raised, the border between Kent and Lambton was to have fallen south of the Sydenham River along the northern border of Chatham and Camden Townships. Zone Township was to have fallen entirely within the County of Lambton, with the county line falling between the Zone and Moravian First Nation lands along the Thames River. The residents were accommodated, and the border was moved. Zone, in its entirety, became part of Kent. However, only portions of Dawn and Sombra Townships were included inside Kent's borders. These southern portions of Dawn and Sombra came to be known as the Gore of Camden and the Gore of Chatham, respectively. As a result, the settlement around the BAI could no longer be described as located in the Township of Dawn; it would have to be described, more accurately, as lying in the Gore of Camden, Kent County, Canada West.

This change seems to have taken place after the new border was declared but before the new names took hold. For instance, the 1852 map showing Essex, Kent, and Lambton Counties (see Figure 9.1) still shows the original borders rather than the amended ones, even though the 1850 Municipal Act had been passed two years earlier. Land registrations were also affected.[26]

Further compounding the difficulties for modern historians is a change that took place in census regions. As late as 1880, the censuses for parts of Camden and Chatham were not registered under their respective counties, but rather under "Bothwell." Even today, searching for census information for residents of Camden and Chatham sometimes requires consulting two sets of census data for each township, because some information is filed under Camden or Chatham and the rest (mainly in the Gore areas) mainly under Bothwell. Archives of Canada microfilm listings appear in the "Bothwell Census" (Lambton County) in 1871 and 1881, a departure from 1861, when Camden's agricultural and personal censuses were filed under "Kent." Genealogists and historians need to understand this eccentricity of local records when they search for data from the latter half of the nineteenth century relating to the area popularly known as the Dawn Settlement.

Reimagining the Dawn Settlement

If "Dawn" does not readily describe a specific village or geographic area, or an institution, how can we understand what contemporaries of the Dawn Settlement meant when they used that term? How are we to understand what the settlement signified to them in terms of the Black Diaspora? These questions challenge us to re-examine previous notions that the Dawn Settlement was a single geographic entity with a single founder (i.e., Henson) or related group of founders (i.e., the board of trustees, Henson and Wilson) whom we can blame for its supposed "failure." A more nuanced understanding of the Dawn Settlement opens up new perspectives on its development and history. It opens up, as it were, the borders of our imagination regarding what constituted the Dawn Settlement – not just where it existed, but when, given that its time frame, like its geographic limits, is no longer tied exclusively to the BAI's time frame and geography.

As we approach the "amorphous and conflicting" evidence of what the Dawn Settlement was, perhaps it is best to begin by setting aside what the Dawn Settlement was *not*. It was definitely *not* the BAI. There is little evidence that a settlement grew up around the school *building* on the institute grounds. The Reverend Hiram Wilson, a co-founder of the institute, is clear on this point in his letter to Henry Bibb's *The Voice of the Fugitive* on 15 July 1852: "The 300 acres of land were purchased ... solely to serve educational purposes and no families have settled upon any part of the tract, except as they were employed about the Institute."[27] That Wilson felt a need to underscore this indicates that the Dawn Settlement's nature and purpose had become a contentious matter by the time he left the institute. It also indicates that even then, there was confusion over the terms for the school (i.e., the Dawn Institute) and the settlement.

The Dawn Settlement was also *not* an adjunct of the institute. Notwithstanding what William H. and Jane Pease suggest, there is plenty of evidence that the enterprise and mission activity in the surrounding settlement was not all linked to the institute:

> "The geography of the settlement was that of the school and its environs, for the *organization of the settlement was largely the administrative arm of the Institute*" (emphasis added). The view of the Institute and other facets of the Dawn Settlement as a homogenous unit does not stand up under the weight of evidence found in land records. This evidence shows hundreds of properties on the borders of the Institute bought and developed under the direction of Black abolitionists who had no known direct link to the Institute or its leadership.[28]

Nor were the missionary institutions in Dresden linked directly to the institute or adjuncts to it. Henson was pastor of the town's British Methodist Episcopal Church and an acknowledged spiritual leader in the area, but there were other churches besides his, most notably that of the Reverend Thomas Hughes, rector of Christ Church, Anglican, a mission funded by Britain and supported locally by Black abolitionists who were heavily invested in the community. There was also the Baptist church and mission, led by the Reverends S.H. Davis and W. Newman, situated on the institute grounds between 1850 and 1853. Land records and other historical evidence indicate that this Baptist church was founded by local people after they had been excluded from the BAI grounds on the arrival of the Reverend John Scoble, former secretary of the BFASS, who in 1853 had been sent by British investors to manage the institute. Thus the Baptist church could not have been an adjunct to the institute.[29]

Dresden and Fairport, both adjacent to the BAI, were mixed communities: Scots-Irish, German, and English. People of African descent also held substantial tracts of land in these communities, however. Fairport remained predominantly White; Dresden, just across Main Street to the north, largely Black. In Dresden between 1854 and 1874, most of the lots in Van Allen Survey 128 and 80 percent of the lots in Survey 127 were Black owned. But even here there is little evidence of formal links between Dresden's Black property owners and the institute.

Indeed, landowners like William Whipper and his family seem to have pointedly avoided the controversies that swirled around the institute, and to have stayed above the fray regarding ownership of the institute grounds that dragged out in the courts between 1853 and 1868.[30] Landowner John Myers, a neighbour of Henson on the 3rd Concession (Lot 1, Conc. 3, Camden Township), was involved, as were a number of other rural neighbours. Myers was loosely connected to the institute's leadership through the Reverend William Newman, but this was in opposition to the management of John Scoble.

Even closer connections to the institute abound among other early Whites in the settlement. William Wright, the Irish-born founder of Fairport, for instance, appears as a witness in a court case, *Scoble vs. Brown*, over the management of the BAI in 1863. He is also reputed, in local historical tradition, to have assisted Henson in the "spiriting away" of equipment from the BAI mill after Scoble arrived in the community.[31] His son-in-law Alex Trerice, soon to be reeve of the Village of Dresden, was the court-appointed receiver of the institute property between 1863 and 1868. Yet there is no evidence that any of these White Dresden and Fairport landowners (as supposed by the Peases' account) took any direction from the institute's leaders or saw their private business concerns as adjuncts to the BAI or as part of any coordinated scheme to develop a Dawn Settlement.

The institute drew the attention of prominent abolitionists – including William Whipper, the Stephen Smith family, and the Purnells, Hills, and Shadds – to the community at Dawn. Yet no evidence exists that any of them developed land at the direction of the institute. In fact, they were carrying out their projects in Dresden precisely at the time of the institute's marked decline and of the subsequent legal battles that would tie up its assets for nearly a decade. These people seem to have planned their own initiatives independently and to have financed them without any direction from Scoble, who by then was managing the site.

If the Dawn Settlement was not the institute grounds themselves, or a series of institutions that grew up near the institute and supported its activities as adjuncts, then what was it? The evidence is that Black-owned properties, businesses, and industries around the institute had existed prior to the founding of the BAI. This concentration seems to be a more likely candidate for the settlement identified as "Dawn" in the public imagination. In the final analysis, trying to define such an "imagined" community with clear boundaries may be an exercise in futility. Yet freeing the Dawn Settlement from its narrow associations with the BAI property frees us to *reimagine* wider borders for the Dawn Settlement in terms of both geography and time.

Doing so also allows us to view the Black community that already existed around the institute and that nurtured its remarkable early growth as part of the Dawn Settlement. Between 1853 and 1868, that community fought to control the institute grounds and to redefine its purpose – actions that led to the founding of the Wilberforce Educational Institute. The community these early settlers created nurtured a broad range of self-directed, privately owned farms, industries, and businesses capable of sustained economic growth and development long after the BAI was dissolved.

Indeed, we could say that the Dawn Settlement was founded when the first Blacks settled in Dawn Township. Land records and other historical evidence suggest that this happened when the Harris/ Willoughby family settled on "the flats" of the Sydenham River just below Dresden. The nucleus of this early community is visible in land records dating to 1825, but there may have been a Black presence in Dawn even before then.[32] This initial settlement had grown to about fifty families by the time the BAI was established in 1841. After that year, the institute, whose activities were widely heralded in the abolitionist press, became a magnet for abolitionists and a catalyst for independent Black investment.[33] From this evidence, we might imagine the Dawn Settlement as a group of unrelated settlements, industries, missions, and institutions radiating out from the institute's three hundred acres, with the institute being part of that group.

But if Dawn began at the institute's borders, where do we draw its outer limits? If the Black settlement mentioned in *Smith's Canadian Gazetteer* refers to settlement in the Township of Dawn, we cannot draw the Dawn Settlement's imagined boundary at the present Lambton County border, but need to research which aspects of the settlement extended north past the county line into today's remnant of the Township of Dawn. The 1971 Shackleton map,[34] and current work by the Dawn Township Historical Society, headed by Lillian Steele,[35] together suggest that Black settlement in Dawn Township extended as far north as Edy's Mills and Dawn Valley in Lambton County. Lambton County newspapers dating from the oil boom mention the burning out of a Black settlement on the Gum Bed line at Oil Springs, and identify some of these residents as having migrated there from the Dawn (and Chatham) settlements.[36]

A review of the Reverend Thomas Hughes's mission work leads us to wonder whether his efforts in and around Dresden indicate that other communities in the region were part of the Dawn Settlement. Hughes's ministry encompassed Dawn Mills to the east and the cluster of settlement on the 11th Concession of Chatham Township, eventually extending as far south as present-day Kent Bridge.[37]

And what of the Dover East community near the now "extinct" Greenway Swamp, noted on at least one early map?[38] Was the settlement in Dover Township, which reached as far south as Lake St Clair, an extension of the Dawn Settlement or of the Chatham Settlement? Or was it an independent settlement area whose history has been lost to us? And what of other concentrations of settlement by people of African descent in the townships of Camden and Chatham and their gores? Do the discoveries of concentrations of freedom seekers and freemen in Kent County as a whole tell us that most settlement in that county existed outside of planned communities, beyond the famous settlements of Dawn and Buxton (and Chatham's "Black Mecca"), and that these people pioneered in many locations unrelated to any plan or specific "settlement"?

The Promised Land Project has searched land records and other surviving primary documents in an attempt to map Black-owned and rented lands in the region.[39] The emerging patterns promise to tell us much about the scope of the Dawn Settlement, but also about the general scope of Black settlement and these pioneers' contributions to the clearing of land and development of agriculture and early industry throughout the region.

Putting borders around Dawn may prove to be as elusive a task as defining the borders of the dreams and hopes of a people. Nonetheless, as we attempt to map Dawn, we may come to appreciate how those dreams and hopes translate into something more than our previous limited imaginings of the Dawn Settlement as a "failed planned colony" could ever inspire.

NOTES

1 Pease and Pease, *Black Utopia*, 65.
2 While some accounts, including the Peases' *Black Utopia*, include the Baptist Mission and the Colonial Mission of the Anglican Church as part of the Dawn Settlement, others do not recognize the existence of these

parallel missions to the BAI in the area of settlement known as the Dawn Settlement.

3 Drew, *A Northside View of Slavery*, 308–9.
4 The institute went into receivership after 1863, but accounts submitted to the courts by the receiver indicate clearly that the institute lands continued to generate rental income from farming. *Brown vs. Scoble*, University of Western Ontario archives, financial accounts of receiver, Alexander Trerice.
5 Drew, *A Northside View of Slavery*, 311.
6 Further complicating our understanding of the institute at the time of Drew's visit is an article by Mary Ann Shadd, written in Shadd's typically aggressive style in the *Provincial Freeman*. In response to Drew's published account, Shadd charges that the British American Institute did not even exist at this time.
7 Dawn Mills is about five miles upriver from the institute, beyond "the rapids" of the Sydenham. It had the area's only post office until 1856.
8 Item #45591, Accessible Archives, 4 January 1853, Frederick Douglass's Papers.
9 Drew, *A Northside View of Slavery*, 309.
10 Survey maps of the British American Institute grounds, Chatham-Kent Land Records files, Chatham.
11 Uncle Tom's Cabin Historic Site is half a mile outside Dresden, which was incorporated into the Municipality of Chatham-Kent after a county-wide amalgamation in the late 1990s.
12 Hill, *The Freedom Seekers*, 171.
13 Winks, *The Blacks in Canada*, 178.
14 This phenomenon of shifting boundaries and renamings is not altogether absent from historical accounts. Drew, for instance, interchanges the new name of the river that bisects the British American Institute lands, the Sydenham River, with the earlier name of the Sydenham's south branch, Big Bear Creek.
15 Walker, *A History of Blacks in Canada*, 80.
16 Walker, *A History of Blacks in Canada*, 80.
17 Partie Occidentale de la Nouvelle France ou du Canada (The Great Lakes in 1790), reproduction of an engraving in the collection of Historic Urban Plans, Ithaca, New York; files of the Kent County Branch of the Ontario Genealogical Society, Kent County OGS Research Room, Chatham-Kent Public Library, Chatham.
18 "North America by Arrowsmith, 1802," Canada at Scale, Government of Canada archives site, http://epe.lac-bac.gc.ca/100/206/301/lac-bac/can ada_at_scale-ef/www.lac-bac.gc.ca/maps/3_0_exp/0514032702_e.html.

19 Carter and Carter, *Stepping Back in Time*, 15. The Native people's presence in the area is also important. It is noted in accounts of the "Dresden Campground Meetings" of the late 1830s. This presence, and the intermarriage that appears to have taken place between Native people and Blacks (as well as Whites), may be a reason why the BAI school deed is careful not to exclude Native people and Whites from the educational purposes of a school clearly understood to be a "Black" educational institute.

20 According to Dr David White of the Council of the Three Fires (Walpole Island Heritage Centre, interview, 2003), the lands in this region at present are the subject of a Native land claim, due to the fact that not all three tribes represented by the Council of the Three Fires signed off on the land deal with the British.

21 *Southwestern Counties of Canada West shewing* [sic] *the principle stations of the free coloured population*, 1855, Weldon Library, University of Western Ontario archives, London.

22 The "Dover East" settlement is a curious "forgotten settlement" of the time that is not explained in any extant accounts. However, through the land record and genealogical work of local Chatham Township historian Frank Vink, it has been confirmed that an extensive Black settlement existed around the Greenway Swamp in Dover Township during this time. This "Dover East Settlement" and similar concentrations of settlement in Chatham Township may be important areas for further investigation if we are to learn the full extent of contributions of people of African descent to the region.

23 Smith, *Smith's Canadian Gazetteer*. The *Smith Gazetteer* was a travel guide that sold for ten shillings and included distance tables, steamboat fares, and information on soil, climate, land agents, and governmental institutions, as well as a "map of the Upper Province."

24 Smith, *Smith's Canadian Gazetteer*, 43.

25 Lauriston, *Romantic Kent*.

26 Counties of Essex, Kent, and Lambton, 1852, Canadian Map Reprint Series no. 1, reproduced from W.H. Smith, *Canada: Past, present and future, being a historical, geological and statistical account of Canada West*, Global Heritage Press, Milton.

27 Wilson's report contradicts that of the Executive Committee of the institute of 1845, which was republished in the *Anti-Slavery Reporter* of 1 May 1856. It states that "several dwellings of modest dimensions have been erected and are now occupied." Without clear and concrete reports of the numbers of dwellings and who occupied them, however, it is impossible

to determine whether these homes were occupied by those who worked at the institute (as Wilson maintains) or by people served by the school.

28 See Marie Carter, "William Whipper's *Lands along the Sydenham*," in this book.
29 "Biography of John Scoble," Canadian Biographies Online, http://www. biographi.ca/en/bio/scoble_john_9E.html.
30 *Scoble vs Brown* court transcripts, UWO archives; *Provincial Freeman*, various accounts of meetings at Dresden and Chatham re the British American Institute; land registry documents for Surveys 127 and 128, Chatham-Kent Land Registry Office; Hiram Wilson Papers, Oberlin Archives.
31 Brandon, *History of Dresden*, 15.
32 Carter and Carter, *Stepping Back in Time*; Brandon, *History of Dresden*; Lauriston, *Romantic Kent*; *Chatham Gleaner*; Chatham-Kent Land Registry deeds to Concession 3, Camden Gore, for the Willoughby-Harris farm, 1825.
33 In his letter to William Still in the 1871 history, *The Underground Railroad*, William Whipper indicates that it was an investigation of his former passengers on the Underground Railroad and their prosperity that enticed him to move north himself. Whipper's brother, in fact, came to Canada to teach at the institute.
34 1877 Map of Kent County drawn from the Shackleton survey, Municipality of Chatham-Kent Archives, Chatham, Ontario.
35 Steele has headed a ten-year project to produce an exhaustive (and as yet unpublished) two-volume history of Dawn Township.
36 Lambton Library Heritage Room archives, clipping files on Oil Springs and Dawn, County Buildings, Wyoming.
37 The diary of the Rev. Thomas Hughes, Diocese of Huron Archives, London.
38 *Southwestern Counties of Canada West shewing* [sic] *the principle stations of the free coloured population*, 1855, Weldon Library, University of Western Ontario archives, London.
39 The mapping of Dresden and Camden Gore and of the Old Survey of Chatham was one of the outcomes of the Promised Land Project. The Promised interactive wiki geomapping with Dresden data and map is also hosted at by the Audiovisual Media Lab for the study of Cultures and Societies at the University of Ottawa (see http://www.plp.uottawa.ca).

Epilogue
Reflections: The Challenges and
Accomplishments of the Promised Land

AFUA COOPER

The Underground Railroad has a way of being used as a stand-in for all four hundred years of Black Canadian history, especially in moments of "multicultural celebrations." And precisely because the UGR's history has not been integrated into the master narrative of Canadian history, it is often caricatured, romanticized, sanitized, and presented as a relic, an object frozen in time. That is how this story has traditionally been presented. For some Black Canadians who are keenly aware that Black history has been relegated to the margins, even the caricatured version of the UGR history is "better than nothing."

Yet the celebratory symbols that have come to dominate this story are only a minor segment of this history. I have spent the greater part of my scholarly life mobilizing knowledge about Black Canadians, especially those associated with the UGR's history. So I know that this history is complex, nuanced, dynamic, and multidimensional. I am not against the UGR history or even the celebratory aspects of it. After all, the African Americans who came to Canada (mainly Ontario) during this period faced great obstacles, not the least of which was racist oppression from White society. Yet in spite of these obstacles they successfully raised families and built communities. They endured, survived, and thrived. Their resilience, strength, and fortitude need to be celebrated. We should all be proud of this history and of the achievements of these history makers.

What I do take issue with is the uncritical nature of this history as it is presented in the media, government, schools, certain books, and other tools of knowledge dissemination. Moreover, there is an unwillingness on the part of certain individuals and institutions to represent this history beyond its "feel good" aspects. It is true that Canada did offer refuge to African American freedom seekers during the antebellum era, but it is also true that for most of these folks, once they arrived here they realized that Canada was not the haven it was touted to be. They faced racism and structural inequalities in almost every area of life. Canada might have been anti-slavery during this period but it also suffered from Negrophobia. Anti-slavery activists like Henry Bibb, Theodore Holly, and Samuel Ringgold Ward commented on this fact and experience in their writings.

Yet current governments, individuals, and certain institutions find this latter point hard to digest. It has been my experience that often-times these groups do not want anyone to say "bad things" about Canada. They are only interested in the "positive" side of the history of the freedom seekers – in the usual narrative of Canada rescuing the poor American slaves.

For a time, I was involved in an initiative to commemorate the 1807 Act passed by the British Parliament to abolish the (British) transatlantic slave trade. Our mandate was to educate the public on slavery, the slave trade, and its aftermath. I wrote pamphlets and articles, gave lectures, curated exhibits, engaged in research, and participated in conferences on Canada's role in slavery and its association with the transatlantic slave trade. The end of this initiative was marked by a closing cere-mony. However, instead of the ceremony engaging with the issue of the British commercial traffic in the bodies of enslaved Africans and the consequences of such trafficking, the main event was a re-enactment of "the Underground Railroad Story" – fugitive slaves escaping to Canada from the United States and finding freedom under "the North Star." Professional actors dressed as fugitives, pioneers, and abolition-ists re-enacted the familiar story. George Brown, White abolitionist and founder of *The Globe* (now the *Globe and Mail*), and Henry Bibb, Black abolitionist and founder and publisher of Canada's first Black news-paper *The Voice of the Fugitive*, made an appearance. The actors played their roles, and the politicians gave their speeches about Canada being a haven and the "last stop on the Underground Railroad." I started to become somewhat disoriented and uneasy, but mainly disorientated. Why had the people in charge of the closing ceremony chosen to have a UGR celebration, one that positioned Canada as the "great.moral lighthouse" on the North American continent, instead of one that we were mandated to present?[1] The pull of the UGR narrative had proved irresistible, and the real theme of the bicentenary had been deliberately left out! The question to ask is, Why is the UGR story so attractive to government and other bodies?

This history took place at a time when Canada/Britain was locked with the United States in a great moral debate over slavery. Britain had successively abolished the slave trade in 1807 and slavery in the colonies, including Canada, in 1834, and now it condemned the United States for upholding slavery. More significant, Britain was offering Canada as a haven to which escaped Americans could flee. And flee they did.

A myth about the UGR was created, replete with trains, conductors, agents, safe houses, the North Star, false-bottomed wagons, kindly Quakers, and, of course, the fleeing fugitives themselves, who on arriving in Canada fell to their knees and gratefully kissed the ground, giving thanks to Britain and her great Queen Victoria. This story shows Britain besting the American Republic and presenting itself as morally superior. It is this romantic history that has come to be most associated with the UGR. Modern governments have latched onto this version because it makes Canada looks good and enables (White) Canadians to believe themselves to be good people who helped others. The image of Canada as the land of refuge for American runaway slaves became a crucial part of the developing Canadian identity. At the beginning of the second decade of the twenty-first century, this enduring image is still used (and dare I say abused) by politicians, the mainstream media, many intellectuals, and members of the economic elite as they invoke Canadian liberalism and moral values.

The uses and abuses of the UGR chronicle tell me that some Black history stories are too hard to hear, bear, or consume. These "indigestible" stories reflect the lives that immigrants actually faced as they settled in Canada. Some of these hard-to-digest stories are about race riots, the colour bar that rose higher and higher, and the Separate School Acts of 1844 and 1850, which denied hundreds of Black children an education.

And why the need to keep labelling these settlers as "fugitives" and "refugees"? When we cast these individuals in these roles, it sets up a scenario where Blacks are always the helpless recipients of charity and Whites always the providers of it. We see this today in television ads in which groups like World Vision show Whites – usually celebrities – as the ones feeding and clothing poor Africans.

It has also dawned on me that some "positive" stories are also indigestible because they give the lie to popular beliefs about fleeing, desperate, and hunted fugitives. As the chapters in this book have shown, most of these individuals were never fugitives or refugees and certainly did not see themselves as such. They had made a conscious decision to come to Canada, prepared for the journey by making inquiries, took their money, furniture, and other goods along with them, relocated their families, bought property once they arrived, and built homes. All of this makes the term "Underground Railroad" problematic because it erases the history of the migration of *free* Black people, who of course did not travel on an underground railroad. They were not runaway slaves (more on this later), yet they are sometimes *transformed* by this discourse into fugitives![2]

What this kind of historiography does is deny the agency of free Blacks who migrated to Canada and also that of the real fugitives who emancipated themselves. These former enslaved Americans oftentimes did not receive any help from kindly Quakers or anyone else but escaped under their own steam.

Then there are the other messy stories of Black Canadian history that the official and sanitized UGR version of history is used to cover up. That is, stories about the enslavement of Africans under the French and British colonial regimes, the mistreatment of the Black loyalists and refugees of the War of 1812, the struggles these groups waged against the British Crown, White-led race riots, anti-Black immigration policies, the hysteria around Black migration to the Canadian prairies, the Ku Klux Klan, Viola Desmond, Africville, and the Priceville Cemetery. The reaction to discussions about Canadian slavery is to minimize its breadth and depth. When my book *The Hanging of Angelique* was published, I was routinely told by academics, journalists, and government officials (after they reluctantly admitted that slavery did exist in Canada) that it was not as bad as American slavery. In fact, they said, Canadian slavery was mild. They insisted on this even when shown that Canadian slaves were often cruelly mistreated and murdered by their owners and the state (in the case of Angelique) and that many ran away rather than endure this "mild" form of slavery.

So it is perfectly understandable that the romantic version of the UGR story was used as a stand-in for the slave trade abolition commemoration: after all, it served the purpose to "deny the significance of slavery, deny its reality as a ... violent system," and deny it had anything to do with Canada.[3]

That is why, when I was asked to write the epilogue for this book, *The Promised Land*, I was cautious at first. Its very title seemed problematic, for it implied that the discussion would be about the old discourse – Canada as haven, as a fugitives' land of milk and honey.

Was it another "celebratory text"? I also wondered whether the title was meant to be ironic. Were the contributors going to show how in fact many Black immigrants did *not* find Canada to be the Promised Land? Were they going to engage the paradox of the Canadian haven – that it was a Promised Land for some but not others?

A quick perusal of the chapters made me realize that this was not another congratulatory text. As I began giving it a thorough read, I became excited, very excited, because I was discovering a real gem – an outstanding compilation based on new research, critical examinations, wonderful analyses, and radical departures. The contributors together have written a bold and creative history. Their chapters are not intended to sanitize, whitewash, or romanticize. Far from focusing on the UGR, the chapters have centred abolitionists, abolitionist activism, and the inheritors of this activism – that is, the Promised Land immigrants.

This book enlarges the history of African Canada, especially of southwestern Ontario, and reveals the transnational nature of that history. As the collection's subtitle implies, the chapters focus on the Black communities that were formed in the middle decades of the nineteenth century, known in popular parlance as the Underground Railroad era. Attention is paid to the lived experiences of those African Americans and their descendants who lived and worked in towns and villages in southwestern Ontario. The study highlights their efforts to end American slavery and to gain more civil rights for the Black people of Ontario. At the core of the praxes articulated by these Promised Land settlers is agency.

This book is part of a larger effort called the Promised Land Project (PLP), which has a bold agenda that I will refer to as the knowledge mobilization of African Canadian history. The collection at hand reflects several aspects to this mobilization: research, data interpretation, writing, and publishing. With regard to the specific research this book offers, the authors shift this history from margins to centre and discover, uncover, recover, and publicize that history, thus rectifying historical amnesia. Lead investigator Boulou Ebanda de B'béri states that the PLP's primary goal has been "to recover, document, analyse, and disseminate the fullness, interconnectedness, and significance of black history in the Promised Land communities." This book succeeds brilliantly at that goal.

Ebanda de B'béri must be commended for noticing the rich possibilities of this history as he toured southwestern Ontario on a camping trip. On his return, he arranged a SSHRC grant (CURA) to realize the project. We in the field often lament that we receive little funding for our work and that funding agencies show little interest in Black Canadian history. By arranging a prestigious SSHRC grant, Ebanda de B'béri laid this complaint to rest – for a while, at least. That this project was carried out with the help of Black communities in the targeted areas is significant because it underscores the importance of bringing those who "own" history into historical research projects. The PLP's overall objective cannot be distanced from the objectives of the book itself, but I will try to confine my comments to the chapters, their historiographical orientation, and the implications for future writings about African Canadian history.

This book developed out of in-depth research (which is continuing) and reflects the PLP's commitment to uncovering and writing new histories of the Black community. It contributes greatly to work that has already been begun by both lay and academic historians.

Ebanda de B'béri, in the introductory chapter "The Politics of Knowledge," discusses the vital need to produce knowledge about Black Canadians and thereby open up spaces in the grand narrative. The stated aim is to move Black history from the sidelines to the centre. The two aims by necessity must be carried out at the same time, given the long absence of Black history from "real" Canadian history. This aim underscores citizenship issues for Black people. The fate of Black history in Canada's official history suggests to me that White authorities have viewed it as illegitimate – as not real or important history. When Black history is seen this way, its subjects are not treated as legitimate, real, or important Canadians. Although this is not stated as a goal, it would seem to me that the PLP in producing this book is attempting to endow Black historical subjects and those in the present time with citizenship rights.

Ebanda de B'béri touches on affective research, and I wish to engage with the implications of this for a moment. Because of this affectivity, there is a tendency for only certain individuals and places to be celebrated within a particular articulation of Black history. A good example involves Henry and Mary Bibb and Mary Ann Shadd Cary. The Bibbs founded and published Canada's first Black newspaper, *The Voice of the Fugitive*; in doing so, they founded the African Canadian press. Yet they are rarely recognized for this. Instead, that honour is usually bestowed on Mary Ann Shadd Cary. So there is a hierarchy of marginalization even *within* sidelined histories. Another example is that of William Whipper and Josiah Henson. Both men were anti-slavery activists, both worked on the UGR, and both were founders of Dresden, yet until now, little has been known about Whipper and his contributions to Canada. This new knowledge comes to us in Marie Carter's chapter on Whipper.

As Ebanda de B'béri points out, affective attachment can prevent researchers and scholars from paying attention to equally worthy contributors. The chapters in this book contribute to a more thorough articulation of Black history, not just in Ontario but across Canada and in the broader Atlantic world. The result is a more textured and critical history.

This brings us to the issue of the "geography of identity" so ably discussed by the lead investigator. The PLP is associated with a particular place and with the creation of a history produced about and by specific communities. I, too, see the cultural authorities, community historians, and experts who are native to these communities as part of the knowledge-producing body. Put another way, the PLP's orientation is towards the Black communities of southwestern Ontario, especially those of Dresden and Chatham and their hinterlands. Surely the PLP team must be aware of the political and historiographical implications of focusing mainly on the Black history of mid-nineteenth-century southwestern Ontario. Is there unease that this history has become the de facto chronicle for all the other Canadian Black histories across time and space? What about the other communities and "Black ethnicities" that do not have ties to a specific place? For example, there are no specific Canadian historical geographies associated with modern Caribbean and African migration in the same way that the Black descendants of nineteenth-century freedom seekers have sites associated with their history and memory. I can only wonder whether the Black people who are not associated with the Promised Land place and time will be paid attention to as worthy subjects of historical inquiry.

Seen in this light, the PLP cannot conceive of itself as a naive and innocent project. As the lead investigator recognizes, it is highly political in its association with the Promised Land communities. The PLP team must be aware that even as it integrates one kind of Black history, it may be sidelining other Black histories.

Handel Kashope Wright makes a salient contribution by offering up this notion of multiple trajectories as he investigates the comings and goings of Black subjects at mid-century and beyond. This is one of the key ideas tying all of the chapters together. Multiple trajectories centre Black people as conscious and empowered historical subjects who exercised agency over their lives. When they needed to change paths, they did, even if it meant travelling across oceans and continents and crossing international frontiers. The history of African Americans who became African Canadians is a history of multiple pathways – of movements of people, ideas, goods, artefacts, traditions, and so on, not just to Ontario but back to the United States, to other parts of Canada, and to West Africa, the Caribbean, and Europe. I took up this matter in my own research on UGR subjects who crossed and recrossed the Canada – US border; I referred to this as the "fluid frontier" to give meaning to the phenomenon of transnational crossings of people and ideas.[4]

One final point about Wright's contribution. He recognizes that the writing of revisionist history can lead to the creation of a new master narrative, a new orthodoxy. He also recognizes that historiographical construction is no easy task and that it is a "political project" of which all the contributors must be aware. "I refuse to fully understand and accept the construction of a new, corrected, coherent historical narrative; I act as a caution against the substitution of a new metanarrative of truth, even a black one whose politics I endorse wholeheartedly, for an older and readily acknowledged racist, exclusionary narrative of truth."

When we create new Black histories in our challenging of mainstream (White) history, we run the risk of sidelining some stories, individuals, and communities in favour of the "right kind of Blacks," those who live in "successful communities" and whose narratives we privilege.

Wright's caution is on point, because the stories our contributors tell are messy, sometimes "incoherent," and never linear. We see that when we engage the other concept Wright introduces: multiculturality before multiculturalism. Even before we look at the interactions among the "three principal races" (Black, First Nation, White) living in the Promised Land communities, we acknowledge the vast cultural diversity among the First Nations. In our geographic region, there were the Six Nations, as well as the Ojibway, Potawatami, and so on, and even within those nations there were cultural and linguistic differences. Among the Six Nations, for example, there were different languages.

When Whites and Blacks arrived in the Promised land communities, the histories they created did not run on separate tracks from that of the First Nations. These three histories often jostled against one another. Many who called themselves "Black" also had First Nations and European heritage. The three communities lived side by side and sometimes intermarried, even as racial tensions marred social relations in the Promised Land communities. Sometimes to find Black history we have to look at White history, as Marie Carter did in her work on Whipper. This abolitionist loaned money to prominent White businessmen in Dresden, although the official White history of Dresden has erased this fact.

The PLP is about researching and writing Black history. Yet as Wright notes, it has also fulfilled an unstated aim, which is to chronicle multiculturality before multiculturalism. The former was an established fact in Canada before this country introduced the latter as the official nation-building policy in 1971.

Nina Reid-Maroney's introductory chapter on history and historiography in the Promised Land Project explores abolitionist Samuel Ringgold Ward's call to research and write Black history beyond the "chains and coffle" story (i.e., slavery). For Ward, the central historiographical issue, with all its inherent tensions, was that Canada was both the land of "Negro hate" and the "great moral lighthouse" on the North American continent. Reid-Maroney fleshes out this historiographical paradox as it was addressed by Ward and generations of other scholars and writers. How did Black freedom seekers deal with Canadian anti-Black racism while holding on to the dream of Canada as beacon (the great moral lighthouse)? She notes that for many Blacks it was not an either/or situation. In trying to make viable lives for themselves, they engaged in a politics of both "rootedness and motion." That is, they built homes, settlements, and institutions and raised families. All of this "was counterbalanced by the idea of movement, setting the world of the Promised Land communities in motion."

In their chapters, Marie Carter and Nina Reid-Maroney write stellar community histories using a biographical frame. Both authors resort to excavation – uncovering new knowledge and bringing it to light. Carter creatively uses land records to explore the Canadian career of William Whipper, an anti-slavery activist, UGR supporter, wealthy businessman and investor, community builder, civic leader, and landowner. Reid-Maroney uses the writings of Parker Theophilus Smith to investigate the rich intellectual tradition that nineteenth-century Black immigrants brought to and developed in Canada.

Until this work by Carter, we knew very little about Whipper's contributions to Canadian community building or his anti-slavery and human rights work. From Carter, we learn that Whipper worked cooperatively with other Black residents to help many poor African Americans whom he had sent to Canada, also, that he owned vast tracts of land in Dresden, established a land investment system with other Black colleagues, invested in several mills, established an inn, built a "Georgian style" house, and – get this – loaned money to White entrepreneurs and held the mortgages on their businesses. Carter reveals that some of the very first industries in Dresden were started by Whipper. Just as important, she reveals his contributions to the struggle for racial equality. Given his significance to the founding and progress of Dresden, he ought to be acknowledged as a founding father.

This research on Whipper explodes the myth that all Blacks were illiterate and impoverished fugitives. Take, for example, the fact that Whipper loaned money to White businesses. The significance of this is not lost on Carter (or on us, the readers). She notes: "These loans challenge the long-accepted notion that Black pioneers depended financially on Whites when they came to Canada. They also call for us to re-examine the assumption that African Americans in the Dawn Settlement were passive recipients of aid from the BAI and other missions. Instead, people of African descent in Dresden contributed actively to community development by establishing businesses and industries, lending money, and building infrastructure."

Whipper's story is not "unique." Reid-Maroney tells a similar one about Parker Smith. This man was an organic intellectual. He owned a farm, and was a carpenter by trade (he built a house for Josiah Henson), and while working at both he developed a praxis that had at its centre Black human freedom. He engaged the existential issues of the day, and through his letters, he disseminated his ideas about Black freedom and human rights to friends, family, and colleagues on North America's abolitionist "circuit." In Dresden, he established a debating and literary society and was active in church circles and civic endeavours. The image of Smith as a reading and thinking man, as a man of letters, is not what we are used to when we think about this era of Black history.

Through these biographies our authors have created a textured community and social history. We are educated about Black life in Dresden at mid-century. We learn about the founding and progress of the town. We learn about race relations. We are offered insights into familial relationships within Black communities and the connections across racial lines. We learn about the vast and intricate abolitionist links that stretched from Dresden and Chatham to other parts of the province, other Canadian provinces, the United States, and Haiti, Jamaica, and other points in the Caribbean. We learn about the fight against slavery and racial injustice conducted by Whipper and Smith and their colleagues. Another startling fact made known is that in mid-nineteenth-century Dresden, Blacks were 40 per cent or more of the population. How do we account for today's Dresden being a White town?

The chapters on Smith and Whipper decentre Josiah Henson as the main generator of Black history in the Dresden area. Black history has been downplayed in the official story of Dresden, and when it is acknowledged, it is Henson's name that is called. Reid-Maroney and Carter make it clear to us that the building of this community did not rest on the shoulders of one person.

Given that much of what these authors have brought to light had been all but forgotten in Dresden, not to mention Canada, this book is tremendously important. It is about more than revising old narratives and making Black history visible again. It is also about restoring that which had been lost.

The chapters in this book seem to have been guided by the maxim "the local is global." This is brought out in Olivette Otele's contribution, which examines how Britain used Canada to activate an abolition program on the North American continent. It did so through Canada's apparent welcome of runaway African Americans to its soil. Moreover, the Crown supported the British and Foreign Anti-Slavery Society, an evangelical abolitionist group, recruiting it to work with Black abolitionists in Canada West. In this, the Crown made religion a central plank in its anti-slavery campaign. The BFASS, working with Black abolitionists in places like Chatham and Dresden, became Britain's "watchdog on slavery." But the Crown's stance towards African Americans was a contradictory one. Even while it "welcomed" them into Canada, it was sealing "profitable commercial agreements" with the United States. Britain struggled with the United States on slavery as a moral issue, yet it lost no sleep in trading with the Americans, often for slave-grown products. This alone compromised the whole idea of the Promised Land and made Britain a dubious friend of the Blacks.

In Canada itself, some Black anti-slavery activists, including Henson, resisted those White abolitionists who sought to impose their own vision of the struggle on Black communities. Blacks took a stand to promote their own vision.

In reflecting on this, we can understand the difficulties African Americans faced as they established families and communities in their new home. Segregated schooling was sanctioned by law, and Blacks faced a multitude of injustices. The Crown and Canada might have been anti-slavery at the official level, but they were also Negrophobic. The fight against slavery was not necessarily a fight for Black people's equality. Otele discusses this in the context of the Promised Land. Perhaps further articulations of the PLP will bring out this point, which is well illustrated by the Black struggle for full civil rights in nineteenth-century Canada, including the Chatham area.

Otele centres the abolitionist movement by probing the BFASS's links with Black and White abolitionists in southern Ontario. Her chapter weaves together the many strands of abolitionist history in Ontario, a history that has been studied too little.

In mid-nineteenth-century Ontario, education was the key issue with regard to whether Canada would live up to its reputation as "haven for the Blacks" or succumb to "Negro hate." Around this time, the Ontario Legislature passed the Separate School Act, which took away schooling for hundreds of Black children. Black communities fought back by founding their own schools, training and hiring their own teachers, and suing school boards for refusing to allow their children to attend local schools. Overall, the Separate School Act had disastrous consequences for the Black community. Here, in Canada, the "Negro hate" so feared by Ward prevailed.

The heroic Black teacher emerged in this context – that is, Black women and men who saw education as the means to Black uplift and who made it their mission to educate Black children. For much of the nineteenth century, teaching was one of the few professions open to Black women. It allowed them to earn a living, gain independence, and contribute to Black progress. During this era, teaching was being "feminized," and as a proportion, more Black than White women were entering the profession. At the end of the nineteenth century and in the first decade of the twentieth, most Black women teachers were employed in segregated schools. Teaching was important to Black women in part because by the end of the nineteenth century in Ontario, the colour bar had been raised higher, limiting social and economic opportunities for Black Canadians.

That is why the diary a young African Canadian teacher kept for four months in 1907 is so important. It is Claudine Bonner's principal source for her chapter about the life and work of Nina Mae Alexander, a young Black woman teacher who taught in a segregated school. This is excavatory work par excellence and keeps to the PLP's overall aim, which is to locate new sources and establish new research databases. In her diary, Nina Mae has come to a new community as a teacher in a segregated school. She negotiates the boundaries between her Black woman self and her teaching, her youth, her religion, and acceptable notions of respectability and sexuality. In keeping a diary, she reveals herself to be a "conscious" thinker. Thankfully, that diary has been preserved, and it provides a window through which to view a young woman, her career choices, and her community and family at least half a century after her ancestors came to Canada West. Alexander is second-generation Promised Land resident. Her history extends beyond the mid-nineteenth century to the early years of the twentieth, and this is crucial because it gives us insight into the history and genealogy of one family over the span of fifty years.

The diary is important to today's historians as we continue working to uncover new sources of history, especially that of African Canadian women. Through Alexander's diary, Bonner fleshes out the history of Black women in Canadian education.

Like some of the other people who receive attention in this book, Alexander and her family were ambitious, literate, and educated. Yet perhaps anticipating a certain question from her readers, Bonner makes the strange statement that Alexander and her family were "likely atypical." I do not understand why she thinks so. This collection has successfully taken apart the myth of the illiterate, impoverished Black. This book offers many examples of respectable, educated, and well-to-do Black families in the Promised Land communities, yet Bonner suggests that the Alexanders were not typical.

Not every Black person, American or Canadian born, enjoyed the privileges and education of Nina Alexander, the wealth of William Whipper, or the intellectual astuteness of Samuel Ringgold Ward. But enough research has been done for us to say that Canada's Black communities were diverse. Gender, economic status, place or origin, status (i.e., slave born or free born), skin colour, and education were organizing principles of community life. And these factors were not static – there was overlapping of all kinds. For example, people with slave origins often married freeborn persons, and there were sliding scales of wealth and literacy. Bonner's chapter on Nina Mae continues the focus on biography, family history, genealogy, and community history that is a hallmark of the collection.

Movement and flow characterized the period of the UGR. Black North Americans moved both across the continent and away from it in their journeys to freedom and equality. Peter Dalleo's chapter captures the energy and the dynamism that seized Delaware's Black freedom-seeking families as they looked beyond the borders of their state. These families developed migratory kinship networks stretching across four geographic regions: Canada West, Liberia, Delaware, and other parts of the United States. As he explores these international familial connections, Dalleo underscores the transnational and transatlantic nature of Canadian Black history. Black families moved across these frontiers and kept in touch with one another through letters, newspaper articles, and visits.

In Dalleo's chapter, we see intellectual, migratory, and political trajectories at work. Black people are shown to be conscious creators of their lives, flushed with agency, energized to create lives for themselves as free as possible from racial oppression. This quest for freedom has sent them packing not only from the United States to Canada but also from Canada back to the United States, from Canada to Liberia, from Canada to Haiti and Jamaica. Their human rights activism spans time, place, generation, and gender.

By focusing on several Delaware anti-slavery families and their migratory trajectories (e.g., the Andersons went to Liberia, the Shadds to Canada, and William Howard Day to Britain), Dalleo reveals how, by creating kinship networks, they shaped a transitional activist culture and politics and helped end slavery and the slave trade. Their activism involved working on the UGR and organizing conferences, conventions, and celebrations. It also entailed entering politics, publishing books, newspapers, and articles, and founding schools and colleges. Still later, activist Delaware families through their international networks continued to agitate for Black people's equality.

This book interrogates history and historiography in Black southwestern Ontario and brings this new history to the fore. It bears witness to the dynamism of Black history and contributes to the production and mobilization of that history. It presents Black history as a moving force. The PLP assigned itself a broad and ambitious mandate, and this collection is one expression of its success at achieving it.

The Promised Land Project has become pan-Canadian by broadening to include studies of Black life and community in Nova Scotia and British Columbia. In 2011, the project was launched in Nova Scotia through a conference at Halifax's Black Cultural Centre titled Revisiting the Promise: Place and Space in African Canadian Communities. A year later, research on the Black experience in BC was showcased at a conference titled Black British Columbians: Race, Space, and Historical Politics of Difference at the US/Canada Border, held at UBC. These conferences have opened up new areas of research on African Canadian history.

But there is much more to be done to mobilize knowledge about the Promised Land communities. I will suggest here new lines of research. In keeping with the transnational nature of Black history and the multiple trajectories described in this book, I suggest that the intellectual trajectory so ably articulated by Reid-Maroney be continued and expanded. Also, because a central aim of the Black abolitionists in Dresden and Chatham was to gain more civil rights for Black people, I suggest that links be drawn between the civil rights movements of the nineteenth and twentieth centuries. This would, for example, underscore the critical work done in the 1940s and 1950s by people like Hugh Burnett, a Dresden resident and descendant of nineteenth-century immigrants. Through his work with the National Unity Association, Burnett challenged legal racial discrimination in Dresden. He himself had been refused service in a Dresden restaurant in 1943. As his work with the NUA makes clear, racial oppression was a fact of life in the Dresden area for African Canadians. The "Dresden Story" made national and international news, and in 1954 the Province of Ontario, after agitation by the NUA and other civil rights groups, passed the Fair Accommodation Practices Act. This was a triumph for the Black community and for other freedom-loving people, yet for Burnett, it was a pyrrhic victory. His carpentry business suffered. Whites in Dresden refused to hire him, so angered were they that he had "exposed" their town. Burnett had to move to London, Ontario, in order to make a living.[5] Working across centuries would allow the PLP to ensure that the activism of people like Burnett was not forgotten. It would also tie the work of anti-slavery advocates like Whipper to that of activists like Burnett.

I also suggest that the PLP consider the twentieth century for new research inquiries. This is the most understudied period of African Canadian history. The twentieth century saw massive Caribbean and African immigration that changed the face of Canada forever by quadrupling the Black population. It was also the century of the Garvey Movement and Pan-Africanism, which swept across Black Canada and the world, and of the continental civil rights movement, the Sir George William University Affair, the demolition of Africville, the rise of the KKK, and official multiculturalism.

This book does more than right the wrong and rescue Black history from obscurity. It functions as a site of remembrance and commemoration. It continues the important tradition of writing about the Black Canadian historical experience. What is exciting about the PLP, however, is that its various resources will enable its members to move the research and writing of this history in directions that had not been taken before. I am certain that the Promised Land Project will change forever the historiographical tradition of African Canadian history and Canadian historical writing. And that is a good thing.

Figure 10.1. Hugh Burnett worked with the National Unity Association
to legally challenge racial discrimination in Dresden. Burnett himself was
refused service in a Dresden restaurant in 1943. Image used with permission
of Patricia Burnett Patzalek.

NOTES

1 Through the initiative, an exhibit *Enslaved Africans in Upper Canada* was
   done in conjunction with the Archives of Ontario. This exhibit did centre the
   experience of Black Upper Canadians who endured slavery in the province

and who sought ways to liberate themselves. One of the five plaques that were erected paid homage to Chloe Cooley, the enslaved Black woman who was sold across the Niagara River from Canada into New York state by her owner in 1793. The plaque recognized Cooley's role in bringing about the Act to Limit Slavery in Upper Canada passed by the Legislature during the same year. Additionally, numerous lectures given by myself and other experts headlined the issue of the abolition of the slave trade, slavery itself, and the various abolitions of slavery. However, at the two events most attended by the press, VIPs, politicians and other dignitaries, the opening and closing ceremonies, the UGR story was used to subvert and minimize the history of enslaved Black people in Canada.

2 There is a tendency in the literature to conflate African Americans free-born people, those who had been living in freedom for a long time, and genuine runaways into an amorphous mass of "fugitive slaves." I once went to an event commemorating Mary Shadd Cary's publishing work. The MC stated that Shadd Cary was a fugitive slave who fled to Canada on the Underground Railroad. The fact is Shadd Cary was a Delaware free-born woman who migrated to Canada with her parents and siblings.

3 Quote from Edward T. Linenthal in Horton and Horton, *Slavery and Public History,* 214.

4 Cooper, "The Fluid Frontier."

5 Hugh Burnett's story is told in Cooper, *Season of Rage.*

Bibliography

Adetugbo, Abiodun. *African Continuities in the Diaspora*. Indianapolis: Indiana University Press, 2008.

Adorno, Theodore. *History and Freedom*. Cambridge: Polity, 1964; 2004.

Ahmed, Sara. *The Cultural Politics of Emotion*. New York: Routledge, 2004.

Akpan, M.B. "Black Imperialism: Americo-Liberian Rule over the African Peoples of Liberia, 1841–1864." *Canadian Journal of African Studies* 7 (1973): 217–326.

Aldrich, R. "The Three Duties of the Historian of Education." *History of Education* 32, no. 2 (2003): 133–43.

Allen, Richard. *The Life, Experience, and Gospel Labours of the Rt. Rev. Richard Allen, To Which Is Annexed the Rise and Progress of the African Methodist Episcopal Church in the United States of America. Containing a Narrative of the Yellow Fever in the Year of Our Lord 1793; With an Address to the People of Colour in the United States*. Philadelphia: 1833.

Anderson, Benedict. *Imagined Communities: Reflections on the Origin and Spread of Nationalism*. London: Verso, 2006.

Apple, Michael W. *Ideology and Curriculum*. 2nd ed. New York: Routledge, 1990.

Backhouse, Constance. *Colour-Coded: A Legal History of Racism in Canada, 1900–1950*. Toronto: University of Toronto Press, 2001.

Barman, Jean, and Mona Gleason, eds. *Children, Teachers, and Schools in the History of British Columbia*. 2nd ed. Calgary: Detselig Enterprises, 2003.

Bayley, Solomon. *A Brief Account of the Colony of Liberia*. Wilmington: Porters and Mitchell, 1833.

Bearden, Jim, and Linda Jean Butler. *The Life and Times of Mary Shadd Cary*. Toronto: NC Press, 1977.

Bell, Howard, ed. *Minutes of the Proceedings of the National Negro Conventions, 1830–1864*. New York: Arno Press, 1969.

Bethel, Elizabeth Rauh. *The Roots of African-American Identity: Memory and History in Antebellum Free Communities*. New York: St Martin's, 1999.

Biddle, Daniel R., and Murray Dubin. *Tasting Freedom: Octavius Catto and the Battle for Equality in Civil War America*. Philadephia: Temple University Press, 2010.

Blackett, Richard J.M. *Beating against the Barriers: Biographical Essays in Nineteenth Century Afro American History*. Baton Rouge: Louisiana State University Press, 1986.

Blight, David, ed. *Passages to Freedom: The Underground Railroad in History and Memory*. Washington: Smithsonian Books, 2004.

Blocker, Jack S. *A Little More Freedom: African Americans Enter the Urban Midwest, 1860–1930*. Columbus: Ohio State University Press, 2008.

Boje, David M. "The Storytelling Organization: A Study of Story Performance in an Office-Supply Firm." *Administrative Science Quarterly* 36 (1991): 104–26.

Brand, Dionne. *No Burden to Carry: Narratives of Black Working Women in Ontario, 1920s to 1950s*. Toronto: Women's Press, 1991.

– "'We Weren't Allowed to Go into Factory Work until Hitler Started the War': The 1920s to the 1940s." In Bristow, *"We're Rooted Here and They Can't Pull Us Up,"* 171–91.

Brandon, Robert. *History of Dresden*. Dresden: n.p., 1951.

Bristow, P., coord. *"We're Rooted Here and They Can't Pull Us Up": Essays in African Canadian Women's History*. Toronto: University of Toronto Press, 1994.

Brown, Christopher. *Moral Capital: Foundations of British Abolitionism*. Chapel Hill: University of North Carolina Press, 2006.

Brown-Kubisch, Linda. *The Queen's Bush Settlement: Black Pioneers, 1839–1865*. Toronto: Natural Heritage Books, 2004.

Buckner, Phillip, ed. *Canada and the British Empire*. Oxford: Oxford University Press, 2008.

Bush, Barbara. *Imperialism and Postcolonialism*. Harlow: Longman, 2006.

Cain, P.J., and A.G. Hopkins. *British Imperialism: 1688–2000*. Harlow: Longman, 2002.

Carey, Brycchan. *British Abolitionism and the Rhetoric of Sensibility*. Basingstoke: Macmillan, 2005.

Carter, Marie. *Building Heritage: A Guide to Historical Houses in Dresden, Ontario* Dresden: Catherine McVean Chapter IODE, 2004.

– "Reimagining the Dawn Settlement." Promised Land Project discussion paper, 2008.

Carter, Marie, and Jeffrey Carter. *Stepping Back in Time: Along Dresden's Trillium Trail in Dresden*. Dresden: Catherine McVean Chapter IODE, 2003.

Carty, Linda. "African Canadian Women and the State: 'Labour Only, Please.'" In Bristow, *"We're Rooted Here and They Can't Pull Us Up,"* 193–229.

Coger, Leslie I., and Melvin R. White. *Readers Theatre Handbook: A Dramatic Approach to Literature*. 3rd ed. Glenview, IL: Scott Foresman, 1982.

Colonial Church and School Society. *Mission to the Fugitive Slaves in Canada ... Report for the Year 1861–62*. London: 1862.

Cooper, Afua. "Black Women and Work in Nineteenth-Century Canada West: Black Woman Teacher Mary Bibb." In Bristow, *We're Rooted Here and They Can't Pull Us Up*," 143–70.

– "The Fluid Frontier: Blacks and the Detroit River Region, 1789–1854, A Focus on Henry Bibb." *Canadian Review of American Studies* 30, no. 2 (Winter 2000): 129–49.

– *The Hanging of Angélique: The Untold Story of Canadian Slavery and the Burning of Old Montreal*. Toronto: HarperCollins, 2006.

– "Nineteenth-Century Black Militant: Octavius V. Catto, 1839–1871." *Pennsylvania History* 44 (1977): 53–76.

Cooper, John. *Season of Rage: Hugh Burnett and the Struggle for Civil Rights*. Toronto: Tundra Books, 2005.

Coulter, Rebecca, and Helen J. Harper, eds. *History Is Hers: Women Educators in Twentieth-Century Ontario*. Calgary: Detselig Enterprises, 2005.

Creese, Gillian. *Negotiating Belonging: Bordered Spaces and Imagined Communities*. Vancouver: Centre of Excellence, Research on Immigration and Integration in the Metropolis, 2005.

– *The New African Diaspora in Vancouver: Migration, Exclusion, and Belonging*. Toronto: University of Toronto Press, 2011.

Dalleo, Peter T. "'Persecuted but Not Forsaken; Cut Down but Not Destroyed': Solomon and Thamar Bayley, Delawarean Emigrants to Liberia." *Delaware History* 31 (2006): 137–78.

– *Researching the Underground Railroad in Delaware: A Select Descriptive Bibliography of African American Fugitive Narratives*. Wilmington: Underground Railroad Coalition of Delaware, 2008.

– "'Thrifty and Intelligent, Moral and Religious': Wilmington's Free African American Community as Portrayed in the Blue Hen's Chicken, 1846–1852." *Delaware History* 28 (1998): 39–71.

Davis, D. Brion. *The Problem of Slavery in the Age of Revolution, 1770–1823*. New York: Oxford University Press, 1999.

Delany, Martin. *The Condition, Elevation, Emigration and Destiny of the Colored People of the United States*. Accessed 19 April 2009. http://www.libraries.wvu.edu/delany/intro.htm.

Delle, J.A. *An Archaeology of Social Space: Analyzing Coffee Plantations in Jamaica's Blue Mountains*. New York: Plenum Press, 1998.

Derrida, Jacques, and Eric Prenowitz. "Archive Fever: A Freudian Impression." *Diacritics* 25, no. 2 (Summer 1995): 9–63.

Dillon, Marmaduke. *Annual Report of the Colonial and Continental Church Society*. London: 1856.

Divine, David. "Voices Waiting to Be Heard and Acknowledged." *Directions* 4 (Winter 2008): 12–14.

Drew, Benjamin. *A Northside View of Slavery. The Refugee, or, The Narrative of Fugitive Slaves in Canada. Related by Themselves with an Account of the History and Condition of the Colored Population of Upper Canada*. Boston: John P. Jewett, 1856.

Ebanda de B'béri, Boulou. *Looking for My Pygmalion: Memoires*. Documentary Film. Directed and produced by Boulou Ebanda de B'béri. Montreal: Globe des Arts Sud-Nord / Orphelin Films, 2001.

– *Mapping Alternative Expressions of Blackness in Cinema: A Horizontal Labyrinth of Transgeographical Practices of Identity*. Germany: Bayreuth African Studies Series, 2006.

– "Transgeographical Practices of Marronage in Some African Films: Peck, Sissako, and Téno, the New Griots of New Times?" Special Issue on Transnationalism and Cultural Studies, edited by Meaghan Morris and Handel K. Wright, *Cultural Studies* 23, no. 5 (2009): 810–30.

Ernest, John. *Liberation Historiography: African American Writers and the Challenge of History, 1794–1861*. Chapel Hill: University of North Carolina Press, 2004.

Essah, Patience. *A House Divided: Slavery and Emancipation in Delaware, 1638–1865*. Charlottesville: University Press of Virginia, 1996.

Este, David C. "Black Canadian Historical Writing, 1970–2006: An Assessment." *Journal of Black Studies* 38, no. 3 (January 2008): 388–406.

Everitt, Joanna. "Public Opinion and Social Movements: The Women's Movement and the Gender Gap in Canada." *Canadian Journal of Political Science* 31, no. 4 (1998): 743–65.

Faires, Nora. "Going across the River: Black Canadians and Detroit before the Great Migration." *Citizenship Studies* 10, no. 1 (2006): 117–34.

Gac, Scott. *Singing for Freedom: The Hutchinson Family Singers and the Nineteenth-Century Culture of Antebellum Reform*. New Haven: Yale University Press, 2007.

Gaddis, John. *The Landscape of History*. New York: Oxford University Press, 2004.

Gallant, Sigrid Nicole. "Perspectives on the Motives for the Migration of African-Americans to and from Ontario, Canada: From the Abolition of Slavery in Canada to the Abolition of Slavery in the United States." *Journal of Negro History* 86, no. 3 (Summer 2001): 391–408.

Garrison, W.L. *Thoughts on African Colonization*. Boston: 1832.

Gaude, Eddie S., Jr. "Pragmatism and Black Identity: An Alternative Approach." *Nepantla: Views from South* 2, no. 2 (2001): 295–316.

Gillard, Denise. "The Black Church in Canada." Accessed December 2007. http://www.mcmaster.ca/mjtm/1-5.htm.

Goldberg, David Theo. *Multiculturalism: A Critical Reader*. Boston: Blackwell Publishers, 1994.

Haedicke, Susan C., and Tobin Nellhaus. *Performing Democracy: International Perspectives on Urban Community-Based Performance*. Ann Arbor: University of Michigan Press, 2001.

Hall, Stuart. "The Culture Gap." *Marxism Today* 28 (January 1984): 18–23.
– "What Is This 'Black' in Black Popular Culture? (Rethinking Race)." *Social Justice* 20 (1993): 104–11.
Hancock, Harold. "Mary Ann Shadd: Negro Editor, Educator, and Lawyer." *Delaware History* 15 (1978): 187–95.
Heike, Paul. "Out of Chatham: Abolitionism on the Canadian Frontier." *Atlantic Studies* 8, no. 2 (2011): 165–88.
Henry, Annette. "Growing Up Black, Female and Working Class: A Teacher's Narrative." *Anthropology and Education Quarterly* 26, no. 3 (September 1995): 279–305.
Henson, Josiah. *The Life of Josiah Henson: Formerly a Slave Now an Inhabitant of Canada, as Narrated by Himself*. Bedford: Applewood Books, 2003.
Higginbotham, Evelyn Brooks. *Righteous Discontent: The Women's Movement in the Black Baptist Church, 1880–1920*. Cambridge: Harvard University Press, 1994.
Hill, Daniel. *The Freedom Seekers: Blacks in Early Canada*. Agincourt: Book Society of Canada, 1981.
Hill, Lawrence. *Any Known Blood*. Toronto: HarperCollins, 1997.
– *Black Berry, Sweet Juice: On Being Black and White in Canada*. Toronto: Harper-Collins, 2001.
– "Zebra: Growing Up Black and White in Canada." In *Talking about Difference: Encounters in Culture, Language, and Identity*, edited by Adrienne Shadd and Carl James. Toronto: HarperCollins, 2001.
Hiller, Amy M. "The Disenfranchisement of Delaware Negroes in the Late Nineteenth Century." *Delaware History* 13 (1968): 124–30.
Hochschild, Adam. *Bury the Chains: The British Struggle to Abolish Slavery*. Basingstoke: Macmillan, 2005.
Hoffecker, Carol. *Delaware: A Bicentennial History*. New York: W.W. Norton, 1977.
– "The Politics of Exclusion: Blacks in Late Nineteenth Century Wilmington, Delaware." *Delaware History* 16 (Spring–Summer 1974): 60–89.
Hopkins, Leroy. "Black Eldorado on the Susquehana: The Emergence of Black Columbia, 1726–1861." *Journal of the Lancaster County Historical Society* 89, no. 4 (1985): 110–32.
Horton, James Oliver, and Lois E. Horton, eds. *Slavery and Public History: The Tough Stuff of American Memory*. New York: New Press, 2006.
Hosseini, Khaled. *The Kite Runner*. New York: Seal Books, 2004.
Howe, Samuel Gridley. *The Refugees from Slavery in Canada West: Report to the Freedmen's Inquiry Commission*. Boston: Wright & Potter, Printers, 1864.
Huggins, Nathan. "Deforming Mirror of Truth: Slavery and the Master Narrative in American History." *Radical History Review* 49 (1991): 25–47.
Hughes, Thomas. *Mission to the Colored Population in Canada*. London: 1869.
Hundey, Ian. *Canada: Builders of the Nation*. Toronto: Macmillan of Canada, 1980.

Irby, Charles. "The Black Settlers on Saltspring Island in the Nineteenth Century." *Phylon* 35, no. 4 (1974): 368–74.
Jensen, J.M. "Not Only Ours but Others: The Quaker Teaching Daughters of
the Mid-Atlantic, 1790–1850." *History of Education Quarterly* 24, no. 1 (Spring
1984): 3–19.
Jun, Helen, H. "Black Orientalism: Nineteenth-Century Narratives of Race
and U.S. Citizenship." *American Quarterly* 58, no. 4 (2006): 1047–66.
Kahn, Charles. *Salt Spring: The Story of an Island*. Madeira Park: Harbour Pub-
lishing, 1998.
Kashatus, William C. *Just Over the Line: Chester County and the Underground
Railroad*, West Chester: Chester County Historical Society, 2002.
Kolchin, Peter. *American Slavery 1619–1877*. New York: Hill and Wang, 1993.
Kuhn, T.S. *The Structure of Scientific Revolutions*. 2nd ed. Chicago: University of
Chicago Press, 1970.
Lacovetta, Franca. "Gendering Trans/National Historiographies: Feminists
Rewriting Canadian History." *Journal of Women's History* 19, no. 1 (2007):
206–13.
Landon, Fred. "The Negro Migration to Canada after the Passing of the Fugi-
tive Slave Act." *Journal of Negro History* 5, no. 1 (1920): 22–36.
– "The Anti-Slavery Society of Canada." *Journal of Negro History* 4, no. 1
(1919): 33–40.
Lang, Marjorie Louise. *Women Who Made the News: Female Journalists in Canada,
1885–1945*. Montreal and Kingston: McGill-Queen's University Press, 1999.
Lapsansky, Emma Jones. "'Discipline to the Mind': Philadelphia's Banneker
Institute, 1854–1872." *Pennsylvania Magazine of History and Biography* 117
(1993): 83–102.
Lauriston, Victor. *Romantic Kent: The Story of a County, 1626–1952*. Chatham:
OHS, 1952 (1988, 1992).
Lechner, Zachary. J. "Black Abolitionist Response to the Kansas Crisis,
1854–1856." *Journal of the Central Plains* 31, no. 1 (Spring 2008): 14–31.
Long, Beverly W., Lee Hudson, and Phillis R. Jeffrey. *Group Performance of
Literature*. Englewood Cliffs, NJ: Prentice-Hall, 1977.
Loomba, Ania. *Colonialism/Postcolonialism*. 2nd ed. Oxford: Routledge, 2005.
Lowenthal, David. *The Heritage Crusade and the Spoils of History*. 2nd ed. Cam-
bridge: Cambridge University Press, 1998.
MacDonald, Cheryl. "Mary Ann Cary in Canada: Last Stop on the Under-
ground Railroad." *The Beaver* 70 (1990): 32–8.
Martin, Tony. "The Banneker Literary Institute of Philadelphia: African Ameri-
can Intellectual Activism before the War of the Slaveholders' Rebellion."
Journal of African American History 87 (2002): 303–22.
Martinello, I.L. *Call Us Canadians*. Toronto: McGraw-Hill Ryerson, 1976.
McCalla, Doug. "Economy and Empire: Britain and Canadian Development,
1783–1971." In *Canada and the British Empire*, ed. Phillip Buckner. Oxford:
Oxford University Press, 2008.

McCormick, Richard P. "William Whipper: Moral Reformer." *Pennsylvania History* 43, no. 3 (1976): 23–46.

Nash, Gary. *First City: Philadelphia and the Forging of Historical Memory*. Philadelphia: University of Pennsylvania Press, 2001.

Nora, Pierre. "Between Memory and History: Les Lieux de Memoire." *Representations* 26 (1989): 7–24.

Olbey, C. "Unfolded Hands: Class Suicide and the Insurgent Intellectual Praxis of Mary Ann Shadd." *Canadian Review of American Studies* 30, no. 2 (2000): 149–72.

Osborne, Brian S. "Landscapes, Memory, Monuments, and the Commemoration: Putting Identity in Its Place." *Canadian Ethnic Studies* 33, no. 2 (2001): 2–48.

Palmer, Beverly Wilson, ed. *Selected Letters of Lucretia Coffin Mott*. Urbana: University of Illinois Press, 2002.

Patterson, Robert S. "Voices from the Past: The Personal and Professional Struggle of Rural School Teachers." In Sheehan et al., *Schools in the West*.

Payne, Daniel Alexander. *Recollections of Seventy Years*. Nashville: AME Sunday School Union, 1888.

Pease, William H., and Jane Pease. *Black Utopia: Negro Communal Experiments in America*. Madison: State Historical Society of Wisconsin, 1963.

Pierce, Yolanda. *Hell without Fires: Slavery, Christianity, and the Antebellum Spiritual Narrative*. Florida: University Press of Florida, 2005.

Poole, Carmen. "And Nobody Wondered and Nobody Understood: Canadian History Textbooks and Canadian Black Identity." Windsor: Windsor University's Faculty of Graduate Studies and Research Thesis Database, 2002.

Prestage, Jewell L. "In Quest of African American Political Woman." *Annals of the American Academy of Political and Social Science* 515, no. 1 (1991): 88–103.

Quamina, Odida T. *All Things Considered: Can We Live Together*. Toronto: Exile Editions, 1996.

Razack, Sherene H., ed. *Race, Space, and the Law: Unmapping a White Settler Society*. Toronto: Between the Lines, 2002.

Reid-Maroney, Nina. "Millennialism and the Church of England's Mission to Fugitive Slaves in Canada." In *Apocalypse and the Millennium: Providential Religion in the Era of the Civil War*, ed. Ben Wright and Zachary Dresser. Baton Rouge: Louisiana State University Press, 2013.

– *The Reverend Jennie Johnson and African Canadian History, 1868–1967*. Rochester: University of Rochester Press, 2013

Rhodes, Jane, *The Black Press and Protest in the Nineteenth Century*. Bloomington: Indiana University Press, 1998.

– "The Contestation over National Identity: Nineteenth-Century Black Americans in Canada." *Canadian Review of American Studies* 30, no. 2 (2000): 173–84.

– *Mary Ann Shadd Cary: The Black Press and Protest in the Nineteenth Century*. Bloomington: Indiana University Press, 1998.

Ripley, C. Peter, et al., eds. *The Black Abolitionist Papers*. 5 vols. Chapel Hill: University of North Carolina Press, 1986.

Robb, Graham. *The Discovery of France*. New York: W.W. Norton, 2007.

Robinson, Gwendolyn, and John W. Robinson. *Seek the Truth: A Story of Chatham's Black Community*. Canada: NP, 1989, 2004, and 2005.

Rollins, Frank A. *Life and Public Services of Martin R. Delany*. Boston: Ayer, [1883]1970.

Rosenberg, Daniel, and Susan Harding, eds. *Histories of the Future*. Durham: Duke University Press, 2005.

Runia, Eelco. "Presence." *History and Theory* 45, no. 1 (2006): 1–29.

Schwalm, Leslie Ann. "'Overrun with Free Negroes': Emancipation and Wartime Migration in the Upper Midwest." *Civil War History* 50, no. 2 (2004): 145–74.

Shadd, Adrienne, Afua Cooper, and Karolyn Smardz Frost. *The Underground Railroad: Next Stop, Toronto!* 2nd ed. Toronto: Natural Heritage Books, 2005.

Shadd-Shreve, Dorothy. *The Africanadian Church: A Stabilizer*. Jordan Station: Paideia Press, 1983.

Shaw, Stephanie J. *What a Woman Ought to Be and Do: Black Professional Women Workers During the Jim Crow Era*. Chicago: University of Chicago Press, 1996.

Sheehan, Nancy M., J. Donald Wilson, and David C. Jones, eds. *Schools in the West: Essays in Canadian Educational History*. Calgary: Detselig Enterprises, 1986.

Shreve, Dorothy Shradd. *The Africanadian Church: A Stabilizer*. Jordan Station: Paideia Press, 1983.

Silcox, Harry. "Nineteenth-Century Black Militant: Octavius V. Catto, 1839–1871." *Pennsylvania History* 44 (1977): 53–76.

– "Philadelphia Negro Educator, Jacob C. White, Jr." *Pennsylvania Magazine of History and Biography* 97 (January 1973): 75–98.

Silverman, Jason H. *Unwelcome Guests: Canada West's Response to American Fugitive Slaves, 1800–1865*. New York: Associated Faculty Press, 1985.

Simmons, Rev. William J. *Men of Mark: Eminent, Progressive, and Rising*. Cleveland: n.p, 1887.

Smedley, Robert Clemens. *History of the Underground Railroad in Chester and Neighboring Counties of Pennsylvania*. Lancaster: Office of the Journal, 1883.

Smith, William Henry. *Smith's Canadian Gazetteer: Comprising Statistical and General Information Respecting All Parts of the Upper Province or Canada West*. Toronto: H. & W. Rowsell, 1846.

Soyinka, Wole. "Telephone Conversation." In *Reading and Writing from Literature*, edited by John E. Schwiebert, 750. Boston: Houghton Mifflin, 2001.

Spearman, Don. *Landmarks of the Past*. Chatham: Chamberlain Mercury Press, 1991.

Still, William. *The Underground Rail Road: A Record of Fact, Authentic Narratives, Letters, & c., Narrating the Hardships Hair Breath Escapes and Death Struggles of the Slaves in Their Efforts for Freedom, as Related By Themselves and Others, or*

Witnessed by the Author: Together with Sketches of Some of the Largest Stockholders, and Most Liberal Aiders and Advisors, of the Road. Philadelphia: Porter & Coates, 1872.

Stouffer, Allen P. *The Light of Nature and the Law of God: Antislavery in Ontario, 1833–1877.* Montreal and Kingston: McGill-Queen's University Press, 1992.

Strong, M. Douglas. *Perfectionist Politics: Abolitionism and the Religious Tensions of American Democracy.* New York: Syracuse University Press, 1999.

Walker, Barrington. *Race on Trial: Black Defendants in Ontario Criminal Courts, 1858–1958.* Toronto: University of Toronto Press, 2010.

Walker, James W. St G. "Allegories and Orientations in African-Canadian Historiography: The Spirit of Africville." *Dalhousie Review* 77, no. 2 (Summer 1997): 155–77.

– *The Black Loyalists: The Search for a Promised Land in Nova Scotia and Sierra Leone, 1783–1870.* Longman Group and Dalhousie University Press, 1992.

– *A History of Blacks in Canada: A Study Guide for Teachers and Students.* Quebec: Canadian Government Publishing Centre, 1980.

– *"Race," Rights, and the Law in the Supreme Court of Canada.* Toronto: Osgoode Society, 1997.

– *Racial Discrimination in Canada: The Black Experience.* Ottawa: Canadian Historical Association Historical Booklet 41, 1985.

Walker, James W. St G., and Patricia Thorvaldson. *Identity: The Black Experience in Canada.* Toronto: Ontario Educational Communications Authority and Gage Educational Publishing, 1979.

Walton, Jonathan. "Blacks in Buxton and Chatham, Ontario, 1830–1890: Did the 49th Parallel Make a Difference?" PhD diss., Princeton University, 1979.

Ward, Samuel Ringgold. *Autobiography of a Fugitive Negro; his Anti-Slavery Labour in the United States, Canada and England* (London: 1855).

Weiler, Kathleen. "Reflections on Writing a History of Women Teachers." *Harvard Educational Review* 67, no. 4 (Winter 1997): 635–57.

Welburn, William C. "To 'Keep the Past in Lively Memory': William C. Bolivar's Efforts to Preserve African American Cultural Heritage." *Libraries and the Cultural Record* 42, no. 2 (2007): 165–79.

Williams, William H. *Slavery and Freedom in Delaware, 1639–1865.* Wilmington: Scholarly Resources, 1996.

Wilson, Carol. *Freedom at Risk: The Kidnapping of Free Blacks in America, 1780–1865.* Lexington: University Press of Kentucky, 1994.

Wilson, J. Donald. "'I Am Ready to Be of Assistance When I Can': Lottie Bowron and Rural Women Teachers in British Columbia." In Barman and Gleason, *Children, Teachers, and Schools in the History of British Columbia,* 2nd ed. Calgary: Detselig Enterprises, 2003.

Winch, Julie, ed. *The Elite of Our People: Joseph Willson's Sketches of Black Upper-Class Life in Ante-Bellum Philadelphia.* University Park: Pennsylvania State University Press, 2000.

– *A Gentleman of Color: The Life of James Forten.* New York: Oxford University Press, 2002.
– *Philadelphia's Black Elite: Activism, Accommodation, and the Struggle for Autonomy, 1787–1848.* Philadelphia: Temple University Press, 1988.
Winks, Robin W. *The Blacks in Canada, A History.* 2nd ed. Montreal and Kingston: McGill-Queen's University Press, 1997.
– "The Making of a Fugitive Slave Narrative: Josiah Henson and Uncle Tom – A Case Study." In *The Slave's Narrative,* edited by Charles T. Davis and Henry Louis Gates, Jr. New York: Oxford University Press, 1985.
– "Negro School Segregation in Ontario and Nova Scotia." *Canadian Historical Review* 50, no. 2 (1969): 164–91.
– "The Canadian Negro: A Historical Assessment – The Negro in the Canadian-American Relationship, Part 1." *Journal of Negro History* 53, no. 4 (1968): 283–300.
Wright, Handel K. "Between Global Demise and National Complacent Hegemony: Canadian Multiculturalism and Multicultural Education in a Moment of Danger." In *Precarious International Multicultural Education: Hegemony, Dissent, and Rising Alternatives,* edited by Handel Kashope Wright, Michael Singh, and Richard Race. New York: Sense Publishers, 2012.
Wright, Handel Kashope, and Afua Cooper. *Black British Columbians: Past and Present* (forthcoming).
Yee, Shirley. J. "Finding a Place: Mary Ann Shadd Cary and the Dilemmas of Black Migration to Canada, 1850–1870." *Frontiers: A Journal of Women Studies* 18, no. 3 (1997): 1–16.
Zimmerman, David. *"William Whipper in the Black Abolitionist Tradition."* http//muweb.millersvillle.edu/!ugrr/resources/Columbia/whipper.html; Underground Railroad Chronology, the Afrolumens Project, accessed 1 February 2006, www.afrolumens.org/ugrr/dwhipper01.htm.

Contributors

Claudine Bonner is an assistant professor at Acadia University. Her research explores the history of African diaspora communities in Canada in the late 19th and early 20th centuries, and she is presently researching and documenting the lived experiences of Caribbean migrant workers in Cape Breton Island, NS, at the turn of the 20th century. One of her recent publications in the *Journal of the Motherhood Initiative for Research and Community Involvement* (4.1) analyses the nature of "Kinship and Community Care."

Marie Carter is a historian living in Dresden, ON. She co-developed interpretive signage, a brochure, and a companion book for the Trillium Trail Historical Walk; a guidebook to local heritage homes (Building Heritage); and the Dawn Settlement Tour before acting as co-investigator of the Promised Land Project. She is a former advisory board member of the Uncle Tom's Cabin Historic Site. Her articles on history, rural issues, and social justice have been printed in specialty publications including *Heritage Matters*. She currently works as the Migrant Workers Ministry Specialist for the Diocese of London, ON.

Afua Cooper is the James Robinson Chair in Black Canadian Studies, an associate professor at Dalhousie University, and the founder of the Black Canadian Studies Association (BCSA). Her research interests are African Canadian studies, with specific attention to the period of enslavement and emancipation in 18th- and 19th-century Canada and the Black Atlantic. She is the author of a national bestseller and the 2006 Governor General's Award nominee for *The Hanging of Angélique* (2006).

Peter T. Dalleo has retired but remains an active researcher and speaker about the African diaspora in Delaware, The Bahamas, and Liberia. He has taught at LeMoyne College, the University of Delaware, and the College of the Bahamas. He is a co-founder of the *Journal of the Bahamas Historical Society*. He regularly contributes articles to *Delaware History* about the African American experience, and he authored *Researching the Underground Railroad in Delaware African-American Fugitive Narratives*. He is currently a member of the Delaware Humanities Forum Speakers Bureau.

Boulou Ebanda de B'béri is the founding director of the Audiovisual Media Lab for the Study of Cultures and Societies (www.lamacs.uOttawa.ca) and a professor of Media, Communication, and Cultural Studies at the University of Ottawa. His research appears in a variety of academic journals, including *Cultural Studies, Journal of International and Intercultural Communication*, and *Critical Arts*. Some of his books include *Les Cultural Studies dans le monde francophone* (2010), *Le "Verbe" au Cinéma* (2013), and *Global Perspectives on the Politics of Multiculturalism* (ed. with F. Mansouri, 2014).

Olivette Otele is a senior lecturer in European Colonial History at Bath Spa University, UK. Her latest publications include "Does Discrimination Shape Identity?" (with R. Latrache, *Journal of Intercultural Studies* [2011]) and "Bristol, Slavery and the Politics of Representation" (*Social Semiotics* [2012]). She is also an editorial board member of the Rowan and Littlefield book series "Critical Perspectives on Theory and Politics."

Nina Reid-Maroney is an associate professor in the Department of History at Huron University College (University of Western Ontario), where she teaches American history. Her recent publications include *The Reverend Jennie Johnson and African Canadian History, 1868–1967* (2013) and several articles that explore the intellectual and religious culture of Canada's antislavery movements in international context.

Handel Kashope Wright is a professor and director of the Centre for Culture, Identity and Education at the University of British Columbia. He is co-editor of the University of Toronto Press book series "African and Diasporic Cultural Studies" and editorial board member of several journals including *Critical Arts, Topia, International Jour-*

nal of Cultural Studies, and *The Canadian Journal of Education.* He has published widely on Africana cultural studies, anti-racism, critical multiculturalism, and qualitative research. His publications include *A Prescience of African Cultural Studies* (2004), *Africa, Cultural Studies and Difference* (2011), and *The Dialectics of African Education and Western Discourses* (2012).

Index

African and Diasporic Cultural Studies